The Bullet
Meant for Me

Broadway Books
New York

The Bullet Meant For Me

a memoir

JAN REID

BROADWAY

Broadway Books titles may be purchased for business or promotional use or for special sales. For information, please write to: Special Markets Department, Random House, Inc., 1540 Broadway, New York, NY 10036.

BROADWAY BOOKS and its logo, a letter B bisected on the diagonal, are trademarks of Broadway Books, a division of Random House, Inc.

Visit our website at www.broadwaybooks.com

PRINTED IN THE UNITED STATES OF AMERICA

Library of Congress Cataloging-in-Publication Data
Reid, Jan.
The bullet meant for me: a memoir / Jan Reid.—1st ed.
p.   cm.
1. Reid, Jan—Health.   2. Paraplegics—Texas—Biography.   I. Title.
RC406.P3 R445   2002
362.4'3'092—dc21
[B]
2001043193

FIRST EDITION

Designed by Claire Vaccaro

ISBN 0-7679-0595-4

1   3   5   7   9   10   8   6   4   2

for Dorothy and Lila

Acknowledgments

Some books you never mean to write. In June 1998, I was finally out of the hospitals and free to countenance the idea of working again. I rolled my wheelchair out to my office with my dogs at the rear, and they circled and settled in on the sofa as if nothing had changed. My wheelchair made a snug fit against the desk; I turned on the computer. I had many years of work invested in two half-finished novels, and my slam dance with mortality made me want to get them done at once. But for a day and then a week I couldn't finish a paragraph. The phone kept ringing: Well-wishers and scheduling with my new doctors and therapists and the friends who had volunteered to drive me about. I got nothing done. I couldn't walk and now I couldn't write. It scared me.

Then an old friend and colleague called. Emily Yoffe told me she was writing now for the on-line magazine *Slate*, and its editors wanted me to take a turn with a feature called "Diary." I would write just three or four hundred words of details and reflections on my new life for five consecutive days. I thought, Well, a good way to knock the rust off is to take on daily deadlines. By Tuesday's piece I was enjoying the exercise. Only one segment wore on long enough that I began to make my editor, Cyrus Krohn, nervous I wouldn't deliver. After reading the first couple of those pieces, my friend Roy Hamric had e-mailed: "Go deeper, if you can." I decided that before getting back to the books I wanted to write one essay about Mexico and my friendship with a deported fighter and how events converged in a cab ride that laid waste to my life and almost finished it. Martin Beiser at GQ was generous enough to take on that piece.

I really thought that would be the end of it. Then from my agent, Jim Hornfischer, I learned that a young editor at Broadway Books, Suzanne Oaks, had seen and admired the *Slate* diaries. Jim asked if he could show her the manuscript of the GQ essay, and later he arranged a phone conversation between us. Suzanne told me she saw a book in this, but that I had to think hard about whether I wanted to write it. I did that, and concluded I needed to take it on. I had no idea how wrenching the work would become. Good editing is often mourned as a lost art these days. That was not my experience here. At times I thought Suzanne was riding an old horse hard. But she got me to focus, trim, and reconsider, and that produced a better book than it would have been. I'm indebted to Suzanne's able and energetic assistant, Claire Johnson. Bill Hauptman, David McCormick, Marcy Garriott, and *Texas Monthly*'s editor, Evan Smith, gave me encouragement and valuable advice along the way. And Dorothy and Lila, my valiant wife and daughter, stuck with it—with me!—until it was finally done.

I must thank some doctors: Roberto Castañeda, Francisco Revilla, James "Red" Duke, Guy Clifton, William Donovan, Kenneth Parsons, David Harris, David Phillips, and Howard Marcus. Therapists Sherry Dunbar, Theresa Gregorio-Torres, Kristin Murphy, Melinda Longtain, and Wendy Kamasaki have my enduring love and gratitude. I received compassionate and first-rate medical care in Mexico. And for all the criticism one hears about managed care in the United States, the medical system worked for me. Norman Chenven, our longtime friend and once our family physician, was in an administrative position to make sure that was the case, every step of the way. I can't imagine how it would have gone without Norman and his dedicated caseworkers, Diane Hosmer and Bobby Claussen.

I will never forget the remarkable gathering of men who walked one by one into my Mexico City hospital room when I first came out of the murk; the colleagues who took it upon themselves to get me back to Texas when time was a critical factor in my rehabilitation and, as soon as I was able, put me back to work; the rich assortment of friends whose common bond is a homely boxing gym; the writers and musicians who shared their talent to lighten the financial strain on me and my family, and on those evenings brought much good rowdy cheer to Austin. I can't begin to name all the friends whose letters, calls, and gestures buoyed me when the outlook was grim. An uncle in West Texas told me recently: "You ought to come out and meet some of the people who were praying for you." Indeed I should. The only way I can repay my debts is to try to be as kind to people as they have been to me. Thanks to them, I can move on now. I can turn the page.

Let me not enter their council,
let me not join their assembly,
for they have killed men in their anger
and hamstrung oxen as they pleased.

GENESIS

In boxing we have this saying: "I'm gonna
put my head on your chest." Means I'm gonna
take the best you got and come right through
all your defenses. In the first fight against
Muhammad, Joe Frazier did that.
To a man as great as Muhammad Ali.
After that, Joe never was quite the same.
What else did he have to prove?

GEORGE FOREMAN

Contents

Prologue

In the lambent sprawl of Plaza Garibaldi mariachis stood about with slim hopes of anyone hiring them. It was a little after one a.m. But the roving beer hawkers were still busy yanking cans from ring-tops of six-packs and offering singles for a few pesos. Mike Hall noticed that we were the only gringos anywhere in sight. I was oblivious to that but I winced on seeing John Spong and David Courtney buy two more Modelos. I was ready to call it a night. I was fifty-three, the only one among us who was married. Mike, the next oldest at forty, was a thin, soft-spoken man who had tanked a small career as a rock song-writer and recording artist so he could make a better living as a maga-zine editor and journalist. His laugh was both soft and explosive, and during the long weekend we had gone from being colleagues to friends; with fine wit he had briefed me on the ups and downs of his life as a musician. The lark in Mexico City had been like that for all of us, except that John and David were already close friends, best friends it seemed. Their banter had that timing, the practiced knowing of what the other was about to say.

The younger of the two, John was a dropout lawyer breaking into magazine work as a fact-checker. John was six feet and slender, with auburn hair and long sideburns. People noticed him; he had the air of a wiseacre, a funnyman. David, a freelance writer who specialized in music, was in the second hour of his thirty-second birthday. He wore a ridiculous straw bowler he had bought on the Zócalo, the city's vast central square. David swigged from a fresh beer and pointed out a troupe of *norteños*—musicians from northern Mexico who were distinguished from the black-clad mariachis by their brown suits. He and John started to amble over and check them out.

We had come to Mexico City to watch a prizefight. The night before, we had watched my young friend Jesus Chavez stop a Mexico City opponent. The arena where he made his Mexican debut was in a dark and dangerous barrio on the periphery of Plaza Garibaldi. I knew we were pushing our luck to come back here. But the others argued that one more night in the Tenampa Bar would give our trip a symmetry—where it began, where it ended. I kept silent, went along, relaxed after downing the first beer and shot of tequila, and soon held up my share of the talk and laughter. But the whole trip had been a bittersweet affair for me. Jesus had gained a number one world ranking the same month the U.S. government ordered him deported. In a few hours we were going home, and I had growing doubts that Jesus ever could.

Watching John and David wander off toward the *norteños*, I said to Mike: "Let's get these guys out of here." He told me later it was the first time he had ever heard me sound impatient, and it was the only time this trip I invoked whatever authority that came with my years.

In Austin I worked out in the boxing gym where Jesus emerged as a contender. These days I did it just for exercise, sparring rarely, but I had sweated and banged myself into the best condition of my life.

Among the young fighters, I was respected as one of the old guys who could make the big bags pop. Jesus lived in a dusty little room at the gym for several months, and it quickly became apparent that we were in the company of a real talent. With undercards that showcased the novelty of skilled women boxing, Jesus's frenetic main events in a converted rock music hall breathed raw excitement into a town with little history in the sport, and for Jesus, with it came the regional titles, then the television, and the climb up the rankings. But Jesus was more than just a star athlete to me, and to him I was more than an aging hanger-on. When I walked in the gym he would call out "Zhann*reeed*," and at the end of the days we often sat on the ring apron talking about things far removed from boxing. Then, suddenly, his dream and prospects were crushed by the Immigration and Naturalization Service and a massive new federal law. Lawyers and federal judges would be analyzing the new immigration guidelines for years, trying to determine exactly what they meant, but one aspect seemed certain: if noncitizens had ever committed a felony in the United States, they not only could be deported—they had to be. The law allowed the INS no discretion, leniency, or, it seemed to me, common sense.

My friend was deported to a country he scarcely knew. He hadn't lived in Mexico since he was ten years old. As the day of his departure got closer, for a couple of hours we could forget and escape it in the gym. Jesus used to train me, and I was fascinated by how much the little guy knew. One day I was trying to make my left uppercut into more than a clumsy shove. "Relax your hand," he told me, "and raise your right heel just a little." The heavy bag popped loudly and danced on the end of the chain. Explain that. Jesus refused to patronize or humor me, though. Calling and taking my punches with gloves that resemble catcher's mitts, he would pop them together loudly, as if to wake me up, and poke me between my heaving ribs and wheezing lungs.

"How you gonna hit me standing way out there?" he ragged me for my cemented footwork. "You've gotta step up in the pocket, then throw that jab."

Those words would come back to haunt me.

I can't remember when I first heard about the peril of the green cabs. It was one of those buzzes that suddenly pervade the conversation of travelers bound for a common destination. In the Mexican capital, drivers remove the passenger bucket seats of old-style Volkswagen Beetles to make room for more fares to pile inside, they paint the cars bright green with white roofs, and hit the streets. You see them by the thousands—unregulated gypsies and, lately, predators in collusion with armed robbers. Residents swore these urban bandits were cops or ex-cops. My friends and I had discussed the hubbub about the green VWs. How much was real, and how much was gringo paranoia? Logistics had divided us and forced us into the green bugs a few times, and nothing had happened. We spoke some Spanish and were veteran travelers. We were big strong guys. We figured we had strength in numbers. We were unaware that the U.S. State Department had just added Mexico City to its list of most dangerous foreign destinations.

Finally all of us were ready to call it a night. Despite my brooding about the immigration policy and my worry about Jesus, we had enjoyed a fine getaway in the Mexican capital. Now it was time to go back to our apartment and sleep and, the next day, board a plane and resume our lives in Texas. With self-assurance John Spong walked out to the line of taxis that served Plaza Garibaldi. He waved on a couple of VWs, then a mostly white Japanese compact pulled up. It looked fairly new and expensive, which made it seem reliable. But the lower fenders and doors were painted green.

I never saw the driver's face. I said hello to him as I slid across the backseat. He stared straight ahead and offered nothing but a vague grunt. We had already taken one cab ride from the plaza to our apartment, and I knew landmarks along the well-lighted way. Soon after leaving the cabstand, this driver made a sharp turn and raced through the dark barrio.

"This doesn't look right," I said.

Why didn't I lock the doors, if my presentiment was so strong? Or just throw my arms around his neck? I could have easily overpowered the guy. But you want it *not* to happen; you want to be wrong. And so you do nothing.

We reemerged on the Paseo de la Reforma and breathed easier. But in the detour we had picked up a tail—one of those green and white Volkswagen Beetle cabs. Mike rode in the front seat of our Nissan; in the back I was squeezed between John and David. The taxi driver carried us almost to our apartment—then stopped abruptly in the middle of a block. Mike had noticed the VW, and he looked back and saw a nightmare. In disbelief's slow motion, two men jumped out and ran toward us holding guns. "Go, go!" Mike cried, turning to the driver, but he was hunkered down, stonefaced. The deliveryman.

The *pistoleros* threw open the doors and vaulted inside; with a lurch our taxi sped off. Both men appeared to be in their thirties. Their guns were old, scarred .38 revolvers. In an instant I went from drunk to sober. A gun in your face does that to you. The robber in the backseat was fat, doughy-faced, and nervous. He forced down the heads of John and David and tried to hide his own face by burrowing into an absurd, rolling semblance of a football pileup.

In the middle, pinned back by their weight, I sat face-to-face with the honcho in front. He had sharp, angular features and black hair combed Elvis-fashion. Possibly a ladies' man. "Shut up! Go to sleep!" he yelled. He sat on Mike's leg and stuck the gun's muzzle in his ear.

The last thing I needed was a lot of eye contact with this guy, but with all the weight and bulk in my lap, forcing me back against the seat, I couldn't avoid it. Responding to my gaze, Honcho leaned over the seat and pistol-whipped me across the cheekbone. He didn't hit me very hard. It was like he was asserting his dominance, controlling an animal. His English was pretty good. He was used to handling a gun and ordering people around. Even odds the robber was a cop.

But he was a bungling thief. Honcho took Mike Hall's watch, then seemed to get distracted. On and on we rode with the second gunman, this wordless, out-of-breath hooligan, in our laps. The preposterousness magnified the terror. I watched Mike lean over until his head touched the driver's shoulder. His expression was that of someone patiently bent on riding this out. For no reason I could determine, Honcho whacked me with the gun again. I was astonished by my calm.

"Well, so much for not taking the green cabs," reflected John. In the hassle and backtalk of telling Honcho that he had spent his last peso on beer, he also got his mouth bloodied by the gun. "I don't know, man," he said in high register, to no one in particular, "this has gone on a long time."

On my right, David was twisted like a pretzel under the second gunman's weight, yet he clung to his dumb straw hat. "I can't breathe, get him off me," David groaned at one point, sounding panicky. Moments later he announced: "I'm gonna open the door and throw this fat fuck out of here."

That's a bold idea, the others of us thought. We wondered what we would do with the driver and Honcho then, and the scenario did not look promising. Watching the muzzle of Honcho's gun, which was an inch away from Mike's temple, John told David, "You might hold up on that."

We careened onto a hellish, lighted freeway that was black with soot and shreds of exploded truck tires. Then we were on an upper deck of the freeway and could see nothing. As the ride carried us deeper into anxiety and unknown sections of the city, our thoughts raced between fright, desperation, and trying to remain calm and think this through. John and David discussed strategies of escape while

I thought, Hasn't anybody noticed that one of these guys knows some English?

"Give us your money!" Honcho screamed at me.

"Well, let me get my hands free!" I yelled back. It was unfortunate and perhaps inevitable; he and I had a relationship now. I struggled and finally came out of the pile with my wallet. Honcho snatched it and tore my cheap watch off my wrist.

Their take from all of us was about $150 and one of my credit cards. I leaned forward and tried to reason with the guy. "We've given you everything. Todo! No tenemos más! What more do you want? What's the point?"

Dismissively, Honcho turned his gaze away. As we came off the freeway into another barrio I heard him say they were going to separate us. If I had been more familiar with Mexico City street crime, I might have thought they meant to take me and my credit card to an ATM machine—where with great displeasure they would have learned that I never set up PIN numbers for cash withdrawals. A bad situation was getting a lot worse. I thought they were going to kill us.

The driver stopped the cab near an intersection. Honcho got out first and ordered the rest of us to follow him. "Screw you, it's our cab," John sassed him. Mike climbed out of the front seat, followed by the gunman in back. Behind me John stepped out on the driver's side. As I emerged last from the car, Honcho grabbed my left arm roughly. But two men were trying to control four.

David cried, "Run, run, scatter!" The fat robber clubbed him on the head with the gun and ripped his clothes, trying to restrain him, but David broke free and sprinted out into the street. I saw or heard none of that. I felt Honcho's grip loosen on my arm, and in reflex I threw his hand off me. After that it was all instinct and adrenaline.

As I backed away, Honcho came after me with a look of fury. I weighed 195 pounds, and in the gym I had learned to throw a hard straight left hand; I guess I meant to stagger the smaller man, then make my escape. But I also felt the pleasure of anger—of striking back at the only real enemy I had ever had.

Yet all that sounds calculated and slow. In fact there was no time for any thought, and in my reacting I failed to heed my friend Jesus's advice: Step up in the pocket, he said, then throw that jab. If I were going to throw a punch at a man with a gun, I damn sure needed to land it. And by inches it fell short.

My friends said Honcho fired once at the ground, as if he were working up his courage or seeing if the old gun worked. It's odd; I have no memory of that. With stone contempt and considered aim he looked me in the eyes and pulled the trigger.

In the air between us a wan flash of lightning appeared, crackling from above his left shoulder to the ground. As the bullet's force threw me backward, I swear I could feel its churning spin: the crude gouge of a screwdriver, with the force of a train. Searing pain in my abdomen and spine was instantaneous and absolute. I cried out to my friends a line that in movies always made me cringe.

"I'm killed."

Houston
some days later

It was just an odd coincidence, a tangle of telephone wires and time.

I lay in a hospital bed diagnosed as a paraplegic. The Mexico City neurosurgeons who removed the bullet from my spinal column had told my wife and daughter I would never walk again, yet panic and despair never seized me in those first days. I was glad just to be alive and removed from that terrible fear and supreme hurt. I had surrendered to the horror and known I was close to dying but had come out the other side. I was in Texas, I was safe. But my life was blown to pieces. How could this have happened to me? Was it random fate, like the man who gets struck by lightning? Or should I have known better than to be standing out in the rain? All my adult life, my judgment had walked shoulder to shoulder with macho confidence. In my work and my enjoyment I skirted risk. Now I could no longer walk at all, and I had to face the possibility that I had tempted fate one time too many. That I had brought this on myself.

I could move my feet slightly—a hopeful sign, my family and I chose to believe. Also, I had pleaded with the Texas doctors to give me something that would knock down the pain. Boy, had they come through. I was lucid at times and then off I'd go—friendless and helpless in strange worlds that seemed to have no use of me at all. I wouldn't recommend morphine as a recreational drug. My nights were zonked but sleepless—hardly ideal for a human body trying to heal. Still, I cherished the fluid periodically allowed to drip down a tube into my arm. Doctors of pain are always asking their patients to rate their discomfort on a scale of one to ten. That night with my back on the pavement and then on the emergency room bed, my pain on that scale was two hundred, ten thousand. A tidal wave of pain reduced my proud manly bearing to that of an inconsolable child. I begged for morphine in Mexico City. And the torture of that night was still a blazing red coal in my mind.

I remember little about the features of the Houston hospital room. Maybe it was the next stop after intensive care. There was a telephone beside my bed, and Dorothy, my wife, had written me instructions on how to make a call and charge it to our calling card. Once so easily memorized, that procedure was beyond my mental reach now. But in some conversation it had gotten through to me that the voice mail on our line in Austin was full and it had been rejecting messages of callers for several days. Dorothy and my daughter, Lila, hadn't been home since their flight to my bedside in Mexico City, followed by a rescue flight to Houston two days later. Dorothy was overwhelmed by all the demands thrown upon her: how to make medical decisions for me and keep a refinance of our house going and assure the care and feeding of our dogs and cat. So with notepad and pen on the bed beside my hip, I cradled the phone between my shoulder and jaw and set out to dispose of one small chore.

There were seventeen calls; I remember just one.

After I was shot and the taxi and the *pistoleros* vanished, Mike had held my head in his lap while John and David ran along the street crying for help. Then Mike rode in the ambulance and gripped my hand, trying to comfort me, as we sped through the streets and my blood soaked his shirt and jeans. "Mike," I told him, "I'd rather die than take this pain, but I want to see Dorothy again."

"Well," he said gently, "there's your reason why."

At the hospital Mike didn't even know how to make a phone call, but at last he found someone who spoke English well enough to tell him how to reach an operator who would accept his U.S. calling card. Mike had met Dorothy once or twice but hardly knew her. His call to her went unanswered, and when the voice mail turned on my drawl—"We'll get back to you as soon as we can"—he left her the most upbeat message he could manage. Afterward he thought, Oh my god, what if she's not there? He fought down his emotions, knowing how close he was to panic. It's nearly three in the morning, he reasoned. She didn't hear it, she must have slept through the call. So he tried again, and this time Dorothy picked up the phone. I can see her rising on an elbow, then lurching up and turning on the lamp. Then when she had hung up and was alone with dogs who were suddenly awake and nervous, pacing, she reached for her cigarettes, her heart slamming within her, and disbelief began to give way to dread and shock.

Now I lay in a hospital bed in Houston, listening to Mike's first call from the emergency room in Mexico City. "Dorothy, this is Mike Hall," he said, voice quavering. "Something has happened to Jan. It's all right, he's going to be okay. But you need to call me right away. . . ." The tremors in his voice belied him. Nothing was all right, nothing was okay. It's a wonder Mike had the composure to say anything coherent. In the receiver I held against my ear, close behind him I could hear the desperation and the horror of my own screams.

Part One

(1)

I believed I was a sane, mature, and peaceful man. It would be easy to attribute the sudden and drastic change in my life to bad luck, to being in "the wrong place at the wrong time." Yet I have to wonder if precepts of manliness, ingrained almost from birth, led me to insert myself in a place and predicament I need never have known. How much of the fault was mine? All my life, had I been riding a fools' train that wouldn't let me off?

The courage of a boy child born in Texas is equated with his balls. It's a crude metaphor but it declines to go away. Male Texans are supposed to be rough, tough, and ready for whatever comes down the pike. In the 1830s the makers of this myth gave up the relative safety of life in the United States and, following the lead of Mexican settlers, they risked all they had on reports of well-watered timberlands and prairies that billowed in the wind like ocean waves. When the Mexican claimants to that wilderness turned out to be bullies and despots, why, Texans licked their army and kicked them out without help from anybody. And then we beat back the ferocious Indians who had denied the Spaniards and Mexicans real settlement of their Texas province for a hundred fifty years. At all costs we stood our ground.

It's a rousing story, true enough, though in the mythological version significant details get left out. As a birthright it's dangerous, and as a code to live by, it's horseshit.

But who would humans be without our myths?

I grew up in rolling mesquite savanna just south of the Red River. Along with bare higher plains in the Texas Panhandle, it was the last stronghold of the Comanches and Kiowas. Except for arrowheads, the nomadic buffalo hunters left few artifacts, no evidence of having been there at all. In the summer, heat mirage spreads like lakes across the highways and makes the horizons in that country shimmer and dance. I used to fancy that hordes of Indians would come howling and riding out of the chimera like Omar Sharif's bedouins in *Lawrence of Arabia*. When I knew more of what really occurred, I could see a few vestiges of that past. Along Red River the little towns of Nocona and Quanah bear the names of famous Comanche war chiefs who were father and son. East of Henrietta is a sloping well-kept pasture where mesquites have never been allowed to take root. I could imagine buffalo grazing there. Farther west, where the Pease River winds toward its mouth in the Red, the Medicine Mounds rise eerily from the plain. From a distance the four conical hills look much bigger than they are—maybe that's part of their magic. They're said to overlook an ancient trail worn in the earth by migrating buffalo, and nearby is a bend of the Pease where a spring-fed creek sweetens the brackish gypsum water. Comanches liked to build their camps there. Young men would go up on the Medicine Mounds to learn their names and behold their visions—see their future, such as it was.

I was born and raised in small Texas cities that sprouted up in the conquered Indian country. The only Indians I ever saw were descendants of the peoples who were chased off to Oklahoma reservations and the squalor that ensued. The climate is famous for tornadoes, ungodly heat, and cold fronts called northers. The wind never stops blowing. The rain is erratic, as cotton farmers soon found, and cattlemen wore out the native grama and bluestem prairies by overstocking them. Gnarled mesquites filled up many pastures to the point that they couldn't be walked through. But rich oil fields were discovered there in the first half of the twentieth century. Suddenly ranching and cowboying were no longer the manliest pursuits. Making money was. Horsehead pumpjacks still rear and nod in the mesquite thickets, sucking out a few barrels a day for the oil companies and landowners who hang on to their mineral rights and hope there might yet be another boom. But no one really believes it. The oil prospectors have gone off to the China Sea and South America. The towns and countryside of my youth look used up, spent.

My dad, Charles Cleon Reid, was a red-haired man of Scotch descent who in his boyhood lived for athletics. He was best at baseball. His father, another Charles Reid, was a Wichita Falls car mechanic who in his later years bought a spudder drilling rig and tried to make a go of it as a wildcatter. Daddy started junior college in the thirties and hoped to move on somewhere and take a degree; he wanted to teach school and coach. But the Depression forced him to quit and find work in oil refineries, which put food on his table the rest of his life. My mother had it harder. Elsie Shelton was one of six children of a tenant cotton farmer. As soon as they were able, every one of them was out in the fields. One fall they brought in their own crop and then moved to another place, where for a little pay they helped pick that farmer's cotton. Mother's home during those weeks was an earthen dugout. She was the valedictorian of her high school class in a village called Bluegrove, but she knew better than to set her marks and hopes too high. The Depression knocked the bottom out of the cotton market, and the programs of the New Deal helped landowners, not tenants. But my grandfather, Dad Shelton, blamed it all on Herbert Hoover. A quick-witted little man and expert whistler, he had to quit farming for a few years, offering himself as a barber in Wichita Falls. After my mother finished school, she too moved to the big town in the area. She cared for an ailing grandmother and got a job as a dime-store salesclerk.

My parents met at a church outing and married in 1940. Daddy was rawboned and muscular, and you could tell by his choice of hats and Chevrolets that he had some vanity and sense of style. Mother was small, pretty, and guided by the Bible. She defied her parents, who were strong Southern Baptists, when she was baptized into another fundamentalist sect, the Church of Christ. Until late in life Daddy declined to join her in that faith; he was a proclaimed Baptist who seldom went to church. They'd grown up wounded by the Depression and now were starting a marriage and family knowing that war was just a matter of time. My sister Lana Gail was born July 14, 1941—Bastille Day in France, and what a bitter one that was, with Paris occupied by the Germans. Daddy had finished a hitch in the National Guard not long before he met Mother; several men in his unit wound up in the Bataan Death March. The walls in Dad and Granny Shelton's farmhouses were filled with portraits of young women with forties hairdos and their husbands in uniform. Mother's brothers, cousins, and brothers-in-law fought in nearly every major campaign of the war. One drove a tank wrecker in Patton's division. Another helped liberate a Nazi death camp. Another had to stand guard over a concentration camp of Japanese-Americans in Oregon. His brother came back from the Pacific with such bitter remarks about the army that it wasn't till he died that relatives found two Bronze Stars and a sheaf of battlefield commendations he'd stored in an old boot box. They all survived it somehow. On those walls my dad was the only one pictured in a coat and tie. He was the only one who didn't have to go.

The draft board in Wichita Falls deferred him because he worked in a defense industry that would be scarcely recognizable today. During the war Daddy's employer, a Texas oil company called Panhandle, sent him out to work in a tiny, undermanned plant in a hamlet named Lueders that had been settled by Swedes. Daddy carried a lunch pail and walked down a short dirt road to the gates of the refinery. They lived in a small rented house and planted a garden behind it every year. Mother kept a hoe close at hand not only to chop weeds but in case she had to do battle with a rattlesnake that slithered in from the pastures. Abilene was just half an hour's drive away; saving ration stamps for butter and sugar, they shopped for groceries there and sometimes took in a picture show. Except for church, in Lueders there was almost nothing to do. But to her surprise, Mother sometimes felt like a golf widow. Daddy and other workers at the refinery chopped, uprooted, and transformed mesquite and cactus of a donated pasture into the fairways of a nine-hole course. Knowing they couldn't keep turf grass alive, they made their greens out of a mixture of sand and crude oil that they raked smooth. You had to hit your putts hard, Daddy told me once, but it would sure grab the spin of a good chip shot.

I was born in the Abilene hospital the evening of March 18, 1945. Daddy put a fair-sized crimp in my boyhood while I still looked scalded. At least Mother claimed the name was mostly his idea. He wanted a fourth-generation Charles if I turned out to be a son, but that could be my middle name. There are fads in naming babies like fads in choosing breeds of dogs. Just after the war great numbers of American couples named their babies Jan. It was my bad luck that about 99 percent of them were daughters. Many people have since assumed that my parents were sophisticates who gave me the European name, pronounced *Yahn*. It's common throughout Scandinavia and Central Europe—there are Czech national heroes named Jan out the kazoo. But nope, Daddy didn't know beans about Europe. He just thought it was a handsome name. I never really blamed him. It's not like all those parents of the baby boomers got together and had a mass consultation. Still, I would be a grown man before I could shrug off some lout sneering, " 'Jan!' That's a *girl's name!*"

My memories of Lueders, of being a villager, are indistinct and few. The images took on sharpness and sequence when Daddy hitched a trailer to his new black Chevrolet and we made the move back to Wichita Falls. It was 1949. We first lived in an apartment house downtown. The units opened onto a central hallway at the end of which was a single bathroom that all the tenants shared. Mother and Daddy hated that. Daddy was consumed with building us a home. He bought a lot on a new street called Keeler that was just four blocks from his dad's broad-porched house on Collins. Though he always voted with labor and the Democrats, my dad was a very conservative man. He wanted Lana and me to grow up exactly the way he had. And before Granddaddy Reid fell victim to heart attacks, it was almost that way for a while.

Granddaddy took us for rides out through the oil leases and in his shaded backyard got us to help him pick up his cherished pecans. At the Collins Street house we got to know our great-grandfather, a tall, thin, blind man in his nineties. In his youth that Charles Reid was a Texas Ranger and had ridden on one of the cattle drives to New Mexico Territory during the time of Billy the Kid and the Lincoln County War. Before a small-town bank failed that had most of his money in it, in central Texas he had a splendid farm and ranch that the Colorado River ran through. On the porch swing at Collins Street he would regale us with his stories, then abruptly he'd throw back his head and howl some song, usually a hymn, like a night rider soothing an anxious herd. Lana and I loved that old man.

My fantasies ran to the past of Texas—open country, cowboy country. I longed for the vacations when we went to see Uncle

Raymond and Aunt Bea on the Shelton side of the family. Mother's brother had married one of her best friends, and since the war they had lived and worked as hired hands on big West Texas ranches. He drove a mud-splattered pickup, rode horses like he was born on them, roped and doctored calves. She cooked three meals a day for the bunkhouse crew. I can see it now as hard, pitiless work, but then it seemed like great romance. The quiver of the horses' flanks when they snorted, the smell of the horseshit mixed with straw—I would have liked to spend my life in those pastures, barns, and corrals.

But that wasn't an escape I could ever make. I was a town kid, like it or not. Without articulating it Daddy tried to shield me from the town's measure of manhood, getting rich. He planned for us to go to grade school at Alamo—built with a brick facade that resembled the iconic Texas fortress—just like he had. Our friends would come from families similar to ours. But Daddy miscalculated: By three blocks, he learned after buying the lot, Keeler was in the district of Ben Franklin, a new school built near the mansions of the Country Club. I started school with kids whose dads were oil millionaires.

There was the problem of my name. I was skinny and had buck teeth. Other kids at school mumbled through a mouthful of braces; I looked in the mirror and saw Bugs Bunny. I was unsteady of emotion and thought I was ugly. We were blue-collar middle class but I thought we were poor. Once I was proud of my dad's '48 Chevy; now it embarrassed me. Every morning in front of the school there was a line of Cadillacs. I was uneasy when my mother took a job in a laundry. Why was our own wash hung out on clotheslines in the backyard? Why didn't we have a washer and dryer like everybody else? At the refinery Daddy wore thick one-piece cotton garments called coveralls. They hung drying from the lines in beheaded mannish forms, twisting their arms in the constant breeze. At night I would square off with the coveralls and pound them with my fists. My mother and sister thought it was funny, and they took snapshots of me doing it. I wasn't pretending to get back at Daddy for some wrong. I think it was more like my first boxing gym. I was trying to work out the anger and fear in my head and turn it into bravery and skill. For sure as sundown, I was going to have to fight.

The fights took place after school in vacant lots and were great fun unless you were one of the fighters. For me they fell into a consistent pattern. I would back up while my opponent walked forward with his fists raised and flung insults and his friends laughed and jeered me. Finally I'd run forward spewing shrill jabber and throwing windmill punches. I lost more fights than I won, but a couple of times my outbursts were so furious that bullies decided to leave me alone. I got in trouble, I eventually noticed, when I started the fights. One foe, Danny Mulligan, was a dark-haired pretty boy who must have been born with a smirk, and he ran with the real toughs. I could be pushed around by that bunch, but I was not afraid of Danny. His scorn of me pissed me off, and I called him out one day right beside the Ben Franklin flagpole. We fought and fought until I staggered around blindly, feeling the blows whang off my head but just not believing the outcome. Finally Danny dropped his hands and said, "Boy, do you want me to make *soup* out of you?"

In a town where athletics was everything, I was a nobody. I came into my teens when Wichita Falls was enjoying its run as the state's kingpins of high school football. Our Coyotes reached the state finals four years in a row and won the title twice. I couldn't play football worth a flip but I wasn't smart enough to walk away from it. I hung on, riding the bench in the games and getting run over by bigger and tougher boys in practice, until a broken collarbone relieved me from a second tour with the B-team. I alienated an assistant coach who managed the baseball team in the spring, so I didn't get the chance to show off my real love and modest talent, playing the outfield. Another coach's invitation to join the track team ended badly; I hadn't the wind or the discipline to run the mile. I quit in a particularly self-demeaning way—pretended to get tripped up by a competing runner, took a fall in the hard sharp cinders, just to put an end to it. I heard the coaches' unsympathetic murmurs, about how I used to fake being hurt in football. Daddy tried to pass on his love of golf but it bored me. All right, bone up for the college entrance exam. Do something constructive. Learn to play the harmonica. But the winter before graduation two friends dared me to join them in a dramatic alternative—boxing.

Joe Haid was the poorest of my friends. His father had died when he was little, and his sweet-natured mother, twice a widow, provided for them by working in a grocery store. But Joe was always first at something—reading Kerouac's *On the Road*, getting up at five in the morning to throw newspapers in the Country Club so he could buy a Cushman Eagle motor scooter that he painted metallic chartreuse, moving on to a pink '57 Chevy that we drag-raced on Kell Boulevard to the limits of its 283 horses and two-barrel carb. Joe found a black man on the east side who would buy us our bottles of Southern Comfort and cherry sloe gin. The parents of Joe's girlfriends always hated him. Joe and his mother scraped together enough money for him to spend his seventeenth summer at the Culver naval school in Chicago, and he returned to us a boxer. He was sort of an effete boxer at first—the footwork they taught him resembled that of fencing—but he was fast with his hands and eager. Wayne Hudgens was a tall, strong, rawboned kid who was game for anything. I was the nervous and glum one in the backseat.

I remember clearly my first awareness of boxing. It was 1953 and I was eight years old. I was playing on the floor of my Shelton grandparents' farmhouse, and their console radio brought on the heavyweight title bout between Rocky Marciano and Jersey Joe Walcott. The exotic names gripped me, then in the static the bell rang, soon the announcer started shrieking, and in seconds it was over, a first-round knockout. Wow! Rocky Marciano. Radio was the perfect medium for boxing; imagining most fights was far more exciting than seeing them. Six years later I jumped around my bedroom and whooped and danced out in the backyard throwing punches when Ingemar Johansson bombed the senses out of Floyd Patterson. Mother came to the kitchen window and stared, wondering what had come over me now. Movie theaters back then showed films of the big fights along with the cartoons and newsreels, and to learn the magic of Ingo's right—his "*toonder* and lightning," his "hammer of Thor"—I watched a Kim Novak picture repeatedly so I could study every move of the fight on the big screen. An usher finally shooed me out.

Johansson had little else but he made the straight right hand look simple. With a dip of the right knee his shoulder, arm, and glove shot out in a perfectly straight line—down the pipe, in the jargon of the game. With a look of near boredom he knocked the heavyweight champ down seven times in one round, and like a robot Patterson kept getting up. But I had just a year of hero worship for the dimpled Swede. In their second fight Patterson knocked him so cold that for a dangerously long time the only part of Ingo moving was a quivering left foot. There is no rational defense of boxing. It regularly maims and kills its contestants, and the professional business of it is a sleazy, rotten mess. But I couldn't help myself. From the start I loved it.

Doing it, though, was another matter. In someone's yard we occasionally laced on gloves and sparred. I found that my only reliable defense was to keep sticking my left hand in the face of the other guy. The jab came to me naturally. But throwing a straight right was not as easy as it looked, and hooks and uppercuts required pivots and timing that were beyond me. To box you had to be in tremendous shape. The real mountain climb, though, was overcoming your fear. Golden Gloves tournaments were well-attended in Wichita Falls. The newspaper gave them good sports-page coverage, and sometimes there were radio broadcasts. Amateur fighters didn't wear headgears then, at least not in Texas. You climbed through those ropes almost naked: More than injury, it was a fear of very public humiliation.

Worse than any of that was the torture of the *chairs*. To get ready for a boxing match you needed to be up moving, breaking a sweat, and maybe banging your own jaw a few times to get the adrenaline flowing. But even at the state tournament in Fort Worth, Golden Glove fighters had to sit quietly in folding chairs beside their opponents. Every time a fight ended, they stood up together and then sat down in the next folding chairs. Did someone decide that instilled sportsmanship? What could you possibly say? Then some man led the other fighter away, and you climbed through the ropes in the red or blue corner, looking at a boy who all at once was an enemy, and the light was as intense as that of an August sun. And if you weren't ready to go when the bell rang, the noise would fade until the only sound you could hear was the thump of gloved fists on your bare head.

Joe Haid researched the teams and declared that we should box for the Pan American Recreation Center. The gym was fashioned from the players' clubhouse of an abandoned minor league stadium called Spudder Park. They had speed bags, a heavy bag, jump ropes, and not much else. The coach was a laconic man who listened as Joe explained how the Culver instructors had taught him to slide his right foot forward as he was throwing his right; that way he was poised to follow with the sweeping left hook. "Sailor told you that, huh," the coach grunted. "Get you knocked on your can, that's what. You've gotta set your feet beneath you."

One day he passed out medical release forms for our parents to sign. It amazes me now that he was going to let me fight the next weekend. I didn't even know how to wrap my hands. All I had done was thump the bags a couple of afternoons and run some laps around the old baseball park. I guess he was of the school that you learn by being thrown in the fire of doing it and that referees know when to jump in and stop a mismatch. Or maybe he was trying to run me off. The challenge thrilled me. This wasn't really sport, it was a fistfight, and if ever there was a way to stand my ground and prove myself, this was it. But as the tournament approached I lay awake at night certain that my fear and the ritual of the chairs would freeze me. When the bell rang I would just stand there skinny, pale, and rigid, broken out with acne, as some boy ran across the ring to knock me out. Yet I wasn't about to tell my friends I couldn't go through with it. Then one day my dad stopped me in the hall when I came in from school. He had the release form in his hand. "Your mother," he said gruffly, having lost the argument. "She doesn't want you boxing. Find something else to do."

Saved! But secretly I was ashamed; I thought I was hiding behind her skirts. Joe and Wayne ragged me about it but they knew my mother—when she said no she meant it. Mother later said she put up with the unpopularity in the household because she'd cringed for years every time a fastball sailed near my skull, she'd gone to get me out of a hospital when I'd suffered a broken bone playing football, and boxing was just too much. But I always thought her veto of boxing was more than simple fear that I might get hurt. It was a moral issue. She knew that violence stirred in that guise easily spills into the street.

Joe and Wayne forged ahead, and they had some success. Joe was a welterweight, Wayne a middleweight, and I was their entourage. Dressed like my idea of a streetfighter, in loafers, jeans, and jacket, I stood before them in the smoky arenas with my bare palms raised, catching light quick punches as they warmed up. Their wins and close defeats thrilled me but made me feel small with envy. In dramatic prose they got their names in the paper. One tournament Wayne drew a more experienced Chicano youth whose best punch was a swift left hook. Wayne caught a rhythm and his jab turned into a spear. The Chicano kid's hooks winged toward him but Wayne's long straight arm got there sooner. The fight brought the crowd to its feet and set up a bout in the finals with Gary Gorham, who had been the star tailback that fall on the Coyote football team. In that town, that credential was the closest thing to royalty. A sportswriter played up the fight as the tourney's main event: The little-known Hudgens had a chance. Joe also had a fight that night, but he was always so cavalier that his bout was all but forgotten as we drove around in the pink '57 Chevy that Saturday. We were intent on psyching up Wayne.

"Gary looked lousy in his fight! You see him? He was so tired he was about to gag on his mouthpiece."

"This ain't football, Wayne, you can do it!"

Then the time came to take their places in the chairs. Joe's opponent was an ugly, slouching boy in red trunks. Trying to make conversation, Joe asked him about school. The boy muttered that he was doing the eighth grade over. Joe remarked lightly that he was a senior.

"What grade's that?" said the boy in the red trunks.

"What grade?" said Joe.

Whatever the senior class was, the boy knew he'd never get there. But half an hour later he came out bobbing his head and shoulders and counterpunching; he whipped my friend like he was an unwanted stray. Joe kept his feet and fought back enough that the referee didn't stop it. In the third round the boy nailed him with a right and Joe was so tired he wobbled and the right he had just let go turned into kind of a lofty backhand wave, like he was shooing flies. When he stomped down the ring steps after the decision his face was puffy and fiery red, and he was in no mood to stick around and cheer for Wayne.

Moments later the bell rang and Wayne came right out to the football star, looking not at all cowed. They touched gloves and Wayne stepped about smartly, holding his gloves high against his temples. Wayne threw out a brisk jab but missed. Gorham moved his left shoulder—a feint—then dipped his knees and drove his right into Wayne's solar plexus. Oh, the worst of all woes: Wayne stood knock-kneed and defenseless, both arms around his midriff, eyes bugged out, trying to breathe. The referee glanced at Gorham, who seemed aston-ished that his coach's strategy had worked with just one punch, but he leapt forward and clubbed Wayne off his feet. The ref waved his arms and stopped it without a count. Then when poor Wayne was stand-ing in the corner trying to get the gloves off and just go hide, his dad had to climb up on the ring apron to see if he was all right. That night I drove away from the arena with my hands clenched on the wheel of the pink Chevy. In the backseat Joe sobbed bitterly with his head in the lap of his girlfriend. Oh Lord, thank you, Momma.

Thuggery's apt to find its way out, no matter how it's stirred. I was engaged by history and English classes in my first year at the hometown college, now called Midwestern State, but my parents didn't have the money to send me away to school, and I resented that. Living at home, I felt like I was missing the college experience. Impressed by the uniform and tan of a friend who came home on leave, I enlisted on a whim in the Marine Corps reserves. The re-cruiter was a tall, thin gunnery sergeant. His calculated indifference was effective. "It'll make a man out of you," he told me with a shrug.

Something would make a *man* out of me. At that I had so far failed, in my estimate. How did I measure this manhood? Sex and vio-lence were about as far as I had thought the concept through. At nineteen I was a mortified virgin. I could hardly cop a feel, at least not from any girl I wanted. In Texas towns there was a simple fix to my dilemma, even if the communities lacked their own house of ill re-pute. All boys had to do was pile in a car with a bunch of beer and drive a thousand miles or so; and in a couple of days, if they didn't kill themselves and somebody else in a head-on collision, they would come back from the Mexican border towns hungover and laid. Our nearest depot was Ciudad Acuña, across the Rio Grande from Del

Rio. *The Last Picture Show,* the movie made from Larry McMurtry's novel, was shot in his hometown of Archer City, a burg in the mesquites twenty-five miles from Wichita Falls, and it devoted a scene to the tradition of horny gringo lads and condescending paeans to Old Mexico. But to me that was just more of the Texas horseshit I was trying to escape. I wanted some girl to fuck me because she liked me, not because she was poor and I paid her. So it seemed that all I could do was wait for the light to shine on me some night and meanwhile wonder what I was doing wrong. Of the brute violence of fistfights I really didn't want more. I desired a knowing and a bearing that would discourage that violence from turning its head on me. Yet when Daddy was on my case one day, I muttered, "Time's coming when you won't wanta talk to me that way."

He looked at me closely and wearily. "Is that why you're doing this?"

Oh, hell, not really. I wanted to get along with him again. But if I could make it as a Marine, I could put all the past humiliations and failures of courage behind me. And, who knows, the year was 1964. It was a plane ticket to California. The culture was ripe with girls who had holes in their jeans, sweet musky odors, and long sunbleached hair. I might get lucky.

Six months later I was back in Wichita Falls, no less a virgin, but with thirty more pounds and a hair-trigger temper I never possessed before. Half a year of being harassed and brutalized will do that. Of course, the Marines were in the stated business of tearing us down and making us into a certain kind of men—men who would kill and risk getting killed if ordered to. Military life fit me not at all, but ironically, my impulsive bolt into its ranks proved to be my way out of Vietnam. The Gulf of Tonkin episode happened while I was in boot camp, and as the ensuing conflict raged, the warmakers decided it would cost them less political capital to fill the divisions with draftees than to call up the reserves. For six years all I had to do was show up at weekend drills once a month and two-week summer camps. And that's all I did—show up.

The oil had played out around Wichita Falls, so the refineries shut down. Daddy looked for another job and couldn't find one, so he took a company transfer to Mount Pleasant, a small town on the edge of the East Texas pines, and they made their home there for thirty years. Living in the house where I had grown up, I attended the hometown college, worked at a seed and feed store, and slouched through the Marines' requirements of my time. I doused too many nights with booze, and sometimes I went looking for trouble.

One Saturday night I found it in Denton, where I was visiting my boxing pal Wayne Hudgens. Outside his apartment I slung my leg over a motorcycle. I was just sitting on it. But from a balcony a collegian yelled, "Hey, you! Get off that bike!"

I glanced over my shoulder and fit my hands around the handlebar grips. "Sorry, Pazz," I mocked him, whatever his name was. "I was just admiring it."

"Get your ass off."

"Oh, now, Pazz."

"I mean it. Get off, it's mine!"

"Sure thing, Pazz. Fine bike you've got. *Roomba.*"

There was a thunder of footsteps on the walkway and stairs above. I wandered into Wayne's kitchen and grew aware of loud male voices at the door. "No, no," someone said. "We want 'Pazz'."

On the kitchen counter was a steel utensil that the brewing industry's pop-top aluminum cans have made obsolete. Liquor stores used to give the beer openers away; we called them church keys. Gripped inside a fist, the hook made a nasty weapon. The uproar out there wasn't Wayne's problem. I swept up the church key and lurched outside to deal with these yahoos.

I wouldn't have taken half the beating if I'd gone out there empty-handed. As the punishment continued I said some dreadfully stupid things.

"I'd like to do this again with the gloves on."

"Are you a Kappa Sig?"

I guess I wanted to slip him the grip.

Some boys never get over the horseshit years. They're rednecks in fact and toughs in their minds the rest of their lives. But if you're lucky you become someone else.

The morning after that fight in Denton, with a wretched hangover I gazed in a mirror and took long stock of myself. Under one eye was a perfectly formed shiner. I wasn't just embarrassed that I would have to go to class and my job looking like that. I was horrified, disgusted. With that church key I could have put that boy's eye out—disgraced my family—gone to prison for maiming him.

Man, grow up, I told myself. And in that regard I did. I didn't throw another punch at a man in anger for thirty-two years.

But that would be a man who held a loaded .38.

(2)

A confirmed bachelor would have to be a scarred and bitter man. No one in his right mind looks longingly at the prospect of a solitary old age. But as I passed thirty-five I thought the statute of limitations must have run out for me. As if to underscore this, one day a package arrived in the mail. My grandmother Shelton made beautiful patchwork quilts, stitching special ones as wedding gifts for her throng of grandchildren. My sister and most of my cousins were married, some of them parents, by the time they were twenty. For years Granny waited, then with an implied air of disgust she gave up and sent me the quilt without a word of comment. I had to ask my mother what this meant.

Not only was I unmarried; in those years I had lived with a woman a grand total of three months. It wasn't that I didn't seek and fall in love. I just half-expected the affairs to end soon and sadly. When I was twenty-four my first love broke my heart, ending the talk of a Russian wedding in a Kansas barn, and no doubt spared us a first divorce. I kept saying I wanted to be a writer, and she kept saying she was a practical person. After that, a procession of well-read young women yanked knots in my brain. In the prime of my youth I went impotent for years that seemed like decades. It took a good psychologist to steer me out of that mess. Eventually I stopped being so hard on myself. And though I still couldn't see why, looking at a mirror, certain women liked having me around.

I was no hermit; Austin and San Antonio, the Texas cities I had come to love, were each fifty miles away, and I had social lives in both. But with a cat and a collie, I lived on a hill overlooking a valley that local folks called Rogues Hollow—outlaws and Confederate deserters and draft-dodgers had once camped there. I had 125 acres to roam and a five-mile view. My rented house consisted of two replicated dogtrot cabins, of the old settlers' style, that were set together in a single structure. Beams of light and cold drafts of the northers came through spaces between the cedar logs. I chopped and chainsawed wood for a potbellied stove. When the day's work was done I went for runs on a winding, up-and-down county road. But I didn't think I was doing enough for my upper body. So I bought a heavy punching bag and hung it from a beam in my office. One day a friend whom I hadn't seen in several years came out for a visit. I noticed her startled frown on seeing the bag; I thought it was just the aversion to boxing that is common in her gender. But later she told me that since we had last seen each other, she had been in a mental hospital and the doctors and attendants had put her in a straitjacket. The first thing they did when they released her from those constraints was to put boxing gloves on her and lock her in a room with a punching bag just like mine. I could understand that. The bag was therapeutic for me. I might spend half an hour working on a single punch, and I began to put together combinations I had never mastered before. The jab the right the hook. The jab the right the hook. Monotonous information and reward, useful to no one but me in the privacy of that moment. But loneliness and hurt were gone, if only for a while, when the room was still except for my heavy breathing and the creak and swing of the big bag's chain.

At night coyotes yipped and yodeled all around, to the aggravation of my collie. In the fall I would look up from my typewriter and admire the spiral and cruise of migrating hawks. The sun moved around so that in winter it came up framed by the window at the foot of my bed—a lovely way to wake up in the morning. In the garden I planted two or three marijuana plants, a year's supply, right beside my tomatoes. They liked the same soil, and I didn't much care who knew about it. Near the garden I dug some horseshoe pits. A friend's divorce made a pool table available; I bought it and placed it in the middle of the living room. I used my dad's four-ten shotgun to hunt doves and kill rattlesnakes, which were plentiful. I compromised some political principles and started keeping the gun loaded. If a thief, lunatic, or rabid animal ran in the house some night, it wouldn't do any good to call 911.

I had reconnected with a rural Texas I remembered fondly as a child. I was as happy as I'd ever been. And as I accepted my bachelorhood I recognized the advantages. There is much to be said for carrying on simultaneous romances without guilt. I could be a considerate, loving companion as long as the going was good, but I had made up my mind to rid myself of emotional conflict. When it began I just walked out. More than once a woman woke up in bed to find me gone. Maybe it was a churlish thing to do, but driving away felt a lot better than the battle of words and thoughts that had kept me awake all night. I don't need this, I would tell myself. I had my work, my pets, my place in the country. Then one day the mail brought an invitation to a birthday party in San Antonio with a stylized graphic of a woman sticking her finger down her throat. "Boogie 'Til Ya Puke" was the caption. September 27, 1980. I still have the piece of cardboard, stained by the years. That was the night I met Dorothy.

.   .   .

The invitation came from Gerry and Chris Goldstein. Gerry was a top young criminal defense lawyer who had become my friend while I was working on a magazine article about a jailbreak of Americans in the bordertown of Piedras Negras, Mexico. Chris, tall, blonde, elegant, and British-born, was turning thirty. The party would begin in their home in a showcase neighborhood of Southwest Victorian architecture called the King William District. After a couple of hours it would move on a few blocks to a little bar called the Friendly Spot. I went to the party alone, and beside the staircase I sipped wine and fell into conversation with Pete Gent. Pete had been a high school and college basketball star in Michigan, then the Dallas Cowboys drafted him to run routes and catch footballs. He played well but took a horrific beating as a wide receiver for a few seasons in the sixties when coach Tom Landry was turning an expansion franchise into a winner. Pete was best known, though, for his roman à clef and movie about the experience, *North Dallas Forty*. He could be a difficult friend, but when his mood was bright, I loved the guy.

"Look what's about to happen," he said philosophically and it seemed happily as we gazed out the door at the street. "In a minute everybody's going to walk out to that sidewalk and turn left, because that's the way to the bar. But I've gotta turn right because I left my gun in the car, and I can't go off in some strange neighborhood without my gun. But the minute I turn right everybody's gonna think, Yep, look, there he goes, he's gonna get his gun out of the car. See what my life is like? You don't have to worry about those kinds of things, because you're not paranoid."

The woman who approached us wore tan pants and a fitted top that complemented short sun-tinged hair, dark lustrous eyes, and a forthright grin. Pete hugged her and they grazed cheeks, then he introduced her to me as Dorothy Brammer. "Browne," she corrected him. After two marriages and divorces she had taken back her family name. Dorothy had grown up amid a family drenched in Southern traditions, in the northeastern Texas town of Tyler. She had come to Austin and the University of Texas as a sorority girl, but she quickly fell into the thrall of classicists, archaeologists, liberal politicians, the magnificent old photographer Russell Lee, and a short, funny, recently divorced novelist named Billie Lee Brammer. He was still aglow in the praise for his 1961 novel *The Gay Place*, which was set in Austin and the ribald world of Texas politics. The book got rave reviews, and his characterization of a Texas governor known as Arthur "Goddam" Fenstemaker had been called the most revealing portrait of Lyndon Johnson—for whom Billie Lee had worked as a senate aide. Dorothy was twenty-three and Billie Lee was thirty-five when they married in 1963. John F. Kennedy had just been assassinated, and Billie Lee had a contract to write a nonfiction book about the new president, but when he and Dorothy arrived in Washington the new administration froze him out—nobody would talk to him. Some people attributed Billie Lee's failure to produce another book to this rejection by Johnson, but the LBJ theory was nonsense; his writing got lost in his zest for the pleasures and excesses of the sixties. Dropping acid and taking speed entertained him more than wrestling with a stubborn chapter. But while he stopped producing, he never stopped giving. After their divorce Billie Lee had been my friend and mentor. I was devastated when he died of an accidental overdose in 1977.

From her subsequent marriage to a handsome, liberal Texas legislator named Arthur Vance, Dorothy had a child, Lila, who was now seven. But as she and I walked toward the San Antonio bar that night I wasn't thinking about who she had been married to. I was just glad she wasn't married to anyone now. Dorothy had come down with an Austin group that included owners of a popular bar and restaurant called the Raw Deal. Fletcher Boone and Lopez Smithum were older

Wichita Falls refugees, and in time we would become close friends. But there was little opportunity to get to know them this night because both were feuding with the women they lived with. Fletcher's argument with his wife, Libby, was especially volatile. No one knew what fueled it except that Fletcher kept referring to women—all women—as "you people."

Libby became distraught enough that Fletcher sent word to Dorothy that they'd better leave. As I trailed them back toward the Goldsteins' house Libby would step into a doorway or alley and wail and sob some more, her face in her hands. San Antonio has the look of an old Mexican town. The streetlight painted a tableau of shadows and adobes, and someone in our company dubbed the walk "the Trail of Tears." At a street corner Dorothy and I sat on a curb and looked at one of the few houses that hadn't been restored. We talked about how it could be done, what colors it might be painted. I wasn't ready to let go of her company, so I offered to take them to their hotel. Lopez had been demanding a cab in a neighborhood where they're not routinely hailed on the street. With a growl he climbed in my backseat and said, "Drive, what do you mean, drive? You can't drive."

"Of course I can," I said. "I'm all right. I can drive."

Several times that night I felt as though I were being auditioned—though for what, exactly, I couldn't say. As the evening proceeded I thought surely the hotel would send someone from security or call the cops. Fletcher roared and clenched his fist at an employee he accused of mismanaging some aspect of the restaurant. Libby would brighten and smile at some story, then start sniffling and soon would be wailing in her hands again. Dorothy and Fletcher got into a playful argument and then a tussle and as he bellowed she bit a blue spot in his ample belly. The night was rowdy. An image of a cutting horse kept going through my mind. If I could just get her away from them. . . .

The next morning, as I heard it, Libby was over whatever had so upset her the night before. She seldom failed to wake up in a gay mood. "What did he say?" she giggled and hooted as they rode back to Austin. "That's so perfect." Later, another of their friends crocheted my remark on a couch pillow. "I really like you, Dorothy, but you sure have some quarrelsome friends."

Dorothy worked for the Texas chapter of the American Civil Liberties Union. When I called her at work the following Monday, she said, "I didn't know if I'd ever hear from you again."

"Yeah, you did," I answered; and so the courtship began.

I would work through the week at my country place and then head for Austin on Friday. We spent many evenings at the Raw Deal, where I caught up on the noise and conviviality I had gone without during my rural hiatus. In Austin I could spend time with writers— Bud Shrake, Gary Cartwright, Bill Wittliff—and a recent acquaintance, Ann Richards, then a local county commissioner. On Sunday the moveable feast settled on Fletcher and Libby Boone's house for food, pro football during that season, and a night of what they called "gonzo bridge."

But I was no bridge player and some nights I fidgeted, bored. There were significant differences between Dorothy and me. Each of her marriages had lasted seven years, while my experience in living with a woman amounted to one short summer. She was four years older than me, and most of her focus was on being a working single mother. Dorothy tried not to impose her lifestyle on mine. On occasion she came out to the cabin on the hill. I loved this place and expected others to like it. One time a young history professor and his wife, a lawyer, came down from Austin with Dorothy; we were going out for a night in San Antonio. The academic took in the punching bag, the pool table, and the rest. "Hmm," he said. "All this needs is some mounted testicles."

I joined in the laughter, but the wisecrack stung.

Another time a norther was blowing through, and I had the stove crammed with wood and ablaze. Still it was freezing. Served with the red wine and fresh bread she brought from town, I made a favorite winter soup called *caldo verde*—white beans, stew beef, rounds of sausage, tomatoes, onions, and shreds of spinach. "Seduction dinner," she murmured later, as we snuggled in the warmth of Granny's quilt, a cat curled against our feet.

Without warning she could turn on me, too. "Look, I'm not into going steady," she said icily one night. "I need to know if this is going anywhere." I gaped at her, stunned, but she had nailed me. I was satisfied with how it had been going, and I would have let it go on that way indefinitely, I suppose. It was my passive nature. Another night she looked at me quizzically and said, "Are you gonna break my heart?"

The matter came to a head on a trip to the Mexican border. In those days it was still possible to catch a train from Austin to Laredo. The extended Raw Deal family booked several cars, piled in books, kids, toys, and suitcases, and took off for another weekend of raucous behavior. I told Dorothy I would pass up the train ride but would drive down there. We all stayed at a nice hotel in Laredo. It had a good swimming pool for the kids, and late in the afternoon a marimba band came out and played. But there was little else to do on the Texas side of the border, so we roamed back and forth across the Rio Grande bridge. "Taxi, taxi!" drivers tried to entice us on the other side. "Wanta see some pretty girls?" *Cabrito*—barbecued kid goat—is a specialty of northern Mexico cuisine. In windows of the restaurants, the grilled naked goats were presented like crucifixions. On sidewalk pallets of cardboard, dark-skinned women with infants held up a hand begging.

Our gang included an attorney named Hugh Lowe and his wife Claudette. Dorothy and Claudette had been roommates their freshman year at the university. They often went to the border as collegians.

Prostitutes roamed the bars in downtown Nuevo Laredo. On one of these visits some Texas boy made a lewd remark to dark-haired and dark-eyed Claudette, mistaking her for one of the whores. Claudette's date jumped up and set off an old-fashioned barroom brawl. Dorothy and Claudette ran for the tourist wagon of their favorite driver, Shorty. His gaunt horse took off at a slow trot but a Mexican cop fired a warning shot over their heads. The gringo collegians spent that night in jail.

From the town where I grew up, it was 390 miles to Ciudad Acuña and its set of whorehouses. Neither I nor my friends ever had a car that reliable, so I missed out on the Texas horseshit of going to "Boys Town," as the red-light districts are called. As an adult I was still uneasy on the Mexican side of the border. Hugh Lowe spoke Spanish well, having grown up around Mexican laborers in South Texas. When we crossed the bridge in my car one night, I let Hugh drive. On a gutted road that rocked wildly he took us to Nuevo Laredo's Boys Town. It proved to be a compound regulated by the government and patrolled by soldiers with rifles slung across their shoulders. The *putas* lined up for sad inspection in front of shacks that contained a bed but looked like little more than two-hole privies.

Bordertown Mexico was as ugly as a dog pound, I thought, but that weekend I explored it happily with Dorothy and her friends. Until the last night. With the marimbas ringing beside the pool, she and I emerged from our room abuzz with tactile and emotional sensation. I thought I could feel every inch of my skin. As the night wore on, one round of margaritas was followed by another. Sometime that night she and I fell back from others while crossing the bridge. "Dorothy," I blurted, "let's get married."

She gazed at the darkness and shook her head sadly. "You're too young," she said, "and you don't have any money."

She had a child to consider, it was true that I lived in self-imposed poverty, and my prospects as a writer were far from certain. She had already been through that once with Billie Lee. And what were the odds of this marriage I proposed? It would pair a woman who had given marriage her best shot twice and a man who had been living alone, essentially, since he left the care of his mother. Still, one minute Dorothy had me feeling that I could vault to the stars. The next minute I wanted to jump off the Rio Grande bridge.

All night I stayed awake or mostly awake, and I helped Dorothy and Lila catch the five a.m. train. As the coach pulled away Dorothy and I continued staring at each other, and, without saying anything, asked: What were we going to do with this? With each other? I went back to the hotel and slept until late morning, then threw my bag in the car and checked out. I was going back to my country place where I belonged. I didn't need this. But the shell inside me cracked. On the interstate highway I was about twenty miles out of Laredo when the tears started pouring, and I couldn't stop them. "Oh, god damn, god damn," I said. Up ahead was the immigration checkpoint, and walking out to greet me and study me rather closely was an agent of the U.S. Border Patrol.

In Texas we walk on ground that was torn from Mexico, and our myth was born in those days. The nineteenth-century adventures are an epic that Texans have every right to be proud of. All the wild and violent history forged a togetherness and attachment to place that residents of many American states seem to lack, and perhaps that makes us richer. But in the swagger and bluster important parts of the story get left out. The tale that most embodies the Texas mythos is the stand and fall of the Alamo, a mission turned fortress where a large Mexican army slaughtered all but a few rebels in 1836. Weeks later, when the Texans surprised the Mexican soldiers in a coastal wetland, their cries of "Remember the Alamo!" were about bloodlust and vengeance, not honor. Texas chauvinists like to boast about the success of our revolution and our past as an independent nation, as big as Spain or France. But the Republic of Texas was bankrupt in a decade, and most of its citizens longed for annexation by the United States, which came in 1848. Mexico never recognized the sovereignty of Texas, much less a border at the Rio Grande. The United States' calculated rescue of Texas guaranteed the Mexican War. Though the war inflicted horrid losses on both sides, it ended quickly; uniformed gringos imposed martial law on Mexico City. All Texans have heard of the Alamo. But few know of the Mexico City schoolboys, martyrs in their country, who fought as cadets against the *norteamericano* invaders, and jumped to their deaths from a citadel rather than surrender.

The spoils of that war were not just the certification of America's claim to Texas and a border at the Rio Grande. For fifteen million dollars and assumption of some Mexican debts, the United States seized New Mexico, Arizona, California, Utah, Wyoming, Nevada, and a part of Colorado; American dominion was at last contiguous from the Atlantic to the Pacific. Mexico lost half its territory to the rampage that the Americans justified as their Manifest Destiny. Mexico's wound was deep and bitter, and it festers still. In Texas the lore has infused a common belief that we're twice-born Americans, heirs to two revolutionary wars, two declarations of independence. When we're in Mexico, we often behave like we own it. The allure that Mexico holds for Texans is almost genetic. We go down there large in stature, loud of voice, flashy and arrogant with our dollars. Danger real or imagined is part of the thrill. Of all the gringos, Texans are resented most. However high and mighty we perceive ourselves to be, to many Mexicans we are still *bárbaros del norte*. Barbarians of the north.

Dorothy and I weathered our crisis of Laredo, and later that summer I won a grant for the novel I was working on. It was just a couple of thousand dollars, but that was enough to float a vacation. Apart from a few crossings to Mexican bordertowns, I had never traveled outside the U.S. It wasn't an aversion to other languages and cultures; I just thought penetrating them would be so complicated and hard. Dorothy took me in hand, and soon we were on a plane to the Mexican resort of Puerto Vallarta.

Shrouded with the rainy season's fog, lush green mountains rose sharply from the Pacific's sand and surf and the cobblestone streets and red-tiled roofs of the town strung along an estuary called the Bay of Banderas. Puerto Vallarta caught on with American tourists after the much-publicized filming of 1964's *The Night of the Iguana*, starring Richard Burton and Ava Gardner. Director John Huston owned a house a few kilometers down the coast in a hamlet called Mismaloya. The moviemaking set off a media frenzy because Elizabeth Taylor flew down to carry on an affair with the still-married Burton. Two decades later, Dorothy and I sat on Mismaloya's quiet beach eating delicate fish smoked on sticks by a man who had put up a lean-to and built a fire in the sand. The wonder, I thought, was that Huston bought the rights to Tennessee Williams' play and brought all those people to so color-drenched a place and then shot the picture in black and white.

We rented a Volkswagen Safari that was square and pokey and had no top. Past Mismaloya that day we climbed the narrow road to a bar called Chico's Paradise. It overlooked a waterfall and rapids that crashed over polished light gray stone. We drove higher until night fell and we were enclosed in fog. Dorothy wore shorts and a striped bow-necked cotton shirt. She clasped her hands between her knees, threw back her head, and yelled, "I'm so happy!" Down the beach from our hotel that night we rolled in the surf, arms and legs entwined, then lay gasping and laughing in the sand and froth as the tide pulled the water back.

Another night I put on my rumpled best and she wore sandals and a dress. We went to a little cafe that had become our favorite. It had a balcony and view of the beachfront street, a plaza, and the ocean. The cafe was named for its owner, who styled himself The Chicago Kid. The owner made it to Golden Chicago, where jobs were so plentiful, then with his small fortune had come back home. He brought us wine and hard rolls and the best black bean soup I'd ever tasted. Below us a large truck and trailer came inching along the narrow street on the water's edge. The driver fought the wheel frantically and swung his head back and forth to his mirrors, for his turn around the little plaza looked impossible. From the truck rose a strange musical tinkling. As the driver swung his rig around on the cobblestone, we saw that the trailer was loaded with countless crates of Coca-Cola.

A small troupe of mariachis approached our table. Dorothy asked if they knew "La Malagueña." The leader smiled and touched the brim of his hat. The fiddler played a prelude and the guitarists set up a procession of chopping chords. The singers rose to their toes to hit the high notes. Though I understood none of the lyrics, it was one of the prettiest songs I'd ever heard. I asked Dorothy what it was about.

She laughed and said, "Love and death. They all are."

Toward the end of our stay we boarded a large boat for a two-hour ride across the mirrorlike bay. Every day the boat unloaded tourists into dugouts whose oarsmen paddled them ashore at a village called Yelapa. The bay water was clear enough for good snorkling, and the tourists scattered through the village, buying what few keepsakes village artisans had for sale. Many came to a waterfall and swimming hole rimmed with ferns. Then at four o'clock the big boat blew a blast of its horn, and most of the tourists were oared back out for their return to the luxury of Puerto Vallarta. Boys from the village ran to the swimming hole and dived to the bottom, coming up with cigarette lighters, rings, and coins spilled from the pockets of the tourists.

In a hotel that consisted of a few thatched-roof huts with mosquito nets and cold-water showers, Dorothy and I spent the night. We sat around the bar, which in the evening was powered by a generator, and ate the fish, beans, and tortillas the kitchen provided. Digging our toes in the sand, we sat at a table playing gin until the bar closed. In our *palapa* we lolled in the same narrow bed for a while, then we parted and set our pillows and arranged our mosquito nets just so. Bugs fluttered and mired themselves in the tallow of the candles. Over the constant gentle splashing of the surf, quiet voices carried from the village.

In Mexico every defense I had put up against Dorothy fell away. Being in love was not new to me, but trusting someone was. I found room for sharing in the masculine citadel I had so long inhabited. And for years that followed, it enchanted us that we had found that happiness and hope in Mexico. Dorothy, who had traveled far abroad, always told me that Mexico was the most foreign place she had ever been. Now it was our place, full of rich secrets known only to us. Mexico is a blend of the mysterious and surreal. And its exoticism was so close, so convenient: to shore up our love and break from the everyday, all we had to do was hop on a plane. Let's go to Mexico—despite the heritage of enmity, for all manner of Texans that has been pleasure's call.

That next morning in Yelapa, before the big boat carrying more tourists arrived, we rented horses from a stable near the beach. A river ran through the village and emptied into the bay. We rode the horses along the river, passing the home of a campesino now and then, gazing at the attempts of slash-and-burn farming on the steep slopes. They hacked out the jungle, then without much success tried to grow corn. Higher up the river ran much faster, and the trail led to a ford. The nags eyed the high water, snorted, rattled their bridles, and refused to cross. But that was all right, because all around us, caressing our arms and necks and faces, was a storm of purple, blue, and gold butterflies.

One morning in 1989, I sat in the garage of our rented house on Possum Trot, waiting for a truck from the Salvation Army. Dorothy, Lila, and I were moving to our new home on Eleventh Street, and we had separated the junk from discards that might have some value. I rubbed my hand over the canvas of the punching bag that had hung in my cabin at Rogues Hollow. The bag had sat in storage so long that it had grown mold. I kept thinking someday, somewhere, I might have a place to hang it. But I couldn't envision one at the new house. Actually I could, but Dorothy was not going to let me hang it under the roof of a structure urbane enough to be called a loggia. Reluctantly and wistfully, I let the bag go. The charity would find a place where kids would use it. I thought I was through with boxing.

An architectural stylist had built our new house in stages, expanding it from its beginnings as a hunting cabin in the woods after World War II. Austin had grown around and far beyond it, leaving a little-known compound, lovely but eccentric, prone to downhill flooding, problematic to maintain. At eleven Lila was in a state of high anxiety about the move; the little house on Possum Trot was the only home she could remember clearly. But buying a house was a milestone for us. Both of Dorothy's previous marriages had lasted seven years. Various friends spoke of a seven-year marital jinx as if it were real. A couple of months earlier we had celebrated our seventh anniversary, and in taking on the mind-boggling mortgage, we were making a statement of confidence and faith in ourselves. Saying boo and begone to that spook.

Dorothy was forty-one when we married, and except for one false alarm, the height of which was a tender, sunbright drive in the country one Easter Sunday, we gave no thought to having children. Maybe we should have. Many times we wished we had. I had never been one of those men who thought he had to pass on his family name and replicate himself with a son. In fact I would have preferred a daughter; the little girls of several women friends had charmed and taken to me along the way. Well, in this marriage here was my chance.

I remember clearly the first time I saw Lila. In a darkened room she was asleep on a bed. She had on jeans and a red pullover, and with her mouth opened slightly she slept with the intent and totality that only children have. She was blonde, and it was striking how much she resembled both her mom and dad. I watched her a long time before I backed away from the door. Trying to win her over, I assigned myself the daily chore of getting her off to school. I packed her lunch, made her favorite breakfast of eggs scrambled with cheese, and though I couldn't intrude on her closeness with her dad—and didn't want to, for Arthur became a good friend—the practical task of rearing her fell to me. I bought her a glove and played catch with her in the backyard the spring she decided to play Little League. She didn't really want to play baseball; it was because a lady in the principal's office told her Little League was just for boys. She spent that night somewhere else. She called me and for the first time said the words, "I love you." I hung up with my cheeks tingling.

Dorothy burned out at the ACLU and took a year off, growing a fine garden. Then she went to work for her old friend Ann Richards, who was now Texas's state treasurer. At the 1988 Democratic National Convention, Ann made her famous keynote speech lampooning the elder George Bush: "Poor George, he can't help it—he was born with a silver *foot* in his mouth." The speech and exposure vaulted her past rival Texas Democrats. Those were giddy times for us. Dorothy and I worked long hours as volunteers in her 1990 campaign for governor, which Ann won handily. Her opponent was a West Texas oilman and rancher who refused to shake her hand, boasted in rodeo slang that he was going "to head her and rope her," joked that rape victims should "just lay back and enjoy it." Ann's election was a rebuke of the time-worn Texas horseshit. She set about rattling the good old boy networks that dominated government in Texas, startling one bunch by naming Dorothy, with her civil liberties past, to high posts in the criminal justice division. Every Christmas Eve, Dorothy, Lila, and I had dinner at the governor's mansion. It was fun while it lasted. Ann was a popular figure, but the suburban electorate poised to dominate Texas politics was overwhelmingly Republican, and George W. Bush had mobilized to prove it. In 1994 he ran a focused, disciplined race, while from the start Ann displayed little of the fire that had driven her against the bumbling cowboy. In her concession speech Ann looked almost relieved. The rest of the nation perceived it as an upset, a backwash of the anti-Clinton tidal wave in that year's congressional elections, but Bush was smooth and hungry—he already had his eyes on the presidency. And even on the losing end it was hard to miss the irony. Ann had made her career with a tongue-lashing of one man and now that man's son had brought her down.

Dorothy scrambled to find another job in government, and I went on staff at *Texas Monthly*, thinking we couldn't afford two free-lancers in the family. After a few months my old friends laid me off in a downsizing. It seemed it would always be like that for us. Dorothy would be up in her work, I would be down in mine, then the situation would reverse; hardly ever were we both up at the same time. But our marriage maintained a fairly even keel. It was based on an equal division of labor. She bought the groceries and cooked one week, I did it the next, and whoever didn't cook cleaned up the kitchen. Sometimes my mopes and her temper got between us. "Passion" was Dorothy's favorite word. Her way of saying it vexed me. I was who I was. I couldn't maintain the intensity and tinge of craziness that drove us when we were falling in love, and the way I heard it, few couples could. I wasn't always easy to live with. Neither was she. Who is?

Storms of adolescence blew through our lives. For a time Lila and I fell into stereotypical roles of conflict—the raging teary child, the resented and resentful stepparent—and Dorothy didn't always help. In the middle of some row I would make a pronouncement. "Forget that," Dorothy would say, then go on with her take on the matter, as-serting rights of guidance to her own child. I would clamp my jaws. One time in the heat of our strife Lila yelled at me, "You are ugly . . . you are stupid . . . and you are boring!" *Boring?* What a well-aimed thrust! At the worst of it an alarm clock sailed out of her room at my head; one night I put her out of the house barefoot and made her walk to a friend's home a few blocks away. You are doing this, I thought, about as badly as it could be done. "Wait and see," said Dorothy. "The day will come when you and Lila are very close." It was hard to believe. But during one argument Lila shouted: "Well, I *am* your daughter!" It stopped me cold and shook me up. I didn't say another word.

Dorothy and I worked hard during the week but guarded our weekends jealously, for then we pushed the work and bill-paying aside and reclaimed our intimacy. Having been a bachelor so long, I won-dered when I repeated my marriage vow if I would really be faithful. But I was faithful, if not always attentive. The longer we lived to-gether, the more knowing and attuned we became in the act of love. We laughed, and how we traveled. With Lila and a friend, we went on a six-week ramble through England, France, and Italy. Then Dorothy and I went to the Pyrenees and Paris, another trip found us far off the beaten track in Ecuador, and then she took me to her beloved Greece. When the funds were tight, without hesitation we headed for Mexico.

Between foreign adventures, I was as stressed and vain as most of the forty-something men I met clumping along the running trails in Austin. More than concerns about health and mortality, those twin spurs kept me working out. I lifted weights, and on free afternoons I got reasonably hooked on pickup basketball games at the YMCA. I enjoyed the guys who kept that going, but my lack of skills embarrassed me; I couldn't dribble or shoot. I could rebound and feed passes to the shooters, though, so I had some value when the sides were chosen. "Man, you can really hack," complained one youth after I fouled him on an attempted layup. That was nothing to be proud of. "You are hurting people, Jan," a graybeard reamed me out one day, "and people aren't liking it." I didn't like him much, now that he brought it up, but I got the message. I scorned the guys who took the floor in a macho huff; and now I stood accused of that, when in fact I was just strong and clumsy. Then I got hurt. I pissed blood for a year and underwent a scary battery of tests in search of some cancer, before the bleeding abruptly stopped and the doctors came back to their first diagnosis—a hard whack in the kidneys while playing hoops. "Basketball's the worst," said Norman Chenven, my friend and doctor of many years. "And softball. All these old farts running like they think they're still twenty."

Why persist at these pointless games? Why not just grow old gracefully? Vanity and escape are part of it. But growing up on playing fields gave me a drive that is hard to satisfy by sedentary games or work. The challenge needs to involve some kind of difficult physical activity. The writer and editor who first published my writing was a like-minded man named Greg Curtis. Though we had our periodic differences, Greg had been my friend since the birth of *Texas Monthly* in 1973. Twenty-five years later he and his wife were hosting a Christmas party for the art and editorial staffs, favored freelancers, and whomever else they wanted to see, and I ran into an old friend, Billy Gammon. Billy was a fight fan, and during a visit out to my cabin years before he and I had banged the bag a little, fooling around. Now Billy pulled Greg and me aside and told us he was doing something that was about the most fun he'd ever had. He was working out in Richard Lord's boxing gym.

I was aware of Richard, though I never saw him fight. Living in Austin, he had run up a record of 28–1 as a professional super feather-weight in the 1980s. The Austin base no doubt hurt him. Austin had no tradition and standing in boxing; despite the city's size—about a million people counting the suburbs—it didn't even host a Golden Gloves tournament. All sports in Austin were dwarfed by the pro-grams and teams of the University of Texas, which did not include boxing. Like many of its residents, Richard had come to Austin to get a degree from the university, and he did. He hoped to compete in the Olympics, but that dream didn't pan out, and he got off to a late start as a pro. Richard could punch, but the hallmark of his career was his outrageous conditioning. He reached the top ten in one world rank-ing, but he never caught on with the major promoters, he couldn't see a world title fight coming, so he hung it up with his health and senses intact. Now he was a terrific trainer, Billy said, and his gym was the hottest workout joint in town. I could tell by the narrowing of Greg's eyes that he was going to be out there the next week.

It took me a little longer—in fact more than a year. I still watched boxing. During those years I seized on certain fighters—Nicaragua's Alexis Arguello, Fort Worth's Donald Curry—and celebrated their triumphs and lamented their downfalls. But doing it myself seemed like an eon behind me. I had lost touch with my high school boxing friends Wayne Hudgens and Joe Haid. I thought of those solitary hours banging the bag in my cabin at Rogues Hollow and wondered if I'd someday pay for it with arthritis in my hands. Still, I had grown bored with my workout routines. Finally I made a date one summer afternoon at Richard Lord's Gym. Billy Gammon normally worked out in the mornings, but he took off to introduce me and get me started. I was forty-five minutes late, and he gave me an irritated look when I appeared. He thought I'd stiffed him. I had been driving around, nervous, thinking this couldn't be the place, and if it were, I might reconsider.

Tucked off beside one of the ugliest intersections in town, the gym consisted of a cramped, metal-sided bin on the back row of units that other tenants used for storage and small manufacturing. It had a fourteen-foot ring with some patches of duct tape and blood splatters, three heavy bags, several speed bags bolted to the walls, cracked mirrors for shadowboxing, a few dumbbells and barbells, a tiny dressing room and toilet, and an office in shambles. A hodgepodge of fight posters and photographs filled the walls. Rock and roll blared from a boombox. Lowering toward a nearby runway, jets roared and beat the air, their shadows flitting in a skylight and slipping across the floor. Dust-caked insulation clung to the walls and ceiling, but a prominent thermometer registered 102 degrees. "Welcome," said Richard, who proved to be a small, muscular, bowlegged man with short hair and a braided ponytail. "We'll turn up the air-conditioning here in a minute."

I had missed the rounds of skipping rope and stretching and abdominal exercises which Richard led at the start of his group sessions. "You know how to wrap your hands?" he asked.

"No, not really," I said. He showed me how to wrap rolls of red cotton cloth around my knuckles, my thumbs, and the bones in my hands, tying them off with Velcro around the wrists. I told him about my false start as a Golden Glover and the little sparring I'd done in the Marines. He told me he had started fighting in the Golden Gloves when he was five. His dad, he said, was a Dallas manager and trainer named Doug Lord; he had a world welterweight champion named Curtis Cokes in the sixties. Curtis Cokes! I had seen Cokes knock out some guy in the main event of a boxing card in Wichita Falls—the only pro fights I'd ever seen in person. He watched me paw at and miss the speed bags a couple of rounds, then he put some tattered sixteen-ounce gloves on my hands and assigned me to one of the heavy bags. Maybe I impressed him some, but I started out throwing as hard as I could, and at the end of just one three-minute round I was gasping and drenched with sweat. After a couple more rounds Richard looked at my running shoes and told me to take them off and climb in the ring in my sock feet. When I stepped through the ropes he picked up a medicine ball and held it against his shoulder. "Aim for the middle," he said, "and watch what you're doing. I'm not wearing my mouthpiece. If you hit me I'm gonna hit you back."

I thought I was in fair shape from the basketball, weights, and running, but in less than an hour of this I was stumbling and faint. Richard said the hand wraps cost five bucks and told me where I could buy some ring shoes. I looked inside my bag to pay him for the wraps and cursed. "My wallet's gone," I said, casting a bitter, accusing glance at the others in the gym. Rip off the old fool. "I should have known better. . . ."

"Well, it's never happened here before," said Richard in his slow, deliberate manner. "I'll get it back for you. You got my word."

Moments later I trudged back in the gym and apologized. I'd left the damn wallet in the car. Dorothy had a notion of a "third place," where friends fell into an important communal order outside family and work. It could be a church, a bar like TV's *Cheers* and our expired

and sorely missed Raw Deal in Austin, a plaza where people of Medi-
terranean tradition gathered for nightly paseo. Or it could be a gym. I
had just found mine.

B asketball was forgotten; boxing was my new addiction. Once
more I fell under the spell of its jargon and tall tales, the body
punchers and cut men and gloriously corrupt promoters. And I loved
the unspoken noise, too. The pops of the big bags, the snaps of jump
ropes striking the floor, the "ta-*tun*-ta-ta-*tun*-ta-ta" when someone
skilled was hitting the speed bag, the sharp, horsey snorts of breath.
Richard was always grooming two or three pros, but it was mostly an
amateur and workout gym. About a third of his clients were young
men who had some degree of ability and ambition. Another third
were women, most of whom were young, and to my initial surprise,
quite a few sparred. Having less power, they worked harder on technique, and some were quite good. Richard was at the vanguard of the
emerging sport of women's boxing, which made him unpopular with
some traditionalists. Amy Miller owned the city's most popular chain
of ice cream parlors. Before she gave it up to have a baby, she worked
out with stamina and skill that awed me, and she had one pro fight,
which she lost by decision to the woman Richard later married. Lori
Lord was a nurse who retired from boxing then got back in shape and
won a world title *after* she had their baby. People were always surprised
by how feminine they were. Anissa "the Assassin" Zamarron was a shy
young woman who didn't know how pretty she was. She looked better in the gym than all but two or three of the men. I had a workout
shirt that said, "I'm not ashamed to admit Anissa kicked my ass."

The other third of Richard's clients were my peers, the geezers.
Billy Gammon, Greg Curtis. A handsome Chicano man whose name
I never learned, for he was deaf and didn't speak. Vince Otto, an FBI
agent, was called into action at the siege of the Branch Davidians, but

I knew him as a skilled light heavyweight who could coach me while sparring with me, which is hard to do. Nobody liked the loudmouths and know-it-alls. Mike Hanchard was a black political science professor, a star academic who would move on from Texas to Harvard and Northwestern—but also a bruising 230-pounder who in his first sparring session held his own with a professional heavyweight. I proposed sparring to Mike; I thought I knew the secret of fighting left-handers. (Straight right hand every time he wiggles.) Mike politely deflected those conversations. He was twenty years younger and forty pounds heavier, and he didn't want to hurt me.

All these people were my friends, and boxing was our contradictory bond. "*Greg* did that to you?" said Dorothy one Saturday when I walked in with a swollen lip. I laughed, not expecting her to understand. We hardly ever talked about our jobs or professions at the gym. It broke an unspoken rule. For an hour or two we disappeared into our bodies and our concentration and release, finding pleasure in a governed kind of violence.

Thirty years too late, I was learning how to fight. The Marines' schooling had revolted me—gouge the other man's eyes and grab him by the balls—although of course that wasn't meant to be sporting. From Danny, a trainer and ex-pro who hung out at Richard's, I learned the trick of giving my jaws some clouts when the gloves were laced on, to get ready. I breathed in deeply and with a whoosh of exhalation snapped my gloves at the floor, unlimbering my elbows and shoulders. It also drove my heartbeat up, and paradoxically, with that came the calm I was seeking. Which is not to say I wasn't scared. More than anything I dreaded the prospect of stopping a hard blow with my nose.

When the bell rang and Richard stepped out of the way, a force I couldn't begin to control barged straight at me and drove me to the ropes. "I like your style," one of the other men said. "It's kind of laid back." He meant it as praise, but in boxing that's not much commendation. Once I'd weathered the opening burst, I either tied the guy up or, as I learned more, fought my way out of the corner. Because it was hard to bend my knees, I stood too straight. My reflexes were too far gone to try slipping punches with movements of my head. But I became pretty good at parrying the blows, blocking or deflecting them with my gloves and forearms. Still, my best defense was the left jab. I remember the first hard jab I landed. The younger man who seconds earlier had bulled me to the ropes went marching backward with this consternated *frown* on his face.

I didn't spar as often as some of my friends did. It was hard for me to jump out of bed for Richard's Saturday morning sessions—one of the best of our crowd, a heavyweight named Sean, likened it to waking up and drinking a martini—and it meant I had to forgo a night of the drinks and wine that were part of the weekend set-asides Dorothy and I held in reserve. Sparring with a hangover was unthinkable. In size and age, Greg was my logical sparring partner. He was more experienced and always in better shape. If someone had been scoring I think he would have won or drawn every time we stepped in the ring. He embarrassed me once, turning me around and leaving me trapped in the tangle of my feet and the claustrophobic headgear, trying to find out where the hell he was. And even if it was just a freelance assignment, he was always, to some extent, my boss. How would he take it if I really went after him? I never found out.

In the spring the gym grew crowded for a few weeks. Richard padded his income by tutoring college boys, most of whom were in fraternities, for an extramural Fight Night that benefited a charity. I ignored most of the youths because I disliked the banal talk. Without being mean about it, Greg preyed on them. He would leave the office early and come out in the afternoons, knowing there might be, as he murmured to me once, "some action." Phi Delts and KAs were shocked to find themselves being belted around the ring by this tall old guy. One time Richard told me to gear up and work into the rotation. Greg and I faced off, and though Richard had been drilling the college boys with two-minute rounds, without telling us he let Greg and me go three minutes. "Look at these old heavyweights!" he cried as we went toe-to-toe at the bell. Afterward we slapped gloves and I threw my arm around Greg's shoulders. It was the best round I ever fought.

In the pantheon of boxing's heavyweights my boyhood hero Ingemar Johansson had diminished to a cipher. Knocked out in two of his three fights with Floyd Patterson, he had finished his career quietly in Europe, a one-fight champion lost in the shadows of subsequent greats and near-greats—Liston, Ali, Frazier, Foreman, Holmes, Tyson, Holyfield. But another nostalgist found Johansson painting a boat in Florida and wrote a piece about him in *Esquire*. He was still a national hero in Sweden, his son said, and that made it hard for him to live there. The old fighter had little to say until the writer asked him how it felt to land one of those right hands. Johansson grinned, patted his fist against his palm, and said, "Ah. That's the best."

One afternoon when Greg and I sparred, I landed my single hardest punch. I threw the right without thinking about it, and it landed where I would have wanted—in the middle of his forehead, against the thickest padding of his headgear. The jolt went through my bones and joints all the way to my jaw. "*Whooo*," he said in compliment, stepping back with a shake of his head.

"Got you with it, didn't he?" said Richard. "You'd been watching it, hanging out with it, and you got complacent." I thought, the Swede's right, it is the best. Later that week I sent Greg a note. I signed it Ingo.

In boxing there's a sorry tradition called the smoker. Best described in Ralph Ellison's *Invisible Man*, kids from one ethnic underclass or another box for town barons who smoke cigars and toss the fighters coins even as they laugh and jeer. I witnessed a variation on this spectacle one spring night. Richard had a Chicano pro whose career had stalled because he kept getting cut. The fighter was trying to make another go of it, and Richard had put him on the card of an invitation-only affair at a hotel in the posh northwest section of town. Richard had some complimentary passes, and he said Muhammad Ali was supposed to be there. "Oh, bullshit," I said.

Richard shrugged. "What they say. They're flying him in."

All the nonboxing people were going to be wearing tuxedos, he added, so we needed to dress well. I put on a suit that night and drove out to the hotel, where a doorman eyed my pass and nodded me through. In a chandeliered room a boxing ring had been set up. What we saw were real pro fights. The fighters had passed physicals and made weight, their bouts had been approved by the state boxing commission, and the outcomes would count on their records. But there were no sportswriters, no photographers, and almost no real fans. In formal wear, men and women stood about drinking cocktails. The men selected cigars from trays carried about by sleekly dressed young women, lit them, and puffed them with the air of big shots. A few studied the fights put on for their pleasure, but most ignored them. They were caught up in their conversations, and I saw several men who pointedly kept their back turned to the ring. When a fight ended and the referee raised a winner's hand, there was only a smattering of applause. But damned if it weren't true: Across the room, seated at a table beside an Austin city councilman, patiently signing autographs, was the most popular human of my generation, Muhammad Ali.

Our contingent from the gym was strung along a wall, taking it in. As faces in the crowd registered I realized what this was. Politics in Austin was ruled by one continual battle: environmentalists against the developers. The builders were having their way in the doing of deals and granting of permits, but they had been taking a beating in public image and at the ballot box. The councilman seated beside Ali wanted to be the mayor, and these folks decked out in tuxes were his power base—the movers and shakers of real estate. If asked, they would have said they were just enjoying the company of their friends, a night away from home. But they were raising money and psyching themselves up to take control of the city, for once and for all.

I was there just for the boxing and the glimpse of a hero. I stood watching the show when a face appeared before me that I knew at once. Charles and I had been schoolmates in Wichita Falls, graduates of the same high school class. We had never been friends exactly, but he knew of my writing and had called me when he moved to Austin, some years back. "What are you doing now, Charles?" I had asked him. "I'm a real estate broker," he drawled. Great, join the crowd. We never had the lunch we proposed but we ran into each other cordially now and then. Now Charles told me of a common friend who had recently dropped dead of a heart attack while jogging. I winced and shook my head. As the hometown chat continued I kept glancing beyond Charles at the fighters in the ring. He noticed the movement of my eyes and stepped so that his face remained in front of mine, blocking the view. He knew what he was doing, and it annoyed me.

"A lot of us don't think much of this," Charles said, moving his head toward the boxers in the ring.

"Then why do it?"

He smiled and didn't answer. "Yeah," he reminisced, "I remember the time Coach Mercer made you and me put on the gloves in gym class at Zundy Junior High. I busted you in that big old nose and you yanked the gloves off and said, 'Boy, I don't want any more of this.' "

"I don't remember that, Charles," I said truthfully. And added, "You wouldn't want to do that now."

"Pugs," he said with a curl of his lip, and moved on.

Richard's fighter won or lost, I can't remember. It didn't matter, because that was his last fight. Richard squirmed to the head of the line and got his picture taken with Muhammad Ali. I leaned against the wall near the exit with Billy Gammon and Vince, the FBI agent. I was about to leave when the councilman took the mike and voiced a brief tribute to Ali. There was a round of applause, then Ali came walking slowly and carefully around the ring. A young man in a suit walked close beside him, poised to catch his elbow if he stumbled. The builders and realtors made way for him as they would for any cripple, some staring, some smiling, others ducking their heads and looking away.

"Aaa*lii!* Aaa*lii!*" I raised the shout he had heard the world around, and others in our bunch joined in.

Ali veered sharply and walked right to us. As he nodded woodenly his gaze roved from face to face. Parkinson's allowed his smile to barely move his lips, but light and humor still danced in his eyes. His hand tremored as he held it out to me. It was a very soft handshake, but when I presumed to grip his bicep it felt a lot firmer than mine. Billy Gammon clapped him on the shoulder and said, "Go get 'em, Champ."

A man named Jim Brewer worked out at the gym on occasion. In his sixties, Jim lived in Los Angeles and came to Austin to visit his mother. He had a boxer's flattened nose and worked the bags with obvious skill, though he took it easy on his hands. Jim and I struck up conversations and a casual friendship as we took breathers. He told me that he couldn't get anywhere fighting out of Austin, so he had moved to Las Vegas and fought fifty-odd pro fights, then he gave it up to be an actor; he said he worked out now at a great gym on one of the studio lots. On Richard's wall was a photograph of a younger Jim in bandana and boots, standing beside John Wayne in similar attire. I asked around and found out his stories were true. In Austin he had been known as "Gentleman Jim." He moved around town with a big entourage and often got the starring roles in local theater. The photo with John Wayne was taken on the set of *The Alamo*. I always liked to see Jim coming; he was my biggest boxing fan. "Man, you had it," he told me once. "You were a little slow, but you had power in both hands, every punch. You could have been a good small heavyweight."

The first summer I started working out at Richard's, Abel Davila was another beginner. He had been a high school football player, and he weighed about 170 pounds when we started. But while my weight stayed the same as I hardened into this kind of shape, pounds fell off Abel. We often worked out with each other in the early days, circling the ring and holding the medicine ball against our shoulder as the other whaled away. Abel started competing in tournaments, and nobody could stay with him. At his peak, as a 145-pound welterweight in 1995, Abel beat everybody he faced in the very competitive San Antonio regional Golden Gloves, and at the state tournament in Fort Worth he didn't lose until the finals. He was a first-class amateur boxer.

Abel hadn't quite reached that level of skill the Saturday morning we sparred. I had about forty pounds on him and considerable reach. We both knew the other's power and we were wary. Abel circled me, slapping my jab away like it was something contemptible, then dropped his hands, stooped, and dared me to hit him with juking movements of his head. But my left kept him distant. Then Abel's eyes would narrow, and when I saw his grimace I knew he was coming in after me. I survived the attacks and held my own until the bell rang at the end of the second round. The gym rule was to fight through the bell, which rang for about fifteen seconds. Still I thought I'd made it, and I relaxed. Abel's right zoomed through my hands and caught me on the jaw halfway between my ear and chin. On the money, as they say in the game.

Abel, a corner post, and the background wavered like the heat mirages that used to fascinate me in North Texas. "Oh, wow, you're hurt, aren't you?" said Richard, putting a hand in the small of my back.

"Sorry, Jan," muttered Abel, dropping his eyes.

If it had happened during a round Richard would have given me a standing eight-count. As it was, I had sixty seconds to recover, and when he asked me if I wanted the last round, I said, "Yeah." It ended with Abel backed into the corner that four minutes earlier had almost eased out of my vision. At the bell we both had our feet planted and were throwing hard. This time I didn't stop till Richard called, "Good finish, both of you."

That night when Dorothy and I went out to a restaurant, it hurt my whole face to chew. My jaw ached for nearly a week, and at times I felt unaccountably angry at Abel. After all, that was what we were in there to do. I sparred on rare impulse after that. My young friend had done me the favor of retiring me, just shy of fifty. Boxing at my age— it was pure hubris. How was I going to go home and tell my wife, Honey, I can't make my half of the house payment this month because I was out there in the ring and now I'm dopey from pain pills and my jaw's wired shut?

(4)

I never had the temperament and nerve of an outlaw. I've spent one night in jail—drunk in public, Graham, Texas, age nineteen—and when my jailers let me out I swore that mug shot would be my last. If such a thing had happened to Lila, I would have worried about her and followed Dorothy's lead, but I wouldn't have held it against her. Easily coaxed by friends and compelled by the rush of half-grownup hormones, teenagers ache to stretch the bonds of acceptability and get in some kind of trouble. They need to rebel but they also want to get away with it. As parents you hope it isn't trouble with the law, and that when the trouble comes it doesn't injure them or someone else, and that it doesn't damage them the rest of their lives. But you also remember how easily you thought your own parents were conned.

One spring day in 1994, Richard Lord saw me walk in the gym and, from his office, he gave me a shout. "I just got off the phone with a trainer in Chicago," he told me. "Irish guy, runs a first-class program for amateurs up there. He says one of their best fighters is living in Austin now, and he may come around to see us. This kid won nearly a hundred fights. He got in some trouble up there and went to jail, but the trainer swears he's a good kid, and he's just looking for someone to give him another chance."

The Chicago Kid, I thought at once, remembering the cafe of that name Dorothy and I had found during our runaway to Puerto Vallarta.

But unlike Richard, I was wary of boxing's oldest story. Paul Newman overdoing the accent of Rocky Graziano in *Somebody Up There Likes Me*. Somebody no doubt liked Sonny Liston, too, but boxing didn't change him; he was still a cheap hood when he was heavyweight champion of the world. A penitentiary and a boxing ring are hard places to find redemption, and nobody, I had found through varied experience, can play a con like a convict or ex-con. In our little gym in Austin, we already had a Chicano bantamweight headed the wrong way down that storyline. A local cable channel had shown him wearing a suit and making a speech one night at the banquet of a civic organization that honored him for his antigang leadership. His first dozen fights got him an audition on ESPN, and he scored a resounding one-punch knockout. Suddenly the phone was ringing nonstop in Richard's office; someone from Don King's operation said they wanted to sign him up. Our bantamweight couldn't handle even that glimpse of success. He disappeared from the gym and went right back to the street. Before we hardly blinked, his face was on a lineup of mug shots in the Austin newspaper—the breakup of a big drug-dealing operation, according to the cops. Our fighter made bond and hung around the gym for a while, looking doleful. There were embarrassed nods of good-bye as he went off to his new home in the Texas department of corrections.

Despite my skepticism, at the gym I found myself eyeing every newcomer of Mexican heritage, trying to judge from his skills if this might be the Chicago Kid. Richard needed another headliner. He had begun to produce some shows in Austin, but the most successful so far had been an all-women affair with the profits donated to a rape crisis center. And now our brightest light was off to prison. When the new fighter at last came to my attention, he carried his boxing gear in a cloth sack and wore jeans and work boots splattered with mud and concrete. He was twenty-two then, hardly a kid. Abel Davila and other youths in the gym called him Gabriel. He was short, just five-six, and weighed 160 pounds. But he was solid; even at that weight he didn't look pudgy. He had short, thick black hair, an olive complexion, muscular jaws, and a dimple in his chin. He had a tic, a habit of quickly blinking his left eye when he frowned in concentration, but nothing else about his appearance or manner marked him as a fighter. When he laughed his eyebrows shot up, and his lips parted over a set of slightly gapped, small, pearly white teeth.

I was in the gym sporadically during those weeks, and didn't see the workouts and sparring sessions that prompted Richard to put him on a crash training schedule. Gabriel had two amateur fights and slimmed down to 135 pounds, then Richard told me one afternoon that they were going down to Houston to turn him pro. He mentioned that Gabriel now wanted to go by his other family names, Jesus Chavez. Good choice, I thought, for a Chicano fighter trying to turn his life around in Texas. The name could be said to honor Cesar Chavez, the farmworkers' organizer and freedom fighter, and certainly Julio César Chávez, the Mexican lightweight champion and national hero, who had a large following in the American Southwest.

But those were my gringo musings. The truth was more complicated than that. Richard took the four-round fight on two days' notice. For a $350 purse, Jesus would be the opponent in the four-round professional debut of Lewis Wood, a national amateur champion who had been a rival of Oscar de la Hoya. Wood's manager had no inkling that the unknown from Austin had run up an amateur record of 90–5–5 while fighting out of Chicago. "Gabriel Sandoval, they would have found out about," Richard told me later, chortling over his bait-and-switch. "But Jesus Chavez? He's got no record, he's from Austin—sure, bring him on."

Despite the short notice, Jesus's parents came down to Houston to watch their son fight. He was so overwhelmed by his need to win that tears spilled down his cheeks as he walked toward the ring. The action was frantic and nonstop. At the end of the first round Jesus told Richard, "I'm having trouble getting my angles. This guy's a left-hander, isn't he?" Richard answered, "Well, yeah." He thought a fighter with his experience would have noticed that at once. But Jesus didn't answer the bell in confusion. He turned around and fought left-handed himself, which bewildered Wood. The furious bout ended with the crowd on its feet. Amid the whoops and applause the referee gathered them at the center of the ring, then raised the arm and glove of Jesus, awarding him the judges' split decision. Wood's handlers couldn't believe they had been suckered, and their heralded prospect had lost his first pro fight.

Two weeks later Richard made a similar match for Jesus. Prominent in Texas boxing circles was an AFL-CIO official who often worked as a ringside judge. He lived in Austin and quickly became one of Jesus's biggest fans. "I worked his second fight in a minor league baseball park in San Antonio," the union man told me. "Rudy Hernandez had been a Texas and national Golden Gloves champion, and this was his first pro fight. It was Rudy Hernandez Night. A big crowd came out. His people were handing out flyers, brought him into the ring with a mariachi band. This other kid comes out with torn trunks, old shoes, a towel over his head—and just destroys him."

Always a little wild in the first round, Jesus fought with unrelenting pressure, continually moving forward. Watching him was like seeing a second coming of young Roberto Duran, except Jesus brought to the ring none of the Panamanian's surliness and macho thuggery.

There was no malice in the way he tore into opponents. Jesus fought like boxing was fun—like he would just as soon do it for free.

But boxing was just one factor in Jesus's name change. If he had failed in the ring, if he had gone on in the anonymity of construction gangs, he might still be slogging around in mud and concrete, spending his paychecks on cigarettes and beer. But he had laid out tracks for himself—one public, the other one covert—that success could only bend into a collision course. The boxer's name was Jesus Gabriel Chavez Sandoval. When he abandoned his past as Gabriel Sandoval and began anew as Jesus Chavez, he wasn't lying to any authorities— those were his real names. But that is a common evasion by Mexican immigrants and other Latinos who have reason to fear the U.S. Immigration and Naturalization Service. The agency's computers are thrown off by multiple surnames. Jesus came to us a proud son of Chicago, but to the INS he was just another illegal alien.

I didn't know Jesus well enough to make judgments about his character, but it was exciting to be around an athlete with so much talent. Jesus had lost only one fight by the time we began to be friends—a disputed eight-round split decision to a Puerto Rican named Carlos Gerena whom promoters had put on a fast track to his world title shots. Richard wasn't bringing our guy along slowly. In San Antonio, Fort Worth, and the Rio Grande Valley, every couple of weeks he matched the kid against the toughest Texas, Mexico, and Louisiana fighters he could find. Word about Jesus was getting around in boxing, but he wasn't making any money yet. Fighters know they're getting somewhere when they're no longer getting paid a hundred bucks a round; it's a hard way to make a living. On one end of the gym, adjoining the toilet and shower stall, was a cramped room where Richard let him live for more than a year. He had a stereo, a TV that seldom worked, a clothes rack, a beanbag chair, a mattress on the floor, and not much else. Jesus had been living with relatives on Austin's east side; moving into the gym enabled him to quit construction work and train for his boxing career full-time. But he knew he was illegal and that anytime authorities might come for him. He didn't want his young nieces and nephews to see him hauled off from that house in handcuffs.

A condition of being allowed to live rent-free in the gym was that Jesus help others with their workouts. Every afternoon he directed the routine of abdominal and stretching exercises that Richard had devised. The sessions were a torment for me; I couldn't touch my toes standing up or sitting down. But I knew that my lack of flexibility was going to catch up with me. Trying to correct that and take some flab off my waistline, I winced and groaned alongside about a dozen others sprawled on towels in the gym's canvas ring, chatting with Jesus as he led the exercises and corrected our form. Then we split up, wrapped our hands, and started our circuits around the light and heavy bags.

For several months Richard had been working me with the gloves that resemble catchers' mitts; by numbers he called out punches and combinations for me to throw and him to catch. "One, two!"— the left jab then the straight right. "One, two, two, hook!"—the same combination, then rocking back quickly for a second right and the twist into the left hook. Pros and trainers use the gloves to warm up before a fight, and I thought I had gotten reasonably good at the drill. Sometimes I threw a punch sharply enough that I knocked a glove flying off Richard's hand. But it never happened with Jesus; he constantly reminded me of my failures and limitations. "You gotta move those feet, JanReid." He always referred to me that way, the two names run together. "Too slow, JanReid. A little baby could get outta the way of that." He stopped me and said, "No, no, that's not a hook. It's a hard punch, but it's not a hook." He set my feet wide and showed me the mechanics of pivoting my hips and knees. "While you're making that pivot, you throw the punch like a slap. See? Exactly like you're slapping somebody. Only it lands with a fist on the end of it, not an open hand."

The bell rang and I dropped my hands, gasping, but he poked me in the chest and made me continue, on through the rest break and yet another three-minute round. A couple of times he pushed me too hard and goaded too much. I wanted to slap him. Probably he was taking out his loneliness and weariness on whomever was in front of him. But it made me feel like a sulking boy. Nothing I could do would please him. I was too old. I wasn't going to play anymore.

Yet I could never stay mad at him for long. His cheer was too infectious. On Fridays, when the gym closed early, we sat on the ring apron at the end of the day and stretched out our legs. The subject of our talk might be music, or scenes from a movie, or the stroll of a young woman coming toward the gym. He told me about his decision to leave Chicago and try to start a new life. And though the circumstance of our lives was vastly different, it reminded me of my desperation to break out of a mold and *do better* when I was a young man.

"When I got back to Chicago I was living at home," Jesus told me. "I loved my family, but it was the same house, the same neighborhood, the same guys hanging out on the street corner. Now they were looking up to me because I'd been in prison. I didn't know nothing about life, but they were looking up to me. I'd see those guys and stop to talk, and they'd want me to hang out. Some of them were either going to prison or they were going to wind up dead. And I'd lie awake at night and could just see where it was going to go for me, if I stayed in Chicago. Man, I already knew what jail was like. After a while I told my parents, 'I can't do this. I can't be here. I've got to go.' "

Texans are accustomed to the presence of Mexican immigrants. Their official status often reveals itself in their dress, their ability to speak English, and their unease with American customs and culture. But Mexican *braceros*, laborers, have so long been a foundation of the economy—harvesting crops, cleaning up hotel rooms, wielding shovels and picks on construction sites—that questions about their status with the INS are seldom asked. If you're a U.S. citizen, the federal law governing that is a thick wall of intricacies and murk, and only zealots, a few of them in Congress, are inclined to raise much fuss about the aliens in our midst. So it was with the fighter in our gym. "I knew Jesus was illegal," Richard told me later. "I just didn't know how illegal he was."

Jesus's path to Austin was unusual only in its circuitousness. He was born in 1972 in Hidalgo del Parral, Chihuahua. A howling force of three hundred Comanches once rode off the Texas plains and sacked the town. A 1916 invasion led by U.S. general John Pershing chased Pancho Villa as far as Parral, and there, seven years later, the Mexican revolutionary was assassinated by a rival gang. Chihuahua and Texas have a great deal in common; they share much history, a long border on the Rio Grande, and a large part of West Texas sprawls across the same desert. Known in Mexico for the quality of its beef and a distinctive style of straw cowboy hat, Chihuahua is ranching country, but much of its wealth has been extracted from coal, gold, silver, and copper mines. Jesus's dad, also named Jesus, rebelled at that dark future and took his only other option—going north to find work. First he labored in southern California, and then he reached the cold Cibola of Chicago—"Golden Chicago," they called it—where few questions were asked and anyone from any country could find a job. The elder Jesus sent for his family when his son was seven. "Wetback" is a Southwestern word that not too many years ago could be found in the titles of official U.S. immigration statutes, but now, like "nigger," it has been assigned a meaning of bigotry. Yet that was how Jesus's family initially tried to come to this country—with him clinging to an uncle's shoulders as they waded the shallow Rio

Grande near El Paso and Ciudad Juárez. That time the Border Patrol caught them and sent them back.

His dad began his American journey as an illegal alien employed by the city of Chicago—he was sent out on maintenance crews to some of the most notorious and murderous public housing projects in the country. When Jesus was ten, his mother, who had been a nurse, came down with the heart trouble that would afflict her the rest of her life. Jesus and his sister Lidia were sent to live with their grandparents, and they attended school in Chihuahua that year. Jesus enjoyed taking karate lessons; when they returned to Chicago he pestered his dad to find him another gym and teacher. Karate was expensive, so the father dropped his boy off at a city recreation center one summer day, to take swimming lessons. Down a hall Jesus heard a bell ringing. He followed the bell to a gym, and there he found his gift. He won his first fight by technical knockout as a 105-pounder. He fell under the spell of three veteran trainers, all of whom were sons of Irish who spoke with the accents and told the stories of their old country.

"Tom O'Shea was a high school English teacher," Jesus told me. "After I met him he opened a gym that was part of a settlement house supported by alumni of Northwestern University. Tom didn't like professional boxing. He got mad at us if anyone talked about turning pro. But he loved amateur boxing. He won a middleweight Golden Gloves title in Chicago when he was a young guy—beat one of my other trainers, Sean Curtin, in the finals. Now they're best friends. Tom used to read us stuff by Ernest Hemingway—stories about bullfighting and courage, things like that. One day this kid said, 'Wow, we must be matadors.' And that became the name of the team and gym."

When Jesus was fifteen his dad registered the family in a federal amnesty program for illegal aliens, and he bought a small two-story house in a north Chicago neighborhood of Latino, black, and Polish families. Jesus—whom everyone knew then as Gabriel Sandoval—

rode buses all over the vast city to work with his trainers and make sparring sessions. When Jesus was seventeen he was voted—as Gabriel Sandoval—Chicago's amateur boxer of the year. He couldn't aspire to the Olympics because he wasn't a U.S. citizen, but O'Shea already had him in line for a scholarship to Northern Michigan University, where other boxing teams that compete internationally are based. Jesus was sure enough about his future that he announced a college major— criminal justice. O'Shea taught at a public high school a few blocks from the Matador Gym, and to spare his protégé so many hours on buses he arranged a transfer for Jesus. It was a favor and a mistake.

"I was a busy kid," Jesus told me one day as we had lunch. "I had school, I had boxing, and I had a job at a McDonald's. On weekends my dad catered Mexican food, and I helped him with that. But at school there was a gang called the Harrison Gents. Older guys in that gang, they were into professional crime—burglary and stealing cars and worse, I guess. But the ones I knew were just smoking dope, dealing a little, and trying real hard to be cool. In the neighborhood they'd help old ladies across the street, trim their lawns for them, stuff like that—so they wouldn't call the cops. I was new to this. I thought, Wow, these guys got clothes, they got money, and they got *all* the girls. I was kind of on the edges of that scene, still checking it out. After I got one of their guys out of trouble in a streetfight, they wanted me, though. They called me Boxer."

Jesus shook his head. "I was seventeen. I had everything going for me. One day I got out of school and this kid said, 'Hey, Boxer, we got this thing to do. You want in?' I listened to them and thought, Yeah, then they'll really like me. It was just dumb, JanReid. There were three of us. We had a sawed-off shotgun and a van, because one kid had a delivery job. I was thinking, What kind of getaway car is this? It smells like a *bakery*. We put on hooded sweatshirts and went in this supermarket. One of the guys stuffed the shotgun in an umbrella; I was backing him up. We went in the office and told this lady to empty a safe, then we ran out and got away. One minute I'm coming out of school with homework in my hands, and the next I'm going off to rob somebody? I had five hundred dollars in my pocket—a McDonald's paycheck I hadn't cashed. I didn't have no business going off to rob a store. I threw away my friends. I threw away my family. I threw away living in the United States."

I t was a boneheaded stunt that could cripple him the rest of his life. They robbed a nearby supermarket where people saw Wells High School students and kids from the Matador Gym all the time. Appropriately enough, Jesus was in his criminal justice class when the police came to the high school. His dad talked to a family member and friends and arranged to borrow the seven thousand dollars needed to make his bail. Jesus had no record of juvenile delinquency, yet there was never any talk of probation; from the start, police and prosecutors said he was facing at least twenty years. "That's too much time, *mi hijo*," said the elder Jesus. Jesus Sr. suggested that maybe the best way out of this was to jump bond, forfeit the seven grand, and run to their family in Mexico. Jesus refused; he said he'd gotten himself into the mess, and he would get himself out. Be a man. He spent the next eighteen months in a savage Cook County Jail wing known as the "gladiator school." It was where the youngest and most violent offenders were locked up. Brutal fights broke out constantly. Just before the trial, Jesus's court-appointed attorney told him that he might be looking at a jury sentence of thirty years, so they copped a plea for seven and a half. At a medium-security prison he got caught smoking pot in his cell. He spent three months in solitary confinement. "Guards would make fun of me; they'd say, 'Hey, why is it they call you Boxer?' I'd be shadow-boxing and crying in the dark. Thinking, *Someday you'll see. Someday I'm gonna be champion of the world.*"

His next stop was Stateville, the maximum-security prison where

Oliver Stone filmed much of *Natural Born Killers*. In the company of murderers and rapists, he was bait—a small, pretty boy. The Harrison Gents did one thing for him; they sent word to members on the inside to look out for him. "They brought me clothes and food and cigarettes. Then one of them handed me a big knife. He said, 'Here you go, you guard that with your life.' I never had to use it, thank God." He met my gaze for a moment. "But at the time I'm sure I would have."

Because of the year spent in Mexico with his grandparents, when his mother was ill, Jesus could not claim ten consecutive years as a legal resident. That gave the INS the legal excuse to deport him. He had no money, so he had no lawyer to fight the proceedings. In April 1994, when he got out of Stateville, the immigration authorities took him straight to a plane bound for Mexico City. He was put off in the Mexico City airport with the clothes on his back and the fifty dollars given all discharged convicts by the State of Illinois.

"How was your Spanish?" I asked.

"It was all right. Good enough. My family spoke it a lot at home."

"What did you do?"

"I knew this was coming, so I'd had some time to think. My grandparents were in Chihuahua. I knew I'd be safe if I could get to them. But that's a big, mean airport in Mexico City. I smoked cigarettes and hung out for a while, just watching, checking everything out. Then I went to the cabstand and found out it would take about all the money I had just to get to the bus depot. A cabbie took pity on me, let me ride with another fare. But I still didn't have enough money for a bus ticket. I hung out some more, and saw a bus driver who looked like a nice man. I talked to him about my problem, and he let me get on board."

I couldn't imagine how I would have fared in that circumstance. "How'd you get back to the States?"

"When I got to my grandparents' house, my dad wired me the

money for a plane ticket. I went to Juárez and just walked across the bridge to El Paso. They asked me a couple of questions, and I talked like an American, so they waved me through."

By going home to his parents he was behaving like any kid in trouble. But he knew he was breaking the law, and the case against him was steadily getting worse. Not only was he an ex-convict and illegal alien; now he was a deportee who had come back into the United States without authorization.

"The flight to Chicago went through Austin," he continued that day at lunch. "It was just a landing, I didn't get off the plane. But as the plane came down, I stared out the window. There were pretty green hills and a narrow winding lake. Then the lake got broader and I could see sailboats down there. People waterskiing. I looked down and thought, What a pretty town. If I could just start my life over, it would be someplace like that."

But his reality was back in Chicago. His parents watched him and worried; finally they had the conversation in which Jesus decided he had to leave. "We talked about where we had family, where I could go. 'Texas,' I said. 'I think I'd like Texas.' They said we had family in Austin, and I remembered how much I liked the look of that place, staring out at the sunshine from that plane."

Jesus said that when he came to Austin, his dreams of fighting for a world title were all but forgotten. He was just looking for a place to work out and get back in shape. But people at an eastside gym told him he was too good to be sparring with their kids. Jesus thought they didn't like him, that they were just trying to get rid of him. He had no inkling he was about to turn pro. "But, man," he said, laughing, "if you'd told me I was going to be a professional painter of houses, I would have done it. Just to be able to say I was *something*." Tom O'Shea made some calls for him, and a few weeks later he walked into Richard Lord's Gym.

Jesus never denied or tried to justify the mistakes he made. In the same predicament I could have seen myself making the same wrong turns. And I knew Jesus wasn't that person anymore. He not only could teach me how to throw a better left hook—why I needed that at fifty, I can't say—but I also thought I could learn a great deal from him about courage. More than ever, I looked forward to going to the gym. I wanted him to succeed as a fighter and be able to watch him do it. But in every way I considered him my friend.

(5)

I often worked out on weekend afternoons, when the gym was mostly empty. One Saturday I was trudging on a stair climber when Jesus came in with a pretty young woman who had short dark hair. He introduced me to Terri Glanger with such pride and formality that she and I laughed as I fumbled for a towel, dried off sweat, then shook her hand. That was the moment I realized Jesus valued our friendship as much as I did.

Terri studied photography at the university. She had worked out at the gym a few times, and one day they shared a ride to a San Antonio Golden Gloves tournament, where she wanted to take pictures. Driving down, he told her about himself, and his prison background startled her. Terri's origins were upper middle class; her Jewish parents, immigrants from South Africa, owned several fitness stores in Texas. But Jesus and Terri started dating. She picked him up at the gym at night as he didn't have a car. She called him Gabriel.

"We'd go out to a restaurant," he told me later, "and I'd ask her to order for me. 'Well, Gabriel, do it yourself.' But that's what prison does to you, man. I was too scared to tell a waitress what I wanted to eat. Terri told me I'd better start to think beyond boxing, and she really

stayed after me to get my GED"—the high school diploma equiva-
lency. "She helped me study for it, and it was okay that while she was
writing papers for college I was doing stuff at an eighth grade level.
She introduced me to a world I'd never known before. Her friends
would say, 'Wow, you're a *boxer?*' But they were cool about it—they
were just interested. Terri and I got to be very close. I went to meet
her parents, and driving up she said she'd told them everything." Jesus
laughed, imagining their reaction. " 'Let's see now. He's Catholic, he's
Mexican, he's been in jail, and he lives in a boxing gym. Way to go,
Terri. You can really pick 'em.' "

In August 1995, Richard started promoting fights in the downtown Austin Music Hall. The "Brawls in the Hall" had two attractions: the novelty of skilled women boxing and the furious pace of
Jesus's main events. Jesus stopped an increasing number of opponents
with body shots; the left hook to the ribs and tender organs beneath
had become his best punch. I was afraid Richard was going to burn
him out with his endless conditioning demands. Every Sunday found
them running up and down the seats of the University of Texas football stadium. And I knew Jesus couldn't get the skilled sparring partners he needed in Austin. Richard arranged sessions with ranked
fighters from Fort Worth, San Antonio, and the army town of
Killeen. If Richard had no one else, he himself would put on headgear
and a padded jacket that protected his midsection, then take a beating
by his own fighter. One day I came out of my proclaimed retirement
and sparred a couple of rounds. Jesus liked to work with heavyweights, and I stepped out of the ring as he was coming in. He said
"JanReid," and with a grin motioned me back in. I was pumped up
enough to do it, but Richard caught my gaze and shook his head
firmly. He didn't want my broken ribs on his conscience.

In August 1996, Jesus fought the Mexican featherweight champion. "Javier Jauregui came in like a really cocky guy," Jesus recalled.
"He had some gold glasses, Ray Bans, gold here and gold there, and

he just thought he was Superman for some reason." The Mexican fighter was in line for a world title shot, and his Chicano promoters from South Texas came in confident he would take care of this kid and they would make off with his big Austin gate. The night of the fight they swaggered into the music hall and ordered paying customers out of the seats they wanted.

And Jauregui could fight. Jesus started fast but after six rounds the scorecards were even. The slender Mexican's left hooks and uppercuts were so fast and came in such a wide arc that Jesus couldn't see them until they landed. "*Damn,* that hurt," he said on the stool after Jauregui's uppercut nailed him square in the nose. "Well, stop letting him hit you with it," Richard replied in his laconic and helpful way. At midfight, with the judge's cards turning away from him, Jesus reached deep and found the courage there. Even through the bedlam of the hometown crowd, his hooks to Jauregui's body sounded like *whomps* of artillery. The Mexican began to sag and wobble. At the end of the tenth Jesus had Jauregui backed up in his corner; as the bell rang Jesus threw a volley of head shots and buckled the Mexican's knees. With admirable reflexes of his own, a cornerman shoved a stool under Jauregui and broke his fall, sparing him a knockdown and its ruinous effect on the scoring. It didn't matter. The bridge of Jesus's nose would ache for months, but he won the unanimous decision going away. The Chicano promoters managed a sickly grin as they gave Jesus a North American championship belt of the World Boxing Council. Four months later, *Ring* magazine ran a story about the fight and proclaimed Jesus a contender for a world title. In Austin, local politicians hustled to be seen with him, and law enforcement officials started bringing him kids in gangs. They were amazed at how he seemed to get through to them. The mayor and city council had a ceremony for him at city hall and commended him for his value to the community. He had recreated himself.

In March 1997, Jesus debuted on the Fox TV network against a smooth and gifted puncher, San Antonio's Louie Leija, the cousin of "Jesse" James Leija. The ex-world champion knew Jesus well from sparring sessions, and he helped his cousin prepare for the fight. Jesus was going up a few pounds to super featherweight; another title of the North American Boxing Federation was on the line. But in Richard's gym we knew that for the first time Jesus had not trained hard. An ancient boxing spook had arisen—conflict between the woman at home and the man in his corner. Jesus moved out of his room in the gym, and one guy heard him raise his voice in Richard's office: "I'm just a puppet on the end of your string." Nobody thought that sounded like Jesus's usual way of expressing himself. "Twenty-three years old," Richard muttered about Terri, "and she thinks she knows everything about boxing promotion."

I went to that fight with much foreboding. Jesus mauled Leija in the first round, but in the third he walked into an uppercut and almost got knocked out. "A big 'ah' went through the whole arena," Jesus described the crowd reaction. " 'Our guy's hurt and we can't do one thing to help him.' But Leija didn't know how bad off I was." Jesus staggered like an alley drunk and hung on to Leija, yet he was dominant again by the bell. In the sixth he unleashed a furious barrage and knocked Leija down twice. When Leija fell the second time the referee stopped it. The Fox commentator yelled: "Jesus Chavez has won the NABF super featherweight championship and a world title very likely will be next. Great finish by Chavez. Jesus Chavez, remember the name, remember the face, you'll probably be seeing both again soon."

After the fight Jesus was interviewed by the ex-heavyweight-contender Tommy Morrison. "Right here in Austin, Texas," Jesus enthused, "we're ready to rock and roll. We'll take on anybody." Fox aired replays of the Leija fight for weeks. The performance sent Jesus soaring in the rankings and won him a contract with a major promoter, Main Events. By then Terri had graduated from the university and moved to New York, where she worked for a prominent fashion photographer. Jesus flew up after each of his fights and Terri took him to Broadway plays, art shows in SoHo. People hailed him on the street. He couldn't believe it. He walked in Central Park and gaped at the skyscrapers and splendor of this country. I thought he was an American success story.

But immigration officials were having none of that. Jesus drove an old black pickup that Richard had loaned him. He got back on the INS radar screen when, at Richard's insistence, he applied for a Texas driver's license and his papers weren't in order. He was in a holding cell and would have been dumped across the Rio Grande that day if Richard hadn't known someone in the system who was a boxing fan. Released on his own recognizance, Jesus hired an eastside lawyer who pursued a strategy of continuance and delay. That could only work so long. Jesus's friends and advocates could argue that the dad who brought him here as a child was now a naturalized U.S. citizen, that Jesus admitted his guilt, that he paid for his crime, that he was deported without legal representation, and that he had since demonstrated abundant signs of being a responsible adult of some value. None of the human nuance mattered. Immigrants from Ireland, Italy, Eastern Europe, Japan, and Vietnam had come into this country and felt the stinging backlash of resentment; now it was the turn of Latin Americans, especially Mexicans. Two massive revisions of U.S. immigration law passed Congress in 1996, and with little news, controversy, or ballyhoo Bill Clinton signed them. Deportations abruptly shot up by half. Three-fourths of them were being sent to Mexico. Two weeks after Jesus knocked out Louie Leija, the first provisions of the new laws went into effect. Jesus was now classified as an aggravated felon, and that provision in the law was applied retroactively; it explicitly forbade judicial review and any discretion or leniency by the INS. Most immigration lawyers refused to represent any aliens who had been convicted of a felony.

The summer of 1997, the Austin lawyer who had been representing Jesus called him and said the INS had summoned him to San Antonio for an "interview." I made some calls to some political friends and was stunned; he would likely be handcuffed and deported on the spot. Jesus had planned to take his little brother along, thinking that might help. "You'd better make plans for getting Jimmy home," I told him in Richard's office at the gym. "Because they're dead serious."

Austin officials made enough calls that Jesus was granted a few weeks to prepare for his deportation. At the same time, he was trying to get ready for a big fight on national TV. His opponent, a Puerto Rican named Wilfredo Negron, was not as experienced, but twelve of his fifteen wins were by knockout. The Austin lawyer withdrew from the case and told Jesus he needed an attorney who was licensed to practice in federal appeals court. Trying to help find Jesus a lawyer, I wound up talking almost daily to Terri Glanger's mother, Karen. The Glangers had been psychologically bruised by the INS when they immigrated from South Africa, and they were outraged that this could happen to the nice young man they knew as Gabriel. But his case seemed hopeless. One lawyer demanded ten thousand dollars up front but was vague about what that would buy. Another warned that if Jesus even questioned the deportation, he could go back to prison for that illegal walk across the El Paso–Juárez bridge. Another told Jesus how families were being separated, people who only came here to work. They were being shackled and hauled off with weeping children clinging to their legs. He asked Jesus: "Where is your tragedy?" He had no answer.

.   .   .

Jesus was in the gym one day, on the highway to a lawyer's office the next. In sparring sessions he was distracted and got belted. Finally he broke the news of his problem to Main Events. The New Jersey promoters steered him to a law firm in Washington, D.C. In a deal struck with the INS, he could stay in the U.S. for two more months and make a debut in Atlantic City on pay-for-view TV, then he would voluntarily leave the country. His lawyer hoped he might qualify for a skilled work visa that would allow him to train in the U.S. and pursue his boxing career. But there was no guarantee of that, his big night in Atlantic City was contingent on his beating Negron, and the deal wasn't finalized until the Friday before they stepped through the ropes of the Austin convention center on Tuesday.

"All that month I wanted to quit," Jesus told me. "But I had to have the money if I was going to be living in Mexico. I couldn't sleep. I was getting up dead, going home dead. And they had me in against this gunner who was knocking everybody out. I was scared. But that night in the dressing room a heavyweight on the card let me use his CD player. I put on the headphones and listened to the Gipsy Kings—good music, and I got into the rhythm. Then I greased up and wrapped up, and before I knew it they brought in my gloves. I looked out and saw the ring and chairs and all those people, still coming in. There it is, man. Let's do it. And then there was nothing left to do but to do it."

Jesus's cornermen now wore shirts that proclaimed him "El Matador"—honoring his Chicago gym and the high school teacher who once read him stories by Hemingway. But in this fight he came out more like a terrier trying to dismember a stork. The crewcut Puerto Rican was five inches taller than Jesus and had a nine-inch reach advantage. Jesus missed often and sometimes badly, but the fight was electrifying. In the second round Jesus threw 108 punches, about forty of them haymakers that landed. Hooks to the ribs, swooping right uppercuts to the chin, and midway through the round he led with a left hook—a risky move against a long-armed right-handed puncher—that momentarily poised Negron on his heels, then surrendered him to tangled legs, gravity, and the seat of his trunks. Now Jesus could spin off with arm upraised in the strut of the matador.

Negron survived the round somehow. In the corner Richard and Lou Duva, the bulldog-faced patriarch of Main Events, yelled at Jesus to settle down. He slowed the pace as instructed, but two rounds later the Puerto Rican again wobbled to his stool. Negron was in such pain his seconds had to wrestle him to get his mouthpiece out, and he kept pitching his head and shoulders between his knees, gasping for air. He couldn't breathe, sit up straight, or answer another bell because one of Jesus's rights had fractured his sternum. It's a cruel game, boxing.

"If I don't win the fight," Jesus reflected, "that big promoter's not going to be so interested. If I'm a losing boxer, how much chance do I have to get that visa?" In his mind, he was fighting for his life.

After the Negron bout, Main Events got him a fight with Troy Dorsey of Dallas on the undercard of the Lennox Lewis–Andrew Golota heavyweight title fight in Atlantic City. A Polish immigrant who lived in Chicago, Golota owed his fame and title shot to two brawls against Riddick Bowe in which he was disqualified for flagrant punches to the groin. The second fight ignited the ugliest riot ever seen in Madison Square Garden. On the way to the Atlantic City fights I passed through Golota's adopted Chicago to get some background on Jesus. I had lunch one day with Sean Curtin at a little Italian cafe that had autographed boxing photos on the walls. Curtin, who refereed fights and was then interim director of the agency that licenses boxing in Illinois, had short curly hair, a bent nose, and a twinkle in his eyes. He reminisced about his own pro career; for several years he fought and drove a cab in Chicago, so he could spend six months of the year enjoying the life of a bohemian in a Barcelona flophouse. He looked up at the waitress and said, "You're Polish, right?"

"Yass."

"Who you like in the big fight this weekend?"

"Ah, Golota," she said with a dreamy sigh, casting the twisted-nosed brute as an erotic hunk.

"You may be right," said Curtin, winking at me.

The boxing administrator talked about his early days with Jesus. "I kept hearing about him," he remembered. "And I thought, Hell, there's lots of tough Mexicans in this town. But I went to see him, and he was everything they said he was. A little Marciano."

Jesus's mentor had flown to Austin to watch the Negron fight, and I asked him what he thought of that performance. "Well, he might try a little defense," Curtin replied. "Jesus is not a devastating puncher—he gets it done with accumulated punches, not one shot—and he's letting himself get hit too much. Guys his weight are the best in the game right now. He's looking at about twelve who are basically as good as he is. He's gotta fight smart. But that's a good place for him, Texas. I like the way Lord's bringing him along."

Jesus Sandoval picked me up at the hotel another day. In his mid-forties, he had a black beard and smiled as easily as his son. He wore jeans and a pair of Chihuahuan cowboy boots. We drove far north through a section called the Ukrainian Village that abruptly changed into a street of store signs offering *comida de Jalisco* and *jugo de papaya*. We talked about the years when he had risked his life making repairs in the housing projects. I asked him why he had come to Chicago in the first place. "Here there is always work," he said. "You can work two, three jobs if you're willing. And Chicago is a long way from that border. The authorities here, they don't look so hard."

The Sandovals' small two-story house sat in a block of neatly kept homes facing a mattress factory. The living room was decorated with family photos and shelves filled with the amateur boxing trophies of

Gabriel Sandoval. They insisted on feeding me; Rosario had cooked her son's favorite dish, *chile relleno*. The elder Jesus led me to a storage building in the backyard and showed me "Matador" painted on a door frame in a little boy's hand. He told me that when his son was locked up, he used to come out here, so the rest of the family wouldn't see him crying. We walked into the front yard as he smoked a cigarette. He asked me if I thought a man his age could find work in Austin. I said I was sure he could; our city was booming. There was a realtor's sign at the curb and a for-sale notice in his van: hopes and plans reliant on a son who was about to be deported. Optimism, I thought, must run in the family. As if to underscore his reasons for wanting to move to Austin, his son Jimmy left a group of friends down the block and pedaled toward us on his bike. Seconds later a police car rolled up, and soon the cops had the other youths propped against a car, patting them down. Eventually they let the kids go.

Jesus Sandoval recalled his reaction to that phone call in 1990. " 'He's accused of *what?*' His mother was crying, and we couldn't find him. We couldn't find out which jail he was in." He looked at me and said without a trace of resentment: "We did what any parents would. When he was in prison, I'd get off work on Christmas Eve and we'd drive all night in ice and snow, then sleep in the car a couple of hours because we only had the money for one night's motel. We didn't want him to be alone in that place on Christmas."

In Atlantic City, Jesus looked fit and ready, but everyone else seemed to have prefight jitters. He had been in Atlantic City once before, stopping a respected ex-champion, Luis Espinosa, but that bout had taken place in a small casino room where gamblers wandered in to take a break. Much more important to Jesus's career, this fight was something of a family affair. Doug Lord was there to help work the corner, as he had when his son Richard was fighting, and his great champion, Curtis Cokes, now trained Jesus's opponent, Troy Dorsey. At thirty-four, Dorsey looked like his pleasure was running headfirst into walls. He had been a world champion kickboxer, and in one fight some years earlier he had pulled off an upset and won a world boxing title. But he had a stony ridge of brow and so much scar tissue over his eyes that he started losing fights on cuts. So he underwent surgery in which the jutting ridge of skull was smoothed off with a file. His boxing record had slipped to 15–9–4, but he was a bigger name than Jesus by far. He was supremely confident.

At the weigh-in they raised their fists and faced off in the ritual pose. Dorsey glared and played the moment for all the advantage it might be worth. Jesus's mouth started working, his eyebrows shot up, and he broke into that innocent's grin. Then he pulled on his clothes and raced through the casino until he reached a pasta restaurant. "Hate being hungry," he said, busy with his fork. He giggled at the thought of the macho staring match. "I try to do it, but I never can."

That afternoon he loosened up in a makeshift gym, then had to do some radio interviews. As I waited for him I listened to Lou Duva, who was in town primarily to steady his headliner Andrew Golota. "One rule you never break in boxing," Duva expounded. "You never fall in love with your fighter. They're all crazy. They all will break your heart. And then there's the matter of what the hell you're talking about. I say to my wife, 'Damn it, I've done it again.' She says, 'What do you *mean* you've fallen in love with your fighter?'"

Darkness gathered as Jesus and I walked to the hotel. Emerging from a casino, a man with a beard and ball cap recognized Jesus and jogged to us. With a burst of Spanish he took Jesus through the complicated handshake ritual of Chicano brotherhood. "Viva México," said the fan, saluting their *madre patria*.

"Sí," my friend replied. "Viva México."

Then the fan was dancing around us, showing off his own hand speed, turning over his wrists in the hooks, uppercuts, and crosses Jesus would need to take care of Dorsey. "Bip! Bip! Bip!" he cried. I looked at Jesus. He rocked back on his heels, gripped the handle of his bag, and laughed quietly, his eyes narrowed to slits. He raised two thumbs to his admirer, then they went through the handshake again, and we walked on.

Farther down the boardwalk, Jesus noticed a sparrow that had strayed inside a yogurt shop and now was fluttering against the glass, panic-stricken. He opened the doors and started trying to shoo the bird out. A youth at the cash register told him the place was closed. "No, we've got to get this out of here," said Jesus, walking around the store and flapping his hand until the sparrow escaped. The kid stared at him, then rolled his eyes. I sensed that it wasn't just that Jesus cared about a small, plain brown bird. He knew what it was like to be trapped in a place where nobody would let him out.

Terri arrived from New York the afternoon of the fight. Richard saw them on the boardwalk and couldn't believe it. He grasped his temples as he told me the story. "I said, 'Jesus, what are you doing? You need to rest. Eat a steak.' 'Well, Terri wants to go shopping.' 'Shopping! What have you had to eat?' 'Tuna sandwich I had in my room.' 'Tuna sandwich!' So he clenches that jaw like he does, and says, 'I'm going shopping with Terri. I'll see you there at seven.' " That night, as we made our way through the big convention hall, Richard said gloomily, "First time I've ever gone to a fight without my fighter." Then Jesus was late. This did not bode well.

But at seven-fifteen he walked in the dressing room, dropped his bag of gear, and flung out his arms like Gene Kelly. "Gonna be a great night, bro's. I am *pumped*, and I just got here!"

The structure was famous as the site of the Miss America pageants.

It filled up this night because of Jesus's Main Events stablemate, Andrew Golota. Britain's Lennox Lewis was a narrow favorite in the heavyweight title fight, but the blacks in the crowd were pulling for him quietly. It was Polish Pride Night in Atlantic City. I wandered into the corridor of a balcony in search of the press section, took one look at vodka-soaked young men who considered me, and quickly turned on my heel. The balconies were full of rowdies who waved red and white Polish flags, wore red and white face paint, and brought the crowd roaring to its feet as they brawled among themselves. One guy took the worst of a pummeling and lashed out with his boots. Bare-chested and painted to their waists, some men raised him and tried to dump him over the rail.

"LOW BLOW! LOW BLOW!" the Poles raised a merry cry.

Lewis's first-round knockout of Golota would turn them into unhappy drunks stumbling meekly in the night. Making matters worse, when Golota left the ring he set out running and staggering; in the locker room he screamed with such anguish that an ambulance crew was summoned. By the time they arrived there was nothing in the balconies but abandoned red and white flags.

But while they were still in full cry, Jesus stepped through the ropes in a new robe and trunks trimmed in Mexico's colors—red, green, and white. He embraced his dad and stepped around the ring throwing punches, loosening up. "Tonight I'm showing my stuff," Jesus had told me. "Tonight I'm gonna dance." At the bell Troy Dorsey charged forward, scarcely moving his head, punctuating his punches with karate-like grunts. Jesus skirted Dorsey's rushes, working off his jab and throwing quick, fluid combinations. One of the TV announcers was light heavyweight champion Roy Jones, one of the two or three best fighters then active in the sport. "Chavez does throw some pretty punches," Jones said in the second round. "Textbook punches. Excellent form."

Dorsey buckled Jesus's knees with a booming right in the third, but Jesus was landing three punches to Dorsey's one. He hurt his left hand in the target practice, so instead of the hook he showcased the right uppercut. Soon Roy Jones was comparing Jesus favorably to himself. From the third round on, a doctor stuck his head through the ropes to check on Dorsey. "Doing fine!" the game fighter barked. "Thank you!"

Dorsey had awed publicists of the fights with his workouts, and he seemed so ferocious that I was dry-mouthed and tight with tension, even as I scribbled notes about the action. I was, as Duva put it, in love with a fighter. There was nothing sexual about it: I didn't want to see Jesus lose; I didn't want to see him hurt. But it soon became apparent that only a lucky punch by Dorsey would derail him this night. Dorsey's surgical reconstruction held up, but he suffered a small cut high on his cheek and both eyes were closing. Jesus didn't go after the damage viciously, as many boxers would. He peppered the cuts, stepped aside, showed off his footwork. He stuck out his tongue, mugging for a friend taking pictures on the ring apron. After the seventh round the doctor stopped it. I heaved a sigh of happiness and relief. It was less a contest than a prime-time recital. As Jesus hugged and kissed Terri, his performance was greeted at ringside with an approving hum. I had written once about George Foreman, and behind me I noticed that George's brother, the promoter Roy Foreman, sat beside Bert Sugar—the legendary former editor of *Ring* magazine. Sugar's signature is an oversized fedora, an unlit cigar, and an air of having seen it all, often to his regret.

Foreman asked Sugar what he thought of Jesus.

Maybe he knew something about Jesus's past, or maybe he saw that Jesus chose not to scar and torture the defenseless Dorsey. Sugar removed his cigar and said: "Too nice a kid."

.   .   .

In October 1997, Jesus left the United States, taking little but clothes, his boxing gear, and his Dalmatian. He went to live with his grandparents in Delicias, Chihuahua. It's a quiet town. Nearby are pecan orchards, impressive stone mountains, and a pretty lake on the Rio Conchos, Mexico's great tributary of the Rio Grande. One day he returned to his birthplace, Hidalgo del Parral. He saw his ninety-six-year-old great-grandmother and checked out the Pancho Villa tourist attractions. "I think I'll be happy," he had said before he left. "Finally I get a chance to rest. Finally I get to kick back and, hell, enjoy a cold Corona."

I thought often of the afternoon I had spent in Chicago with his trainer Tom O'Shea. Sean Curtin had dropped me off at the Matador Gym on his way home from the office. Curtin hung around for a while; his friend was late for our appointment. "Tom's getting a little forgetful," he said with a sly smile and a slow right cross. "I hit him pretty good that time we fought in the Golden Gloves." With two boxing rings and matched bright red leather bags, the Matador Gym was gleaming and spotless—nothing like Richard Lord's Gym in Austin. In the trophy case was a small exhibit devoted to Jesus. O'Shea walked in peeling off a windbreaker and, after getting some grade school boys organized and started, he walked to me and apologized. We pulled up chairs and talked. Retired from teaching now, O'Shea had salt-and-pepper hair and spoke like an Irish tenor about to break into song. "At the end of his career, I wonder where he'll be?" he said of Jesus, whom he still called Gabriel. "Five percent of the boxers make eighty-five percent of the money in the pros. Those are lousy numbers, especially for the little guys. Boxing is experiencing its last gasp. All the grand heroes are gone. Ah, but Gabriel, my wife and I talk of him still. Everyone is fearful, but he went in the ring with such alacrity. He had this joy—the joy of the warrior. I read about great generals and battles and see ones like him marching in the ranks."

As much as Dorothy had helped me escape myself and place faith in others, Jesus had coaxed from me feelings of both awe and care. I called my old friend Gerry Goldstein, at whose San Antonio party I had first met Dorothy. Gerry was a criminal defense lawyer, but I thought he might have some good advice. As he listened he said, "You really like this kid, don't you?"

"Hell, I'd adopt him if it would do any good."

Even as I blurted that, it struck me how important Jesus had become to me emotionally. That was one hell of a presumption, considering that he had real and loving parents in Chicago. Jesus represented everything I wished I had been as an athlete. He had youth, good looks, ebullience, and more important, he seemed to go through life with an absolute lack of fear. To me the balance and striving he maintained were heroic. Our relationship would extend far beyond boxing. In my devotion to this fighter and the helpless panic I felt when he was being deported, I realized that I had made him into the son I never had.

(6)

When Dorothy was away overnight I turned up rock and roll and shadowboxed in the dark. The dogs barked and leaped, overjoyed by our game. My devotion to boxing was no more aggressive than that. It was hard to go on fancying myself a heavyweight fighter when the mail besieged me with advice on how to pay for my long-term nursing home care. I had a firm grip on my temper and a good eye for situations that might get out of hand. I never dreamed that real violence could come my way again.

I hardly ever watched the major fights because they were scheduled on Saturday nights, and Dorothy and I reserved that time for each other. But she understood the mental release and camaraderie that can come with a routine of exercise; she enjoyed that herself. She didn't mind what the boxing workouts had done for my body. And for years, both inside and outside government, her working life had revolved around social justice. She didn't have to be a boxing fan to understand my anguish over what had happened to Jesus.

Six months passed before the magazine piece I had decided to do on Jesus worked into the lineup of *Texas Monthly*. My editor was Mike Hall, a soft-spoken man whom I liked at once. In the eighties

Mike had written a magazine profile of Richard Lord when he was a world-ranked pro fighter. But then he went off into his rock and roll career. Like many American musicians, he enjoyed much of his success in Europe, but in Austin he still had a cult following. Mike had sharp features, an almost delicate nose and chin, with a spray of freckles across his cheeks. He told me with a laugh that in his days as a punk rocker he accused Lyle Lovett of stealing his haircut.

John Spong did the fact-checking for my story about Jesus. John was six feet tall and slender, with curly auburn hair and sideburns. For some reason I imagined him as a frontier preacher in a dusty black frock. He came from a family of Episcopalian clerics. His father Will taught at a local seminary and in the pulpit was renowned as a raconteur and showman. On the subject of his brother, though, Will was careful about what he said. John's Uncle Jack had been a controversial bishop of Newark; retired but still outspoken, the elder John Spong had championed women and gays as officiaries of the faith. "For Dad it's either 'Your brother's famous' or 'Your brother's a cockroach,' " said John, chuckling.

John practiced law for only a few months. He took ironic satisfaction in having his name attached to the largest losing judgment ever awarded in the county. John wanted to write, and despite the long hours and low pay, his job as a fact-checker was a good way to get his foot in the door. Every story he checked for accuracy fed him new material. Another writer starting to make headway was his friend David Courtney. Before he finished his degree in psychology, David took a long break in Austin "flipping burgers," as he put it with a grin. His drawl was so slow it could sound like a record played at the wrong speed. He was the only intern I ever saw at *Texas Monthly* wearing a cowboy hat.

The issue containing my story about Jesus was at the printer when Mike Hall called. "Hey," he said. "You want to go to Mexico?"

For Texans, much devilment and danger are contained in those words. From the heritage of boys roaming bordertown red-light districts to the John Huston–Humphrey Bogart movie *Treasure of the Sierra Madre* to the droll thrill-seeking cowpokes in the fiction of Cormac McCarthy, the culture can be found in countless songs, books, and movies; and it is a particularly male tradition.

"Why?" I asked Mike. "Where? What's going on?"

"Mexico City," he answered. "Your guy's got a fight."

In Chihuahua, Jesus was in a quandary and funk. He enjoyed his grandparents' company, but his lifeline was the telephone. He thought his romance with Terri Glanger was over, that they were just friends now, but they had trouble acting like the fire was really out. It was an impossible situation for any relationship. Jesus had gone down there thinking he might be back in Texas in a couple of months, but now his Washington lawyer held out little hope of getting him home anytime soon.

At first Jesus flatly refused to fight in Mexico. He had grossed fifty thousand dollars against Troy Dorsey in Atlantic City; now his promoters wanted him to fight for just fifteen hundred. Main Events had been blindsided by Jesus's deportation. When they signed him they had envisioned a series of televised fights that would showcase him amid his rowdy following in Austin. Now his whole career was entangled in immigration statutes and policies, and all they knew of that was what the law firm told them. Their investment in Jesus had turned into billable hours. Still his manager and trainer, Richard Lord didn't know how to advise him either. Jesus was ranked number one in the super featherweight class by the World Boxing Council— one of the fractured sport's three major governing authorities—and he had the WBC's North American title, so he couldn't be written off completely. But to keep that ranking he had to stay busy, and on occasion he had to defend his regional title. Jesus could travel on a

Mexican passport. Main Events could have kept him busy fighting in
Canada, the Caribbean, and Europe. But except for one fight in
Poland, on the undercard of a homecoming by Main Events' problem
child Andrew Golota, those matches were never made. The best Jesus
could get now was a fight in Mexico City against a local journeyman
named Moises Rodriguez.

In theory a number one ranking guaranteed that Jesus would
someday get his shot at a world title. But his ranking was really meaningless. No champion would be forced to fight him because the
money in boxing relied on American television, and no U.S. network
would produce a championship fight in Mexico. That wasn't just because of ratings. It was fear. In March 1998 the flamboyant boxing
promoter Don King had gone to Mexico City for a world title fight
involving the Mexican national hero Julio César Chávez. A robber
stuck a gun in King's face and relieved him of a diamond-studded
Rolex watch worth, he said, one hundred thousand dollars. "A shiny
little doodad," King showboated afterward for the press. "A gaudy little thing that sparkles—nothing of significance." But a month later, as
our Jesus was training for the Rodriguez fight, a CNN crew went to
Tlatelolco, a Mexico City suburb, to cover a conference on the U.S.-
Mexico drug war. While Mexican police watched, robbers got off
with a van full of cameras and other costly equipment. Confronted by
reporters, the cops shrugged and explained that the robbers had them
outgunned.

The same month the U.S. State Department added Mexico City
to its list of most dangerous foreign destinations. Street crime in the
capital seemed out of control. "Express" kidnappings were the latest
rage; people were snatched by men who had researched their finances
and demanded their liquid assets by the end of the day. One gang,
run by an ex-cop, had a modus operandi of cutting off victims' fingers
and ears and sending them to families to speed up the transactions.

But nothing informed Americans more about Mexico City than the December 1997 shooting of a man named Peter Zarate. An ex-Navy SEAL, Zarate worked for an American corporation. He and his family had made Mexico City their home for four years. In his wealthy neighborhood Zarate caught a ride with a cabdriver working with *pistoleros*—one of the most common scams. Emboldened by his commando training, Zarate unwisely tried to fight his robbers. They shot and killed him and dumped his body in the street. Five men confessed to the police, but after two weeks a judge said they were coerced by police torture, released them, and called the gang's leader a "modern-day Robin Hood."

My colleagues and I—all reporters—could have easily discovered all of this and more. But if we had bothered to find out, I doubt that would have stopped us. We would have thought we could handle it. We had a cheap airfare, and a friend of John was going to let us use his apartment in the Polanco, one of the prettiest parts of the city. What the hell? Why not? Heading down to Mexico is a ritual that American men—especially Texans—are born to. It goes back to the Texas Revolution, the Mexican War, and the Mexican revolution of the early twentieth century. John Reed and Ambrose Bierce chasing after the hijinks of Pancho Villa. Bierce, recall, did not make it back. Our nonchalance about entering an unsafe area wasn't exactly racist, but implicit in the ritual was an assumption that we were a bit superior. Within me there was a residue of foolish, youthful arrogance: We weren't bulletproof, but by our size and wits and numbers we were confident we could take on anything. Of course Mexico was full of danger. That was part of the appeal.

"Oh, I want to go," said Dorothy. Just two years earlier we had gone to Mexico City with our friends Gary and Phyllis Cartwright, and we had a great time roaming the vast old city. But this time I hedged. Jesus's fight was to be in the Arena Coliseo, the Madison

Square Garden of Mexican boxing. Of this place our travel guide said: "The atmosphere is rough. Don't be surprised if a lit cigarette lands in your lap or a firecracker goes off over your head."

"You don't want me to go," Dorothy chided me.

"No, no, we'd have fun. But, you know, in the middle of it there'd be a day of boxing. Which you don't like too much. We'd have Friday night and then all day Sunday to do whatever we want. We'd have fun." Then I had to add: "But this place where he's fighting is supposed to be, um, rowdy."

A day or so later she said, "Oh, go on. I shouldn't spend the money. And this sounds like a *guy thing*."

On the flight from San Antonio I put a magazine aside and thought of Mexico City. In the fifties two friends, Fletcher Boone and Lopez Smithum, had connived a way to live in the Mexican capital, which they considered one of the world's great bohemian enclaves. Living off their GI Bill payments, they went to college and danced the nights away in jazz clubs—reviving the Charleston, showing off the dirty bop. Fletcher described one joint whose patrons filled a table six inches deep in voluntarily surrendered knives and guns, but even there they never felt endangered. It snowed one time, he said, and for three days the ancient lakebed lay cloaked in sootless white. I never expected to see that Mexico City. The first morning I ever awoke there, people walked to work with handkerchiefs pressed to their watering eyes because of the horrid air pollution. But one afternoon a front blew through, and it was as if the heel of a giant hand pushed the muck away. For just one cool day I could see what a glorious place it once must have been.

At the airport in Mexico City we got our bags and cleared customs. The first greeting of Mexico is the smell—mingled odors of smoke, sewage, things fried in lard. We took one of the airport's sanctioned cabs and alternated between excited jabber and just staring. It's a beautiful city at night. The driver left us on the curb in the Polanco. The apartment was small but functional—the place of a well-heeled bachelor who came in and out of the city in his work.

It was still early, about nine o'clock, and we hit the streets. In the valley of the Aztecs it was a warm spring night. The streets were broad and well lighted, the sidewalks lined with poplars, but the Polanco was a neighborhood concealed by gates and walls. Nothing was going on. We walked about a dozen blocks, unwinding and getting our bearings. Several drivers of the green and white Volkswagen cabs slowed down for us. These were the gypsy cabs that were causing such a furor. Stay out of the green and white Beetles, we had been warned repeatedly. Hell, the four of us couldn't have gotten our legs in one of those things. At my ambling pace I lagged along behind. John stepped out and spoke to the driver of one of the Beetles, trying to get some directions. When the cab pulled away, a Ford Explorer made a sharp U-turn and pulled up to us. In it was an attractive young couple, a bearded man and dark-haired woman. "What are you *doing*?" the woman chewed us out in English. "You can't make yourselves targets like that. You have to understand—this can be a very dangerous place for you."

I looked around in bafflement. The Polanco is a virtual country club.

John told them we were thinking about going to Plaza Garibaldi and hear some music. In chorus they said it was too dangerous; they were animated and vehement. The woman gave us directions to a Hard Rock Cafe. Across the street, she said, was a hotel with the best mariachis we could ever hope to hear. I thanked them for their advice, and with smiles and waves they drove on.

Before our trip I had never heard of Plaza Garibaldi. In Mexico it's the equivalent of Bourbon Street, and John and Mike had their minds made up to go. We found the Hard Rock Cafe and the hotel across the street. Lined up in front of the hotel were cabs with red paint. These were licensed and regulated cabs and were supposed to be safe. John asked one driver if Plaza Garibaldi was too dangerous to go there. No, no, the driver scoffed. But he was just as vehement. We had to listen to him, he said. He would take us to one place, where we would stay all evening, and he would return for us at exactly one a.m.

As advertised, Plaza Garibaldi was full of mariachis. The driver walked us past them to the doorman of the plaza's most famous bar, the Tenampa. "A las uno," the driver said again, holding an index finger in the air. We smiled and said, "Sí. A las uno," and raised our fingers. The bar was crowded and noisy, and the mariachis lived up to their billing. We told stories and chased tequila with beer. Near our table was a booth occupied by two young Mexican couples. Seated on the outside, the men were drinking, gesturing with sweeps of their arms, and smoking cigars. Suddenly one man turned his head, leaned over, and vomited on the floor. His wife or date and the other couple did not react at all. The sick man sat still for a moment, then inhaled from his cigar and turned back to their conversation. An attendant strolled over and, without a word to the customers, tossed some janitorial absorbent on the puke, swept it brusquely into a long-handled dustpan, and that was that.

At one o'clock we spilled out of the Tenampa like puppies released from a basket. Our driver ran across the plaza, rounded us up, steered us to the red cab, and as we mumbled happily, he took us safely home. A man of honor. We thanked him profusely.

The next morning the phone rang exactly at eleven a.m.—our driver of the red cab. He took us to a different part of the city, a commercial district with little commerce, and unfortunately that was the last we saw of him. The buildings were squat and grimy. Solitary people hurried along sidewalks beside vacant lots where walls of boards had been put up; the boards were cluttered with handbills and graffiti. The small hotel where Jesus had been staying sat back from the street. With a tiled and gurgling fountain, it was a hotel for the Mexican middle class—hardly a flophouse. In the coffee shop Jesus beamed on seeing me, we embraced, then I introduced him to my friends. After reading about him and talking to him on the phone, they were all stunned to see how small he was.

Everybody in the coffee shop but the cook and waiter had some connection to the fight. Robert and Marcy Garriott had flown down in their plane from Austin. Sons of an astronaut, Robert and his brother Richard were founders of a video game company called Origin Systems Inc. Robert had cashed out of the company in recent years; he spent his time learning Spanish, flying his plane, and doing anything else he wanted to do. Marcy had spent several years working as an executive with a telecommunications company. Now, after making a couple of short educational videos, she had announced she was going to make a documentary about Jesus, his past, and his predicament. Marcy had a smile that glowed with even white teeth. Robert wore his hair in a crewcut and spoke with the self-assurance of someone who had gone to MIT and made a fortune. They were very nice and very straight. Parked outside was a luxury American sedan they had rented and a driver hired to escort them whenever they left their hotel. Marcy's documentary, "Split Decision," would ultimately do far more for Jesus than my magazine piece ever could, and in time she and I became close friends and allies. But on first impression I pegged her wrongly as a dilettante.

Main Events had no real presence in Latin America, despite all its great boxing champions. The promoters assigned a man named Lou Mesorana to look out for Jesus and protect their investment while he was in Mexico. Lou offered himself as a friend to Jesus when the boxer was going through a discouraging, lonely time. A New Jersey guy who had wound up in Corpus Christi, Texas, Lou was an old hand in boxing; he had managed a little, carried the bags a lot, and he was angling for a piece of this action. He and Richard Lord had no use for each other. Richard anguished over what had happened to Jesus, but their professional relationship was on the rocks. After the Leija and Negron fights a cable company had proposed a series of prime-time fights that would showcase Jesus, his presumed world title, and the boisterous Austin crowds. "We were this close, this close," Richard told me, holding his thumb and forefinger an inch apart, from a run in boxing that could have made them both rich.

But it hadn't happened. Richard had a thriving business in his Austin gym, and he also had a wife and infant son. He couldn't be down in Mexico trying to manage Jesus's career. However, Lou Mesorana had arranged his life so he could. Jesus was angry at Richard for never calling him. Richard claimed he had a handful of telephone bill receipts that would prove how often he had called and had been told Jesus wasn't in his room. Richard believed that Lou and some Mexico City promoters were trying to drive a wedge between him and his fighter, and deal him out. It was a boxing soap opera.

Another figure on hand was a dark-haired young man I had known since I started working out at Richard's gym. Wayne Harrison had average talent and zeal in the ring, but his eyes were always darting, a half-smile on his lips. Not your ordinary business major. After looking around Thailand and volunteering in George Bush's campaign against Bill Clinton, Wayne had found a Mexico City couple who were skilled at making punching bags and other equipment. Now he lived there and marketed their products. He met a Mexican girl named Patty on the subway and they moved in together. He also watched the Mexico City fights with a keen eye. Son of a Fort Worth boxing promoter, Wayne had grown up around the sport. Now he supplied Richard with Mexican fighters for his cards at the music hall in Austin. They were hungry and tough guys who would, as Richard put it, take a beating for a hundred bucks.

It was time to go to the weigh-in; everybody started arranging rides. Wayne nodded at me, and on the street outside he raised his hand at one of the green and white Volkswagens. David Courtney hollered and trotted up to join us. At almost our first opportunity we were breaking our vow to stay out of the Beetles. But Wayne lived in Mexico City, and he got in the cab as casually as he crossed the street. As the cab bumped along, David filled me in on Origin's pioneering of the video game industry. Wayne listened with his pensive smile and watched the Garriotts' driver, who soon got lost. Wayne spoke to our driver in Spanish and had him pull around the big sedan, which he signaled to a halt. Wayne told the driver to follow us, and eventually we pulled up to a gray structure that looked like it had been inspired by a cubist painting.

Inside we encountered none of the posturing and gibberish that afflicts boxing weigh-ins in the States. Waiting to be called into an office by a doctor, the fighters sat on sofas looking very young and trim. Most wore slacks and cheap long-sleeved shirts. Unlike American boxers, none of the Mexicans looked like they spent any time training with weights. Speaking quietly, Wayne pointed out two or three who he thought could fight. Jesus's opponent, "Moy" Rodriguez, was tall and curly-haired. His slumping posture gave him the appearance of having a concave chest. Wayne said he might be fourth or fifth best at his weight in the city, but not all of Mexico. Still, he was capable.

In his underwear Jesus made weight—132 pounds—but he didn't look as solid as he had in Atlantic City. He took the doctor's cursory physical and answered his questions, slipped back into his jeans, shirt, and running shoes, then spoke with a Mexican sportswriter. The other fighters watched Jesus with curiosity but no apparent resentment that the reporter ignored them. The writer asked Jesus if he thought his troubles with American immigration authorities could be resolved. "Pues, no sé," he began. He didn't know. After listening to the interview, Moy Rodriguez, the journeyman opponent, cornered

Jesus and lectured him. "Listen, you can't say that. You must look at things in a positive way. You have to believe that God is with you, and that you'll get to go back to Texas and have the life you want."

What a nice guy, Jesus thought. In seven hours they would be trying to take each other's head off.

After the weigh-in, Wayne led us down to a subway station. We rode the car for a few stops, then got off and followed him to a sidewalk cafe in the Zona Rosa. He hadn't seen my story about Jesus yet, and I told him I'd send him a copy. Like many Americans living in Mexico, Wayne had an air of streetwise bravado. He mentioned that this place tonight, the Arena Coliseo, was in a rough part of town. The last four times he and his girlfriend had gone there, they had been attacked.

I blinked. "Damn, Wayne. What did you do?"

"Ran from them twice. Another time I had some Mace. Other time I had some scissors"—with a spoon he demonstrated how they fit between the fingers of his fist—"and I, uh, popped a guy one."

I made a mental note to address the magazine to "Scissorhands" Harrison. But I thought if I couldn't find a safer place to watch the fights, I'd check out the *fútbol* or jai alai.

Back at the apartment, when it was time to go we called a taxi service in the phone book—a recommended way to get around safely. Once more the rendezvous was at Jesus's hotel, and Wayne again took command of our transit. I rode from there to the Arena Coliseo in the backseat of another green bug, chatting in Spanish with his girlfriend Patty. She said she couldn't visit Texas with Wayne because the U.S. *migras* would not grant her a visa. In rush hour we arrived at the arena, which looked like a run-down movie house. Cars were backed up, their drivers honking in boredom. In the bright afternoon light nothing about the street looked sinister. Jesus,

Richard, his dad, and other members of the fighter's team emerged from a van. The Garriotts unloaded camera gear from their sedan, which in that traffic stood out like an aircraft carrier. Across the street from the Coliseo, my friends descended on a street vendor of tacos, which he cooked over a charcoal brazier. David carried a camera, and he lined up Mike, John, and me with the storied old Texas trainer, Doug Lord. I think a lot of that photograph—keep it framed in my office. Wearing a cap with a bill pulled to his nose, John raises his sideburns and chin with his usual insouciance, Mike drapes his arms across Doug's and my shoulders in a Kerouac-like slouch, Doug offers his dimpled chin and old charmer's grin. It's the last picture I have of myself standing easily, hands in my khaki pockets, unconscious of the act of standing up.

et's go! Now!" Richard barked. We followed him through a door held open by a dark-skinned mestizo who inspected us without ever looking us in the eyes. "Periodistas," journalists, Richard explained to us all. Inside, the seats on the first floor were metal chairs painted yellow, purple, red, aqua. The arena was arranged conically; the first and second balconies were built so that spectators could look almost straight down at the ring. The balconies were sealed off with chicken wire to keep spectators from throwing objects at the fighters. It looked like an elaborate pit for cockfights.

The bouts went off at a rapid clip; the referees were much quicker to stop a fight than they were in the States. Between rounds music blared a sort of Mexican rap. Wearing blue cotton stretch garments advertising Corona beer, girls in high heels prissed and strutted around the ring with the round cards, each of them pulling at hems of skirts that did not quite reach the clefts of their buttocks. The crowd whistled and stomped. A formidable *dama* waited at the foot of the stairs. As the card girls came down, she raised their hands like they were ballerinas, and walked them past anyone who might doubt their virtue.

Jesus told me later that this woman was one of the foremost powers in Mexico boxing. Fighters prospered and were protected if they caught her eye and won her favor. They called her *la Madre*.

Moving around the ring aprons as the fights proceeded, Robert and Marcy Garriott shot with video cameras worth about five thousand dollars each. Wearing a blouse and khakis, Marcy was game—I had to give her that. No protocol or annoyed ring official could keep her from climbing anywhere she wanted.

Jesus's fight, the main event, came up fairly quickly. Jesus, Richard, a Mexican trainer, and Jesus's Uncle Julio from Delicias walked down the short aisle. Jesus's left eye blinked in his nervous tic. He wore his familiar red and blue shoes, a T-shirt, his North American Boxing Federation championship belt, and a pair of white trunks stitched with tributes to his new home, Chihuahua. When the bell rang Jesus looked sluggish. He had been told that Rodriguez had a weak chin, and he tried too hard to finish the fight early. Rodriguez's arsenal was a jab followed by the straight right and occasional uppercut. With longer arms, he popped Jesus often with his jab. Jesus missed wildly with a left hook aimed at the body, and paid for it—Rodriguez whacked him with a good right cross. The journeyman probably won the first round on the cards. In the corner Richard told Jesus to settle down, relax.

In the second round Jesus began to get his rhythm back. He rose up on his toes and pressed forward with combinations of body shots. Rodriguez grunted a couple of times; Jesus was getting to him. Mike Hall and I slouched beside each other on the first row. A longhaired American expatriate shouted beerily in my ear. "I've been watching boxing a long time! This guy's got it! This guy's a Hagler!" Shouts popped out of the crowd: "Matador! Matador!" The nickname born in a Chicago gym had found a receptive audience.

"Sharpen up your punches a little," Richard told Jesus on the stool after the second round. "Let's get this guy out of here." Jesus nodded and grinned, watching a card girl prancing and pulling at her skirt. He came out in command and was just beginning to get warmed up. A minute into the round he landed a hard left hook to the ribs, which brought Rodriguez's hands down, then blasted the Mexican with a straight right that turned his head almost all the way around.

Rodriguez touched his gloves to the canvas to stay up, then wandered off in a tangle-legged stagger. The touch of the gloves counted as a knockdown, and as the referee called out the standing eight-count, he didn't like what he saw in Rodriguez's eyes. He stopped the fight. Jesus walked around the ring with his arms raised, his first win in Mexico under his belt.

Afterward Jesus was mobbed by children, autograph seekers. The boxing card came to an end after another couple of fights, and the arena emptied quickly. We hung around the small dressing rooms with Jesus and with Moy Rodriguez, a pleasant man and gracious loser. "How you doing, JanReid?" said Jesus with his hand on my shoulder. "What did you think?"

"You looked a little rusty, but you took care of him," I said, pulling him close and hugging him. "Man, it's good to see you."

"I've missed you, JanReid. Thank you guys for coming down here. It means a lot to me."

"I'm going to come see you in Chihuahua."

"You better do that, my man."

Meanwhile Richard grimly waited for payment from the promoter, and Marcy and Robert Garriott sudddenly realized the predicament they were in. Their video cameras and gear were laid out in large, conspicuous cases. The street that had been so bright and merry at five in the afternoon had a harshly different look at eleven p.m. They had to call their sedan driver and had just assumed there would be a public pay phone at the coliseum, if one were not available in the business office. But this was Mexico. In a panic Marcy started stuffing tapes of footage in her clothing. Then she saw someone on the street with a cell phone. "Señor, por favor," Marcy cried. "Podría usar su teléfono?"

As she busily punched in the number of their driver, Richard hurried through the arena, waving for all of us to come on. He had finally gotten Jesus paid, and though the cash purse was pathetic, he didn't want to stick around.

A party after the fight was scheduled at a restaurant in the Zona Rosa. The only vehicles this time were the van and the Garriotts' sedan, which filled up quickly. John climbed in the van with Jesus and his cornermen, Mike in the sedan with the Garriotts. I stood on the sidewalk feeling large and stupid. Holding Patty's hand, Wayne shot glances at the darkness and told David and me that it was a bad idea to hail a cab. Even if the driver was all right, the one-way street would force him to turn back through places we did not want to visit. Anticipating that we might need an extra hand, Richard had asked a young man named Matt Rodriguez to come to Mexico City. Matt had been a university student when he started coming to Richard's gym. The light heavyweight was so mild-mannered that opponents were often badly startled when they got in the ring with him. As a teenager Matt had been schooled by Roy Harris, who enjoyed his brief fame more for his hometown of Cut and Shoot, Texas, than for his losing performance in a 1958 heavyweight title fight against Floyd Patterson. Richard had asked Matt to come along for one reason— muscle—and he asked him to walk with us. Matt sauntered toward us, broad-shouldered and grinning.

"It's four blocks," said Wayne. "When we get to the lights we're okay. Stay together in one line. Keep walking." His stories about having to fight his way out of the Arena Coliseo echoed in my mind. I took the other end of the line from Matt. From a doorway I saw some men eyeing us, and for a moment thought I heard mutters and the scrape of shoes behind us. I remembered our guidebook's cheerful description of our destination: "As evening falls lots of people come to stroll or sit, catching some of the music or trying their hands at one of the stands where they can bust a balloon. . . ." Bust a balloon and put a knife in my spleen! How many were we going to have to fight? How would they be armed? It was the scariest short fast walk of my life. Finally we burst into the glare of light. Across the busy street was Wayne's safe haven—Plaza Garibaldi.

(7)

When we woke the next morning Jesus, the Garriotts, and all the boxing people were gone. It was our day just to be tourists. Our apartment wasn't far from the sprawling Chapultepec Park, and Mike wanted to go there and tour the anthropology museum. We stopped at a stand in the park and bought soft drinks. The smog had closed in early. Leaves hung limply from the park's towering trees, as if stricken by the lack of oxygen. Above the trees was a steel pole with a set of leather loops attached near the top. Four Indians in tribal dress shimmied up the pole, set the loops around their heads and necks, stretched out their arms, and as the pole revolved, the centrifugal force hung them feet outward in the sky. The pole swung around so slowly the sight was incongruous—four Indians doing bored laps in the gray sky.

As we watched them a young woman approached me. She asked if we were Americans, and I said we were. In slow, careful English she told me she was a student at a business college, and she had an assignment to interview someone in English. Would I do that for her?

"Sure, claro," I said.

Mike sat nearby, listening. The young woman wore a plain navy blue dress and seemed self-conscious. On lined paper she had a hand-written script of questions, and she held a minicassette recorder near my face. Where did I live? Was I married? What were the names of my wife and children? My dog and cat? She read from the page, "What is your religion?"

"None."

She looked at me as if that were an odd or inappropriate answer.

"Lo siento," I apologized. "I have none. I'm not religious." I shrugged.

I kept answering her questions partly or wholly in Spanish, which frustrated her. I tried to stop doing it.

"What is your favorite baseball team?"

"The Cleveland Indians."

"What is your opinion of Mexico City?"

"Well, it's one of the world's great cities, or it was. But it's so polluted now. And all the crime. It's a shame. I hope your government can turn it around—that it's not too late."

She frowned and stared at me. I couldn't tell if she had not understood my English or if she was offended. "Don't you think?" I said. "Don't you agree?"

The young woman turned off the recorder, gathered up her things, murmured her thanks, and walked away.

I looked at Mike and said, "Am I wrong, or was that weird?"

"Definitely weird," he said. "Like she was going to wig out in some way, at any moment."

The strange interview stirred in me a vague unease; it was one of those surreal, fleeting encounters that abound in Mexico.

We spent over an hour in the National Museum of Anthropology. Afterward, while waiting for the others I sat on a stone wall under a fragrant shade tree covered with gorgeous, deep purple wisteria.

Thin-legged little girls paraded back and forth in Sunday finery—
white dresses with flared skirts and crocheted embellishments. They
wore patent leather shoes and carried purses or baskets, which they
filled with the flowers. The little girls were very pretty, in that
ephemeral prepubescent way, and they knew it. After admiring
them awhile I realized what this show was about. In essence, they had
been sent out by their parents to beg. I gestured at the one who had
been flirting the most with me. She walked toward me swinging her
basket. I laid some pesos in it. She spun on her heel and walked off
without giving me another glance.

We walked and walked that afternoon. We crossed under a freeway and doubled back to Chapultepec Castle. But long lines wound
from the castle doors to the sculpture of torches honoring *El Niños*,
the cadets who jumped to their deaths rather than surrender to U.S.
Marines in the Mexican War. What did they call that war? I wondered. For a few moments we watched a mime perform, then headed
back down the hillside. Mike had taken a special interest in a painter
at an art show in a park during a recent trip to Mexico City. He knew
the art show reassembled every Sunday; he wanted to go back and, if
possible, buy a painting he had seen the first time. We wandered across
long blocks downtown, and because it was Sunday, absolutely nothing
was open. Except for passing cars we saw almost no one. Though
Mike grew frustrated and embarrassed, we didn't give him too much
grief. We encountered a man with a newspaper rolled under his arm.
He walked with a limp. Mike stopped him and asked him if he knew
about the art show. The man thought a moment then pointed and
told us to keep walking. In time we should see the park on the left.
We walked on a hundred yards, then heard the man call out to us. In
his uneven gait he hurried back to us. He pointed down the street to
our immediate left, and with a sweeping motion of his arm, he indi-
cated a section of the city.

"No vayas allí," he said. "Es peligroso."

Don't go there, it's dangerous.

We found the art show but the painter who appealed to Mike had moved on. As the show shut down we caught a cab to the Zócalo. Political groups and artisans were spread across the vast plaza. A big Mexican flag popped and rang its chain in the breeze, and periodically some anthem burst from the recording system. Indians pounded drums and kept up a daylong dance. John wanted to find a painting of the Zapatistas' *Subcomandante* Marcos on black velvet. Peculiar to the culture along the Rio Grande, the usual subjects of the folk art on velvet are bullfights, raging stallions, and Elvis in his rotund Vegas phase. We rummaged through the Zapatista stuff at length. There were choleric pamphlets, also a band, standing in somewhat military formation, that was pitiful—one of the players tried to blow notes out of a trombone without a slide.

John bought some T-shirts, then we drifted on, looking at cowboy hats, colorful blankets, silver jewelry. David spied the ridiculous hat, the brown straw bowler, and couldn't live without it. Leaving them to their shopping, Mike and I walked through the cathedral. The elaborate exterior of the sixteenth-century church wears a permanent smudge of dark smoke stain, and inside, because the weight of the structure has sunk it into the old lakebed, every column is now enclosed by a supporting brace of steel. Glass cabinets contained the usual likenesses of Christ, the Virgin, and the saints, and toward the front a mass was in progress, but to me the Mexico City church captured everything about that faith that is dark and forbidding.

We all reconvened and climbed stairs to the roof of the Majestic Hotel. At first there were no tables available out on the patio. We settled happily in the bar, alone with a soccer game on TV and an attentive bartender. At sundown we were called out to a table in the rooftop cafe, and with the national anthem blaring we watched a detail of soldiers bring down and fold the flag. We had dinner and more drinks on the rooftop cafe. The sky above the Zócalo was a lovely mauve dusk.

I was the only one, I discovered later, who had any qualms about going back to Plaza Garibaldi. I was tired from all the walking, and the night before, the experience outside the boxing arena had set off loud alarms in my head. I wanted to go back to our apartment, have a drink on our own patio, and get in bed with a book. But I said nothing about it—I didn't want to be the old grump. And it felt like some force was pulling us along, keeping us out in the city.

I did speak up when they started talking about how to get to the plaza. John noticed that below us a street sign pointed to it. But I knew that following that path would take us back into the unlighted streets around the Arena Coliseo. I got out a map, and said we had to follow the Avenida 16th de Septiembre to its end, where on turning right we would see a park called the Alameda. On a major street, San Juan de Letran, in a few blocks we would arrive at the plaza.

It was fully dark when we set out. When we reached San Juan de Letran we set out north, and suddenly we plunged into a sidewalk bazaar. We weaved around racks of clothing and pots of soup cooked on charcoal fires. Smells of cumin, peppers, smoke, and sweat. It was claustrophobic and frightening. I told the others I had to cross the street, where there were bus stops and storefronts. Then we saw lights and open space and once more we heaved sighs and walked through the plaza.

Away from the street, it was encircled by bars with large neon signs proclaiming their names and Mexican labels of beer. Before each one a hawker claimed their mariachis were the best. But mariachis were everywhere on the plaza. Some with elaborate sombreros strapped around their necks, resting on their shoulders, the black-clad musicians stood, strolled, and played, hoping something about their looks or their skill with a guitar would prompt the tourists or locals to hire them on the spot. It was a pleasant bedlam of singing and strumming.

Then like a school of fish some in the crowd suddenly veered off in pursuit of what we determined was a running fight. We jogged along with the others and watched the show. A mariachi fled from a dark-haired woman who screeched at him. He was panicky, desperate to escape her shrieks. He made a mistake and stopped in a gazebo; the crowd cut off his escape. Now along with the tongue-lashing she flailed at him with her fists and tried to claw him with her nails. Encircled by the grinning crowd, he fended her off as best he could. I half expected him to coldcock her, just to shut her up. But his machismo was already in shreds and puddles. There was no way out.

We could still hear her screeches when we greeted the Tenampa's doorman. The bar was not as crowded and lively as it had been on Friday night, yet despite my initial reluctance to brave the plaza, this evening was making us all laugh and enjoy ourselves. We started drinking about ten o'clock and at least three times agreed this was the last round, only to order another. Mike was still a working musician, I had written a book about the Austin music scene of the 1970s, and John and David were friends of young Texas musicians who were having some success, so the talk soon turned to music, its nightlife and casualties. We drank to songs and memories of B. W. Stevenson, Townes Van Zandt. Then I got off on regaling everyone with my great underreported Texas stories. I told them about the convict who murdered his warden, drowned him with his bare hands, but the jury acquitted him. They couldn't believe it. In Texas? What could that warden have possibly done? I told them about the high school foot-ball coach whose teams won a state championship. He became a pillar of his community, then was charged with using cheerleaders in a call girl ring. The coach quickly disappeared, and so did the story. Come on, the others joshed. "I was there, I remember it," I said. "Or maybe I dreamed it."

At midnight David looked at his watch and announced it was now his thirty-second birthday. We whooped in surprise, clapped him on the back, and ordered another round. Half a dozen groups of mariachis stood around the half-empty bar, and we started putting them to work. "La Negra" and "Las Mañanitas" and "Cucurrucucu," the onomatopoeic cry of a lovelorn dove. I told my young bachelor friends the story about how I fell in love with Dorothy on the trip to Puerto Vallarta: the horseback ride through the storm of butterflies and the intimate cafe called the Chicago Kid. A couple of groups shook their heads when I requested our love song, "La Malagueña." Not because they didn't know it; the song was too hard to sing. The most numerous and fastidiously attired group gathered around us with antique guitars, violins, and trumpets. At my request their leader said, "Claro que sí," and bowed.

The guitarists kept up a rhythmic strumming of chords, the trumpeters came in with blasts of emphasis, while the fiddlers roamed over and under the man's voice. The girl's given name implies an origin in the Spanish province of Málaga, and she's a dancer, alive to music. The poor boy has nothing to offer her but his *corazón*, his heart. The singer had to start low and in the chorus, range high—almost rolling the highest note and the boy's plea into a yodel.

Malagueña salerosa

Besar tus labios quisiera	I would love to kiss your lips
Besar tus labios quisiera	I would love to kiss your lips

Malagueña salerosa

Y decir que niña hermosa	And to say what a beautiful girl
Eres linda y hechisera	You're pretty and enchanting
Eres linda y hechisera	You're pretty and enchanting
Como el calor de una rosa	Like the passion of a rose

Outside we again walked among the crowd. In one of the stalls of the flea market a fight erupted; a man tore off his shirt and stormed after a rival, but somehow the violence seemed to spill toward and focus on us. Mike and I skipped out of the way and looked around for John and David. I saw they had bought more beers. David announced that he had seen a group of *norteño* musicians who were set apart from the mariachis by their brown suits. He and John ambled off in that direction.

I looked at Mike and said, "Let's get these guys out of here."

They had no objections; all of us had drunk enough. John walked out to the cabstand and waved on the green VW. Then the Japanese compact pulled up. We saw the stripe of green paint, but the car looked new and substantial enough that it seemed the driver would be reliable. He offered a cheaper fare, fifty pesos, than we had paid before. I spoke to the driver, who kept his gaze fixed straight ahead, and I slid into the cab's backseat.

When the driver took his dark fast detour I fueled the others' fears by saying, "This doesn't look right." But then we seemed to be back on the right street, which was broad and brightly lit, and the driver took us into the Polanco, down our now-familiar street, and I said no more. Then the driver jammed on the brakes. Mike looked around and saw the *pistoleros* coming. For about ten minutes after Honcho vaulted into the front seat, he kept the muzzle of his gun in Mike's ear. Don't do anything stupid, Mike was thinking. But this tough guy in the bright red shirt sat in his lap and issued inane orders: "Shut up! Close your eyes! Go to sleep!" What a bunch of losers, Mike thought. Amateurs. He bet the guns weren't even loaded.

None of the rest of us even considered that.

There was nothing to do about the pistol-whipping but sit still and take it. This is going to be unpleasant for a little while, John thought—then we'll be all right. "Well, so much for not taking the green cabs," he said, affecting a droll sigh. But when the cab sped onto the hideous freeway, tension began to swell like heat in a balloon.

"I don't know, man," John said now. "This has gone on a long time."

When David said he was going to open the door and throw the fat one out, he meant it. Yeah, right, thought Mike. In a B-movie he does that and I grab this guy's gun and it all goes off like clockwork— except it's us, and we'll all be dead. John's warning as he watched the gun aimed at Mike's head did not convince David. His plan was foiled because he couldn't quite reach the door handle. But in the end he used his head better than any of us. The *pistolero* in the backseat wore a soiled T-shirt that didn't meet his jeans, which were slipping off his ass, and he smelled bad. The pileup was suffocating David. He struggled until he got his head free of the slob and could breathe. What the hell's going on here? David thought. If these guys were just going to rob us, they could have done that a long time ago. A TV show flashed through his mind—some cop saying that the second stop was when people usually got killed by hijackers. Take your chances the first time they let you out of the car. Never get in the trunk.

My friends said later that Honcho and I spoke a great deal of Spanish. I don't remember that. They also said it grew heated between us, that it became personal. Maybe sarcasm leaked into my voice, the set of my lips and eyes. It's true I yelled at Honcho. "Give me your money!" he shouted. "Well, let me get my hands free!" I yelled back. I twisted around under the ridiculous pile of weight until I could finally get my wallet; he tore it out of my hand, then caught my wrist and ripped off the watch. It's a Timex, asshole, I thought. No Rolexes here.

Their robbery was a bust. I was the only one who had any money—about $150 in pesos and a bank credit card. Honcho had hopes for that credit card, probably, but we could not have gotten any money out of it in Mexico City. Maybe he would have killed me beside some ATM machine, when I couldn't give him a PIN number and make the machine drop cash in his hands. I thought I was appealing to reason when I leaned forward and argued that we'd done everything he asked. For an instant I thought Honcho was hearing me, acknowledging me, but then he threw me a look of contempt and turned his head back to the road.

The cabdriver wheeled off the expressway into a barrio. I was the only one who heard Honcho say they were going to separate us. Did he say it in Spanish? Or did he say it at all? It doesn't matter. I knew with certainty that nothing good awaited us. Adrenaline was racing through Honcho, too, and he had felt the power of making us cringe. He had terrified and humiliated us with that gun. He was crazed with that power; he didn't intend to thank us kindly and let us go. Sooner or later Honcho meant to kill me. All of us. I was sure of it. Somebody had to do something, throw this train off course.

We came to a four-way intersection, then the driver turned and stopped. Mike was almost certain they were going to let us go. If they kill us, he thought, they'll just pop us all in the head, standing beside the car. Mike breathed a prayer as the cab stopped. When we were ordered out of the car John said, "Screw you, it's our cab." I don't know if John realized that was a comic remark, for he went on with pleas that were meaningless to the *pistoleros*. "We don't know where we are, we've got no money, we can't get home. . . ."

David must have gotten out and hesitated, for I had time to step out behind him. Honcho grabbed me roughly by my left arm. I was clearly the one he wanted. John had the brass to step out on the driver's side. He was free! He had put the car between himself and the guns. All he had to do was duck and run. But he wasn't thinking clearly, because he strolled around the trunk to join us, to check things out. "Run, run, scatter!" cried David, fighting off the fat guy and running around the car and out into the street. The gunman clubbed a big knot on his head and tried to tackle him, tearing his pants down the seam. Yet David never let go of that dumb straw derby. Mike was immobile, frozen, standing beside the car.

That's the only way I can visualize the sequence of movement, because I was aware of none of it. David's breakaway must have distracted Honcho, for I felt his grip loosen on my arm. In reflex I threw his hand off me. If I had then just turned and run, could he have wheeled and aimed and shot me in the back? Or if I'd had the speed and reflexes of my friend Jesus, the real boxer, I could have pivoted and knocked Honcho down with a right hand, for he was smaller than me and he was looking away. "I don't know, Jan," a friend at the gym named Mario would say, shaking his head. "If you'd hurt him, cut him, he might have emptied that gun on you." Yes, he might have. But all the what ifs came later. There was no time for any reasoning. It was survival instinct, the dilemma of all creatures since the dawn of time—fight or flee.

Except I didn't quite do either. Honcho lurched at me in a rage. The punch I threw at him was as hard, fast, and angry as any I'd ever thrown, but I miscalculated the distance and the left came up short. Then I stood my ground. I was up on my toes—glaring at murder. Dunderhead! Now it was too late for me to flee. I backed away from Honcho, raising my arm at the gun. Mike said that Honcho fired one time at the pavement—how could I have no memory of that? Then immediately he raised the gun at me. His eyes were full of hate and revulsion. *So you want to fight me, gringo.* He took careful aim at my vital organs, looked me in the eyes, and pulled the trigger.

I wrote a novel once that had a gunfight at night in the story. I'd never seen such a thing, so I got a friend who owned pistols to go out in the country with me. From a few paces away he fired two bullets over my head. Both muzzle flashes looked like jagged, spear-shaped blooms of flame, pistils of white heat narrowing from the bore. But Honcho's beat-up old .38 threw out an eerie, pale crackle of lightning that wobbled left and right and reached from above his shoulder to the ground. The bullet broke both bones in my raised left arm, which must have slowed it down. But it tore through me like a drill stem, a big hot churning screw. The force of it hurled me on my back, and I knew at once I was gravely hurt. "I'm killed," I said, thinking I might not have time to say anything longer.

The taxi and the *pistoleros* vanished from our lives. I was in agony, and furious at myself. *You had a good life, a good marriage, and you come down here and get yourself wasted by some chickenshit thug.* I was embarrassed by what I had said. Such a bad Hollywood line. Mike thought it was so trite it must be a signal of triumph: I had staged a comic pratfall to make them go away. My groans soon disabused him of that. I had worn jeans and my favorite Mexican shirt that night, a Oaxacan long-sleeved white cotton shirt with a pleated front. At first the blood flowed inward, not out. They pulled up my shirt and finally found the wound. David said it looked like a dime, just below my left rib cage.

This can't be happening, David thought. *It can't be happening.* While Mike held my head David and John ran opposite ways down the street, calling out for help. David's Spanish was better: "Ayúdame!

Ayúdame! Mi amigo . . ." They ran to the ends of the block, then back toward me, still seeing nothing but boarded up windows. Then an old woman opened a door and motioned at John to come inside. But when he asked, she said she had no telephone.

"Ambulancia!" David cried out.

"Sí, sí," some woman answered him. One had been called.

The intersection was well-lighted, and I looked up at a clearly defined ring of faces. They would have looked the same if it happened on your street or mine. Their expressions were frightened, anxious, wondering how they could help. Then the first godsend came to my aid.

A paramedic in his thirties, he lived in the barrio. My friends thought maybe he was still wearing his work clothes; they were unsure. But he pushed through the crowd and took over at once. He checked my pulse and asked me a couple of questions, then shooed away an old woman who kept trying to give me the water I desperately craved. As they waited for the ambulance, Mike cradled my head in his lap and John and David held each of my hands. I was bleeding more now, and it began to soak in Mike's clothes. They were surprised at how quickly the ambulance and a police patrol unit arrived. The paramedic briefed his peers from the ambulance on my condition and told them to take me to the American British Cowdray Hospital. He stressed it—Hospital ABC. As my stretcher was being raised to the back of the ambulance, John stepped out from the crowd and said: "Hey, Jan, it's gonna make a *great story*."

Oh, fuck you!

John would explain that he was just trying to elevate the mood. You know, lighten up. It might help. But David barked angrily at his friend. Mike said later, "That's when I remembered we were drunk."

The medics in the ambulance were businesslike but not particularly friendly. Maybe they resented me being sent to the best hospital in the city. This is going to cost a lot of money, they stressed to Mike. A lot of money.

The pain was unimaginable. I clung to Mike's hand and said, "Mike, I'd rather die than take this pain, but I want to see Dorothy again."

I remember his voice was very soft. "Well, there's your reason why."

That snatch of dialogue found its way into the Austin newspaper, and suddenly people would make us into Tracy and Hepburn, Bogie and Bacall. Not so widely known, Mike told me when we could both laugh, was my final wish. "You said, 'If I die, tell Dorothy . . . oh, you know what to tell her.' "

I n the emergency room I screamed with every breath. "Tranquilo, tranquilo," said a doctor with a sharp nose and black mustache. Calm down. If he was questioning my courage, forget it. That was used up, spent. I looked the doctor in the eyes and screamed again.

I was lucky. It was a slow night, the early morning hours of a Monday, and practically everyone in the emergency room could pay attention to me. But the endlessness of such pain astonished me. I thought shock was supposed to relieve it. I kept hoping I'd pass out. I asked one of the doctors for morphine.

"No la tenemos," he answered.

They don't have morphine?

They probably did have a small supply in the hospital. But for whatever reason, Mexican doctors and hospitals prefer a synthetic substitute, and believe me, it's just not the same.

Mike said they had me lying naked on a steel table. I complained of being cold. He said I screamed continually, "Oh, God!" I remember that I thought about praying. I believed I still knew how. But I found I had no religious faith. There's no solace in that. Some time later I gazed at the dark eyes of the nurse. She had been there for a while, and she was pretty. I was tired and scared beyond all limits of my being. "Me estoy muriendo?" I asked her. Am I dying? "No, no, estarás bien," she said, putting a hand on my arm, and in Spanish she talked me through that dark passage of surrender and despair. She persuaded me I could hang on.

A paramedic living in a tough side of town and an emergency room nurse on the night shift. Guardian angels, and I'll never know their names.

(8)

I f I hadn't feared and felt the nearness of dying I wouldn't have uttered that cry. Death's air was melancholy, and it pulled like tidewash loosening beach sand under my feet. I had been calm in the taxi and brave with Honcho in the street, but now I was frantic with this pain, unhinged by it. For God's sake, I thought between screams. Just let me pass out. And at last I let go of consciousness, or it let go of me.

A vascular specialist, Roberto Castañeda, led the first team of surgeons. Dr. Castañeda found me very pale, my heart beating rapidly, and while I was still conscious I had complained of intense burning pain in my legs, with some pain in my abdomen. Dr. Castañeda opened my abdominal wall and found the peritoneal cavity awash with two and a half liters of blood. Scarce wonder I was pale—I had lost a third of my blood supply. Perforations in my small intestine accounted for most of the bleeding. Dr. Castañeda removed some intestine and rejoined the ends. The bullet had narrowly missed the aorta, a grand central station of blood vessels. If the aorta had burst, I would have died in minutes.

Dr. Castañeda watched me closely in recovery. He noticed some small movements that he thought were voluntary—I flexed my toes and the soles of my feet—but my legs appeared to be paralyzed. When he was confident I was stable, he turned me over to a team of neurosurgeons headed by Francisco Revilla. After studying the results of a CT scan and MRI, Dr. Revilla and his colleagues opened my spinal column from the rear. They found the bullet had fractured my twelfth thoracic vertebra and had come to rest nose down in the *cauda equina*—"horse's tail" in Latin—which is a flaring bundle of nerves at the base of the spinal cord. Dr. Revilla removed the bullet, then with a surgical microscope inspected the spinal canal. The spinal cord appeared to be whole, though an unknown number of nerves in the *cauda equina* were destroyed or damaged by the blast of heat and shock. Unlike the cord, some of those nerves might be able to heal and regenerate themselves.

Barring some rampage of infection, I was almost out of danger. But the MRI had not looked good to Dr. Revilla. And throughout the surgery he had administered a test called a Somato-Sensorial Evoked Potential Recording. The neurosurgeons in the Mexico City hospital placed a great deal of faith in that test of my movement capability, and it registered a completely flat line.

While I was in neurosurgery, Dorothy and Lila arrived at the Mexico City airport jangled, distraught, terrified, and sleepless. Lila did not even know I had gone to Mexico until her mother called her. Then an airlines clerk said Lila's passport had expired; only some frantic driving by her boyfriend, Greg Wilson, let her present her birth certificate and board the plane. They cleared customs in Mexico City and were exasperated that the only way to get to the hospital was to catch a cab. They didn't know what to expect; Texans were always hearing horror stories about medical care in Mexico. But the American British Cowdray looked like any modern, first-rate hospital in the States. They met Mike, David, and John in the waiting room where they had tried to sleep. It was awkward as they talked. Mike's clothes were stained with dried blood. "It's so bizarre it could have happened like that," Mike told them. "Because he—all of us—had such a great time."

They were exhausted, devastated. While Mike accompanied me in the ambulance, a pair of Mexico City cops had given John and David a ride to the apartment, where John got my passport and a credit card, and then had taken them to the hospital. The cops asked them what happened, but with an air of curiosity, not investigation. During the night no police had disturbed them. No cops ever came to question them at all. "Listen," Dorothy told them, "there's nothing you can do here. You guys go home."

Roberto Castañeda was horrified that such a thing could happen in the city where he made his home, a city he loved. Having saved my life, he swept Dorothy and Lila into his emotional care. With short brushed hair, a widely bridged nose, and black-rimmed glasses, he was the smart, caring man we want all doctors to be. He had kept my wedding ring buckled to his watch. In almost fluent English, he told them what he had done and all he knew about my condition. "The neurosurgeons will probably tell you he'll be paralyzed," he tried to prepare them. "They'll paint the bleakest possible picture. That's just how neurosurgeons are." Dr. Castañeda would write in his own report that my prospects for complete recovery were very poor. Still he told them, "Remember, I saw him move his toes voluntarily. I saw that. Don't lose hope."

Dr. Castañeda left them in the care of a gracious hospital volunteer. Administrators provided them with a room I was not yet ready to occupy. Dorothy knew she needed help; as she packed she had called our friend Ty Fain and asked him to come. Ty had worked for the

State Department and an assortment of Texas agencies that had relations with official Mexico, and he spoke Spanish with a diplomat's
confidence and ease. He arrived during the afternoon and took over
the welter of calls. Reporters were calling from all over Texas and
Mexico. Dorothy and Lila were amazed by Ty's aplomb. He would be
talking into the hospital phone, then the cell phone he had brought
from Texas, one call in English, another in Spanish, all the while taking notes.

Later that afternoon the neurosurgeons came to the room. They
were all freshly groomed and dressed in black suits. Lila and Dorothy
later nicknamed them "the Crows." Dr. Revilla was solemn, proper,
and frank. A few minutes later Lila was standing outside the hospital
when John and David arrived in a cab. They had gone to the Polanco
apartment to pack for the trip home. As they neared Lila, John saw
that she was sobbing. She told them, "They just said he'll never walk
again."

Dorothy and Lila thought Dr. Revilla was somewhat aloof. Of
course, he couldn't tell them anything they wanted to hear. But suddenly he reappeared, and this time he was smiling, animated. Dr.
Castañeda had been right. In the recovery room I had been coming
out from the anesthesia, and one of the doctors scratched my foot and
shin with a plastic card, a routine way of testing sensory responses. It
wasn't much voluntary movement, but I yelped with pain and gave a
feeble kick.

Unaware that anything had changed, Mike, John, and David went
by the U.S. embassy on the way to the airport. Ignored by the
Mexico City police, Mike wanted to be sure they told the story to
someone of official capacity before they left the country. As they left,
other friends were arriving. Dick Reavis happened to be in Mexico
City on a freelance magazine assignment. When I first knew Dick,

he was going up in the Sierra Madres alone to interview guerrillas. A friend from the Mexico City bureau of the *Houston Chronicle* had called him at his hotel and told him about me. Dick said, "My first thought was, Holy shit! That should have been me! All the times I'd jumped in a Mexico City street cab . . ." Dick came to the hospital but found no one he knew; he left Dorothy a card offering to help. When she called, she asked him to relieve Ty with the phones.

Other friends from Austin and Dallas arrived throughout the day. Late that afternoon, the doctors said I could receive visitors one at a time, for just a minute or two.

"You came," I said to Dorothy, as if that surprised me.

At a loss, Lila asked me if I needed anything.

"An aspirin," I replied.

I don't remember seeing either of them or saying those things. But soon after that, I became aware of lying in a bed that seemed to float in olive green ether. Through an oval in this fog came a procession of several close friends. Roy Hamric, Gary Cartwright, David Lindsey, Robert Draper, Dick Reavis, Ty Fain, Jim Crump. A handshake, a smile, a few words, and then they were gone. What a fine-looking bunch of middle-aged men! How nattily dressed they were!

I was pretty sure I was alive, but couldn't this be like dying?

In Austin, *Texas Monthly*'s frenetic publisher, Mike Levy, lived for such a crisis. Soon after hearing about it, he tracked down his friend, Dr. Red Duke. Red Duke had been a Texas A&M Aggie, an officer in the Army Rangers, a Baptist seminarian, and he was the surgeon who treated Texas governor John Connally at Dallas's Parkland Hospital after the John F. Kennedy assassination. But he was famous in Texas because of his folksy programs of health advice that ran on the news of local TV stations. A tall, bony man with a droopy cowboy mustache, he was as familiar to his audience as a pair of jeans and roughout boots. Red Duke was also a world-renowned trauma specialist, and he administered a service that dispatched jets all over the world to rescue people.

Monitoring the storm of calls for us was another friend of twenty-five years, Norman Chenven. He had been our family doctor, then had retired from his practice to help found the HMO that served our insurance plan. When Norman heard about the shooting, he assigned his top caseworker, a young woman named Diane Hosmer. Diane had already lined up a jet when she learned of Mike Levy's efforts. "But there was an element of Indiana Jones working now," chuckled Norman, who knew Mike well. As a doctor Norman thought it was a little premature to move me, but he left the decision to my wife. "Dorothy was angry," Diane said later. "Angry at what happened and where it happened. She said, 'I don't want him, I don't want us, to be here.' "

Dick Reavis, my friend who had been in Mexico City on a magazine assignment, was a small, mustachioed man who, as he aged, more and more resembled the weathered ranch hands on the Panhandle plains where he grew up. A drunk had once crashed a car into his motorcycle on a Texas highway, and Mike Levy had come to Dick's rescue, visiting him in the hospital daily and making sure his medical bills were covered. Dick thought this was a time of paying back and taking his turn. Patiently he kept answering the phone. He took one call from Jesus Chavez, who was castigating himself. Lila went in the hospital room alone to talk to Dick about the possibility that I might not survive a flight to Texas. The hurry was that spinal injury specialists in Texas were saying every day of expert rehabilitation could be critical at this stage. "If it was me," Dick told her, "and it meant I might walk, I'd probably take the chance."

"I want a daddy who can walk," she told Dick. "But more than that I want a daddy." Friends from *Texas Monthly* were telling Dorothy that a rescue jet from Houston was available, but the clock was running. If we didn't use it, somebody else would. My wife felt like her head was about to explode; she was under horrendous pressure. Then, with the agreement and consent of the neurosurgeons, thirty-six hours after I was shot, Dr. Castañeda wrote a report that my condition was good and I could be transferred to the States as soon as my family wanted. Dorothy took a deep breath and said, "Let's go."

But hours dragged on as they waited for the jet and its rescue team. Several parties of cops had come to the hospital by then, doggedly asking questions of people who had no knowledge of what had happened. Then the higher-ups arrived. These police had cell phones and a security entourage, and one lugged a heavy office typewriter to the waiting room. "They were mad," said Dick, "mad that the press knew about this, and mad that the other guys had left Mexico." The cops' leader told Dick: "He's not going anywhere until he makes a statement to us."

"He *can't* make a statement," Dick replied.

The cop looked around, exasperated. Finally someone suggested that an interview of Dick might do. Half an hour passed while the top cop batted the idea back and forth with his superiors. At last Dick's statement was approved. In the waiting room, the cop with the typewriter placed it on the counter of the nurses' station and rolled in several sheets of paper and carbons.

"You understand that I saw none of this," said Dick. "The only one here who did see it is unconscious. Anything I say is based on what I have been told secondhand or have read in the American press."

One cop nodded, and another started typing.

It was close to midnight when the rescue team—one nurse and one paramedic—reached the American British Cowdray Hospital.

I had a lucid moment. The leader was a feisty woman with curly hair and happy-people stickers on her stethoscope. "Mr. Reid," she said, her face close above me. "You're going to Houston! Tonight!"

I grinned at her, goofily no doubt, then once more sank into the murk.

During the ordeal a medical technician at the hospital had told Dorothy and Lila, "I'm so ashamed." And now as they said good-bye to Dr. Castañeda, the surgeon implored them, "Please don't hate my country."

The ambulance made slow progress up a winding, bumpy road to the outlying town of Toluca. The American technicians knew about my pain difficulties and they had brought morphine. Our plane took off with me bound tightly to a stretcher. The flight to Houston was short and free of weather bumps, but it was nerveracking for Dorothy and Lila. I snored loudly with my eyes wide open. That's not a good sign, I've since been told. I was at the first tier of descent into a coma.

When the plane came to a stop at the Hobby Airport in Houston, the woman in charge strode up to Dorothy, her voice charged with tension. "Ms. Browne, we're having trouble waking him up."

Right after that I stopped breathing. As they forced tubes down my throat and began to inflate my lungs, Dorothy and Lila were hustled off the plane. In the darkness Lila cried out in fear and accusation: "They OD'ed him!"

Dorothy said in bitter despair: "Lila, don't ever put your life in my hands."

I resumed breathing and for a moment was conscious again. Something uncomfortable was clamped over my nose and mouth, and I struggled, fought it. The face of the woman in charge appeared above me. "Mr. Reid, you know me. We talked two hours ago in Mexico City. You're in Houston now. And"—I swear she said this—"you're *blowing it!*"

.   .   .

On the tarmac the rescue team stood around waiting for an ambulance. "Get a helicopter in here," Dorothy yelled at them. They jumped to and made the call. As the aircraft rose with me and veered north toward the sprawling Houston Medical Center, Dorothy and Lila were in the racing ambulance. For all they knew I was dead. Dorothy had been told I would be under the care of a Houston neurosurgeon named Guy Clifton. When the ambulance reached the emergency room of Hermann Hospital, they ran inside. They encountered a tall old guy with a rusty-colored mustache that covered most of his mouth. He wore hospital greens and scratched himself. Dorothy burst upon him, blurting my name and demanding to see Dr. Clifton. The old-timer answered in a reassuring drawl. "I'm Dr. Red Duke. I'm gonna be your doctor, and I'm gonna be your mother."

As they plunged into sleep in the hotel room he booked for them, I floated in an eerie kind of remove, half-aware. "We're afraid you're going to lose the mobility of your legs," a Mexican doctor had said, phrasing it gently. I'm paralyzed, I thought, but I'm alive. I'll deal with paralysis. Then I saw my friend Norman Chenven. I thought it was night and I was outside; Norman stood among a crowd pressing against a chain-link fence. (He was actually beside my hospital bed.) He told me in his matter-of-fact way that paralysis was just one possible effect of a lower spine injury. "The bladder and bowel and sexual function—we'll just have to wait and see about that." Bladder and bowel and sexual function! I could be incontinent and impotent, too? I took that harder than being told I was paralyzed. I felt like my manhood had been chopped off at the waist.

.   .   .

There's a line from an old Rolling Stones song: "Please, Sister Morphine, turn my nightmare into dreams." In the first of my dreams
I was riding in a truck being driven by an Asian woman. It was early
in the morning, the sun just up. I wanted to trust this woman, but she
ignored me. On a country road she stopped at a store with grimy
windows and a dusty soda pop machine on the porch. After a moment she came back out, started the truck, and we drove off. Still she
said nothing; she had an air of making her daily rounds. We came to
a river that was running brown and high. It was up to the throats of
the water buffalo. *Water buffalo!* Where was I? The woman sent the
truck down the bank toward the swollen river. She was going to try
to ford it.

"Listen here," I cried. "You get me back to Dr. Red Duke. Right
now. He's supposed to be taking care of me." It would be several days
before I enjoyed Red Duke's company, but I invoked his name like a
protective chant.

My days were spent in paranoid tedium. I lay in a bed staring at a
ceiling. I heard voices on the other side of the walls. People were va-
cationing on a seashore. I could hear the gulls. They talked about children and meals and laundry. Their mundane chat and their comings
and goings were maddening. I lay helpless, abandoned. Every now and
then a woman came in with a bucket and mop. She answered my
pleas with a disinterested grunt.

The editors at *Esquire* sent flowers. I know this happened because
I still have their card. But a nurse told me I couldn't have the flowers. I
was being moved to a room of less intensive care. The beds of several
patients in serious condition were arranged with the usual monitoring screens and nurses close at hand. But I believed I was in a ward
where the beds were plugged into a dock like tractor trailers. The talk

that drifted over from the next cubicle was black English, cool and tart. Profane. Two women were trying to bolster the spirits of a professional athlete. He was paid to be on the field catching passes, but he had broken his leg, fooling around, and the front office was furious. The team had him on ice, immobilized. "This is where they bring the football players," I informed Lila one day. She looked around at my fellow patients and thought it sure was an elderly team.

One night I was in a house. I could see and hear a man and woman moving about. They spoke English with French accents. They had contracted with the state to care for me, but they were con artists, and their fraud had been discovered. They took their time packing, but they meant to be gone by dawn.

"Wait!" I cried. "You can't just leave me here. Please. You've got to find Red Duke."

Ignoring me, the man carried things to a car in the garage. The woman stood by my bed and watched me for a moment, coolly smoking a cigarette.

"Do you know what's happened to you?" she asked.

Another dream took on aspects of a novel I had been working on. For generations there had been rumors and lore of a great lost house on the Brazos River. A sort of Texas Camelot. It was the home of Sam Houston's family, the patriarchs, and I had found it. The large front room had a marble staircase, bookcases, and oil portraits of elders. I was in this house, and I could walk. I moved around freely and enjoyed myself. Sam Houston was there, ragging his son Temple for being drunk all the time. "You're one to talk," Temple shot back, pouring himself another. It was a rowdy gathering. Tall, striking old women flung good-natured taunts at the men.

The Houston family seemed to have merged with the Parkers,

another prominent Texas clan. The family gathered proudly on the staircase to be photographed by a man who stooped at the rear of a camera and tripod.

"Wait," one of the women insisted, and the uproar resumed. Quanah Parker deserved to be in the picture, the sisters maintained. He was blood kin, even if he was a half-breed Comanche.

In the flesh, I was in that room. Then the voices receded, and the focus narrowed, leaving the staircase blurred. I saw my friend Jim Anderson. Tall and slender, he greeted me and said, "Jan," with a nod.

And I greeted him, thinking, Jim, what are you doing here? It was entirely seamless. Jim handed me a telephone, and I found myself talking to my sister Lana in Wichita Falls.

Very much for real. For the first time since Mexico City.

"Mother's all right," Lana told me. "She's just very shocked. She needs to hear your voice."

My eighty-two-year-old mother. In my absence I had gone from being as fit as a fighter and younger than my years to the limbo of a patient in constant need of others' care. And in this mindblown condition I must try to talk to my ailing mom. I thought, Man, you'd better rally. Because you're not going to reassure her very much at all.

Part Two

(9)

When I came to my senses I was in the bright glare of a media frenzy. I was bewildered. I couldn't understand the furor—people get robbed and shot *all the time*. Part of it lay in growing public awareness of the violence in Mexico, awareness that some of it was directed against Americans. I was on the cusp of a breaking national story. But the fascination with my looping trail of choice and chance was more personal than that. In the communities that responded most, it tapped into the strained union and past of Texas and Mexico. This was how the popular version played: Trying to save the lives of his friends, the unarmed Texan looks down the barrel of the glaring Mexican *pistolero*. In a desperate act of bravery, one man stands his ground. I got cards and letters conveying a belligerent attitude of Us against Them. Remember the Alamo and the Punitive Expedition against Pancho Villa. I got fraternal calls from old Wichita Falls streetfighters who treated me like a bony nerd in their heyday. "We're going to send down a posse to get him," one teased a baffled Lila, answering the phone at the hospital in Mexico City. "Tell them Meskins they better look out!"

The chauvinistic embrace of my struggle was Texas horseshit. The faceoff with Honcho was my first streetfight in more than thirty years.

Through travel and reading and writing I had been trying to escape and rise above an ethic that equated manhood with hooliganism. But the jocular messages continued to come from men—always men—who were half-serious. With language lifted from his own decoration ceremony, one Vietnam veteran awarded me a photocopy of a Purple Heart. It was touching but absurd. Nobody was at war with Mexico. I went down there because I was a devoted friend of a young man of Mexican heritage. Mexicans saved my life.

Of course, most of the reaction was decent, intelligent, and compassionate. The first card I opened, from a girlfriend of years past, said: "Dear Jan, Never go to a gunfight without a gun." I laughed out loud. That part of me still worked. Women friends cheered me up with inflatable plastic tulips and a toy green Volkswagen Beetle. The avalanche of letters would go on for months—would awe and inspire me and fill me with guilt that I could never answer them all. Total strangers, a young hospital fund-raiser and her attorney husband, gave Dorothy and Lila use of an apartment in a pleasant area just five minutes from the Houston Medical Center, sparing us the cost of hotels and the stress of Houston's traffic. Thousands of dollars poured into a Rescue Fund drive that would allay my loss of income and help cover medical expenses. One day brought a check for five thousand dollars and a warm personal note from the boxing promoter Don King, who had endured his own Mexico City holdup and was moved by my connection to the fights. Dorothy's boss told her to stay with me as long as she needed—the job would be waiting when she returned. Dorothy and Lila were holding up, but they were still running on adrenaline, inured by lingering shock. It was as if a hand grenade had crashed through a window and gone off under our dinner table.

We weren't the only victims of the crime. Though physically they suffered no more than knots and bruises, my friends had been terrorized and brutalized, and they weren't being given time and space to recover. "What you did was brave but stupid," Mike Hall told me later.

Brave but stupid, I thought. How bluntly he cut to the truth of the matter! "But what I did was nothing," he went on. "I froze up. I called my parents and said I needed to talk. But my dad is career Army; he's seen combat in three wars. His attitude was 'You move on.' Whatever happens, you move on. I kept trying to talk to him about what happened to me, what happened to you. He said, 'You're not hurt. Your friend's alive. Forget it. Move on.' It wound up with him getting really mad at me. He hung up on me, slammed down the phone."

I knew they all had to heal from this experience, and it was unfair for them to be harried by endless questions about me. Hermann Hospital's public relations director came to my room and said their phone lines were swamped. She offered to set up a press conference in my room with one TV camera and a pool of reporters. "You're going to do *what?*" said Dorothy when she and Lila came back to the hospital. Not long before this I had been talking about the ward full of football players. But five days after the shooting, three after I had stopped breathing on the airport runway, about twenty reporters crowded into the room. I said I was going to make a statement but would take no questions. I told them about my friendship with Jesus Chavez, the story I'd written about him, how my colleagues and I had gone to Mexico City to watch him fight, then had gone to Plaza Garibaldi and climbed in the wrong cab. Dorothy was thunderstruck. "It's like you clicked into overdrive," she later said. " 'Press . . . I know that—it's what I am'. . . so you hit that button, and that's what played."

My peers were respectful, but as it usually happens they did call out some questions, and I answered a few. One asked how I thought my medical challenge would turn out. "I don't know," I said. "Some days it seems like I'm going to be fine, and some days it seems like I'm climbing Mount Everest."

At the side of my bed was a table and a telephone. Every time the phone rang I answered it. I knew better, but the phone was a channel out of this frightful state I was in. Before, my life had conformed to a practiced, familiar routine. I had good days and bad days, but nothing much surprised me. Now, everything before me was a black hole of unknowing and fear. I didn't know if I were brave enough to overcome and find dignity in what lay ahead. I didn't know if I were *man enough*.

During that time I dialed our voice mail in Austin and heard the recording of my emergency room screams. "He's all right," said Mike, his voice breaking, and in recognizing my voice and realizing what this was, I heard the cry of a dying animal. I listened to it, frozen. With morbid fascination I started to play it again, but the moment I again heard the voices, I erased it, flung it to oblivion, nobody was ever going to hear that again.

Except when I played it over and over again, in my mind.

A reporter from a Texas newspaper had been calling the room. Patiently and then not so patiently Dorothy turned her away. A day or two after the press conference the phone rang, and I picked it up. The reporter's deadline was pressing, and she didn't mean to be denied. "I've got all the others," she said of her story and my friends. "I really need your perspective."

She sounded very young. "Look," I said. "I'm under sedation and I can't talk to you. Get a copy of that videotape. It's got everything I have to say now."

I didn't think I ought to have to lie in a hospital bed and lecture her on our professional ethics. But she persisted. "The others said there was something personal between you and that guy. I just want to know where all this *anger* came from."

My jaw dropped. "Well, he pistol-whipped me. Twice."

The reporter's question was my first awareness that I would stand judged on grounds of gender: I had brought all this ruin on myself and my family because in a moment calling for calm and calculating acquiescence, I had found that in the deepest heart of me was a macho fool. A Cuban-born friend who has known too much violence and hurt in her life told me later that she had taken a poll of our Austin circle of friends. Every man, she said, admired me for what I did.

Every woman thought I was insane. When I began to write again, from editorial precincts I heard the conceptual phrase "inappropriate male response." I laughed at that one, but the insinuations of reproach did not go away. At least I got the feminist vote that counted. "It's the same argument that our defense attorney friends use against rape victims," responded Dorothy. "The victim caused it. 'What were you doing in a place like that? Why were you wearing such a short skirt?' "

I can only speculate on how things would have turned out if I hadn't rebelled when the thugs got us out of the car. But I'm confident that if I'd gone quietly I would have been killed. I acted in a split second when action seemed required. I felt more courage that night than I would have ever dreamed I possessed. But I couldn't see much heroism in it. Heroism was the judgment of others; it wasn't an anointment I could ever pour on my head. And the inference that I stepped up to take a bullet to spare my friends just wasn't how it happened. Not exactly. Of course I wanted them to be safe, but in that split second I didn't even know where they were. I saw no one but Honcho. It was a vicious and very short streetfight. Now when I was alone my thoughts leaped from mournfulness to anger. If I was going to throw that first punch, I should have thrown two or three more. I should have gone after him, risked everything, tried to put him down. But that was my friend and teacher Jesus Chavez's style, not mine. I was always sliding, jabbing, looking for the chance to catch the other guy coming in. And you can't very well counterpunch when the other guy has a gun.

Then my racing thoughts turned on me. What am I doing, lying here with no feeling beneath my waist, thinking about *boxing?* A man's solution—fighting with your fists. I didn't feel like a hero. I felt stupid. In those first days Dorothy never cut a glance or made one remark of accusation or recrimination. Lila refused to go home. Every day she came in and made me do the exercises that would keep my hand from freezing up as the bones in my arm and wrist healed. Their behavior was just as instinctive as mine had been, only it was another kind of bravery. Theirs was the bravery of dealing with the wreckage that comes after violence. Their support buoyed me, but when they were gone I lay in anguish and shame. This never should have happened. Why couldn't I act my age? What have I done?

As long as my family and friends were around, I played the cheery, grateful survivor. At night the morphine held the pain at bay, but it wouldn't let me sleep and forget. I obsessed about magazine assignments and thought if I just had a laptop computer I could get them done. Why they mattered anymore, I can't say. I watched NBA playoff games that I had no interest in. One night I pondered Christianity. I decided my reconversion would take place in a tiny Episcopal church near our home. In large type their yard sign stressed that they used the 1928 edition of the Book of Common Prayer. I saw myself strolling to church on a bright sunny day in bowtie, shirtsleeves, and suspenders, fanning my face with a straw boater. Then I dozed, and when I woke my reborn faith was gone. Another trick of the mind and drug.

Meanwhile my strange notoriety continued to grow. ABC's *20/20* spliced a segment of my press conference into a story about Mexican violence that was finished and ready to air. Far more gripping than anything I had to say was a videotape of a robbery and brutal beating that took place in daylight while a uniformed cop casually turned his back a hundred yards away. Afterward two night shift nurses, who were black, came into my room with their eyes widened. (I had recently been moved from the intermediate care unit to a private room.) "Was that you on that show tonight?" one said.

"Yes ma'am. Afraid so."

Before that, their care of me had been professional but fairly impersonal. Now one crossed her arms and leaned against the wall, and the other propped her hip beside me on the bed. "Lord have mercy," said the one standing. "What's this world coming to?"

The nurse on the bed was squat and strong. She had a broad face with expressive features. "Oh, honey, I'm so sorry," she said. She cocked her head and studied me. I could tell she wanted to reach out and touch my face, as she would a child.

"I'll be all right. All you folks helping me."

"Ain't just Mexico City," said the one standing. "People killing for the sake of killing right here in Houston. Westheimer Boulevard they opened a poor girl's car door at a stoplight and just shot her in the head. Then threw her out and ran over her, stealing her car. She wasn't doing nothing but driving home from work to her kids."

"Ain't nobody safe," agreed the one on the bed. "I was in a restaurant with my child about a year ago. Boy come in there just crazy on dope, waving a gun around. Robbing people one by one, then he got it in his mind they called the police. Woman at the register crying, 'Don't shoot! You been watching me the whole time! I never touched that phone!' Then he come to us and said he was gonna take my child, hold him hostage. Ten years old, he's seeing, hearing all this. I said, 'Please, please, don't take him. Please don't. I'll go with you. Take me!' "

The little boy was spared, but the stories of outrage and malice flowed on and on. The women ducked their heads toward me and I tilted mine toward them. The bullet meant I had been ushered into a brotherhood and sisterhood for whom violence is a commonplace. As they left I told the nurse, "I'm sorry that happened to you and your son."

They came back on the shift a couple of nights later. The broad-faced nurse inspected the bedding and found that I had fouled the sheets. I didn't even know, which humiliated me all the more. Her features returned to an impassive mask. Without another word to me, she and the other nurse logrolled me from side to side, cleaning me up and changing the sheets. That's the word they use for moving someone who's paralyzed.

Logrolling.

.   .   .

Every afternoon Red Duke came to see me and it was a huge boost to my morale. He disliked the new breed of doctors who couldn't write a coherent sentence, wanted nothing personal to do with their patients, and jealously worshiped their "lifestyles," a word he voiced like an oath. Slouched in a chair with one long leg crossed over the other, Red said the bullet had so narrowly missed my "business district" that it was pretty much a miracle we were having these conversations. He said the bullet's force had "slapped" my spinal cord pretty good. It had to be injured. But he told me not to worry too much about the changes forced upon me. Having to use a catheter to piss, for instance. He said he ran across an old cowboy who lost his bladder control to prostate woes. The old fellow had figured out that his catheter tube made a perfect fit in the crease in the crown of his Stetson. Whenever the time came to empty his bladder, the gear was right there in his hat.

When Red wasn't practicing medicine, he was teaching it. He slept most nights at the hospital, but he had all the ego required to match his celebrity. Just shooting the bull with him had a kind of healing power. He reminisced about growing up around Willie Nelson and Texas' cantankerous lieutenant governor, Bob Bullock. "Had the chance to kill Bob Bullock," he half-jokingly remarked. He told me about his love for riding and packing high in the mountains of Alaska to hunt bighorn sheep, while I shared with him my admiration for mules, which I used to ride on broken-country trail rides with a cowboy lawyer friend from Amarillo. Which led Red to come back the next day and perform a dramatic reading from the novel *Run with the Horsemen*, written by a Georgia doctor, Ferrol Sams. Stroking his mustache and wiping tears of laughter from his eyes, at length he read about a boy in the Depression who was provoked into putting a match to the farted gas of a spoiled plowing mule.

" 'A flame leaped out as long as a man's arm. There was a clear zone between the source and the beginning of the flame. The blaze was blue, and it hissed and crackled and had long, feathery projections on the upper side of it, and it kept on and on and it was altogether awe-inspiring to witness. Pet's reactions were the swiftest in a decade of laziness. First she tried to clap her tail down to cover the flame, but apparently this was painful, for she raised it again with alacrity. Still with her haunches hunkered, she jerked around, eyes rolling so that the whites gleamed in alarming exophthalmus, and beheld the great blue torch over which she had no control. With a loud snort that expressed wonder, disbelief, terror, and rage, she lowered her head, kicked both hind feet straight back into the plowstock, crouched, then launched herself into a furious gallop. The boy was never sure when the fire went out.' "

At the end of these affairs Red would put his hands on his thighs, push himself up, and say, "Be back tomorrow." Then he would amble down the hall, nurses tittering. It didn't seem possible he was seventy years old.

The doctors wanted to give me a new MRI. The complicating factor, much discussed in my presence, was the external fixator holding my left wrist in place. It was steel, and the doctors and technicians were very careful about removing rings, watches, coins, and other metal from patients before sliding them into the long tube. The reason, a technician told me, was that the magnets producing the imagery could jerk metal this direction or that and cause injury. I looked at the steel bow the Mexican orthopedist had screwed into my hand and arm and said, "What?"

Twice the MRI was scheduled then postponed for that reason. Finally, late one night, nurses shifted me from my bed to a stretcher. The nurse on duty told me to ask for a Valium. Some people thought the tube was claustrophobic, and the pill would make the time pass easier. "But what about this?" I said, raising my arm and the fixator.

"They say it'll be all right. With that kind of metal."

"Who's they?"

"I don't know."

I looked at the orderly, a young black man who had strapped me in and was preparing to roll me down the hall. "I don't know nothin' about it," he said.

"Of course."

The ride took me into the bowels of the hospital; the technician greeted me perfunctorily. "Can I have a Valium?" I asked him.

"Not unless a doctor prescribed it. And there's nothing on your chart."

Sometimes I'm blessed with great patience. After the test began, I gripped the fixator, and the alloyed steel felt inert and cool to the touch. I was fine. I was in no danger and in no pain. I simply had to lie still for a while in a long pipe that sounded like it was being beaten by a drummer with two ball peen hammers. I followed the patterns and smiled. The ultimate in heavy metal.

The next afternoon Guy Clifton swept into my room with the results of the MRI. The neurosurgeon was upbeat; the Mexican doctors had done an excellent job, he said. He wouldn't have to operate on me again.

"You may walk and you may not," the surgeon told me. "This is going to take a year to eighteen months to play out. If you have to get around in a wheelchair, you know you're going to have at least some movement of your legs. You can still work. You can drive. You can get on an airplane."

"A productive life," I said, trying to match his enthusiasm.

"But there's nothing on here," he said, tapping the MRI's manila folder, "that says you *can't* walk."

Then he said, "Now. We're going to get you sitting up."

"Right," I said with a sort of laugh.

Soon after the doctor left, nurses wheeled in a contraption that looked like a heavily padded stretcher. When they slid me over to it and hit a switch, the stretcher turned into a chair that groaned and vaulted me upright. They rolled me out into a waiting area where Lila gaped in surprise, grinned, and said, "Hey." From the windows I could see the tops of trees and bright sky afloat with summer clouds. I was woozy from the abrupt change in altitude, but they let me sit up for half an hour. I watched the changing colors of the trees and sky and felt serene. Still, I couldn't entirely dispel an image that assailed me when the nurse got me up. I happened to glance down, and I saw something pink that flopped like a salmon thrown on a bin of ice. It was, I realized, my right foot.

I always thought of myself as the eternal pessimist. On matters small and large I was always saying this won't work, I can't do that. It drove Dorothy crazy. I had a history of intermittent depression; over the years I had seen psychologists for it a couple of times. I don't know why I had this inner darkness. But I was the kid who signed up for the Golden Gloves and was secretly glad when his mom wouldn't let him go through with it. The bachelor who walled up in a cabin and believed no love could last. The boxer with some talent who never got over his fear of getting hit in the nose.

If I had somehow known a bullet was going to come to rest in my spine, I would have predicted I'd wallow in depression and then slowly begin to deal with it. But that's not what happened. My thoughts of those Mexicans trying to save my life, the bundles of mail put on my bed every day, the love and steadiness of Dorothy and Lila, and Red Duke's earthy straightness vaulted me out of gloom and self-pity, in the manner of that hydraulic chair.

The bullet meant I was a cripple. But I could wiggle my toes; some of the wiring still worked. I had a vote in how crippled I would be. When Dr. Clifton raised that MRI and said, "There's nothing on here that says you *can't* walk," something in me decided I would.

(10)

On Norman Chenven's advice, Dorothy and I decided I would remain in Houston a good while longer. Tucked away in the Houston Medical Center is a small hospital called The Institute for Rehabilitation and Research. Known by its acronym TIRR, as in weeping, the facility is considered one of the premier rehab hospitals in the country. On May 1, 1998, I left Hermann Hospital and the care of Red Duke for an ambulance ride of five or six blocks. It was the first time I'd been outside. Like a released prisoner I stared at patterns of tiled roofs, the brilliant greens of ordinary grass, a couple in shorts jogging with a baby carriage. Pushed along in a wheelchair, I arrived on my floor in the early afternoon. Two of the therapists came up to greet us and at once put us at ease. I happened to be wearing an old T-shirt that advertised Richard Lord's Gym. An occupational therapist, Theresa Gregorio-Torres, told me with much enthusiasm and rolling of her fists about her recent first night at the fights. A number of TIRR employees had gone to cheer for a speech therapist who was also a professional middleweight known as "the Waxahachie Kid."

My daily uniform consisted of athletic shoes, socks, sweatpants, and a T-shirt. I had a number of shirts printed with images of Jesus Chavez and other fighters. From the start, in a teasing, encouraging way, the TIRR staff identified me as the fighter. Anything to laugh about was a plus, and in a way boxing prepared me for rehabilitation. The schedule was unrelenting. Every morning and every afternoon, therapists had me straining against the bonds of my injury. The work was hard, frustrating, and repetitive. Some patients didn't respond, and they were quickly discharged to their homes and outpatient programs. The screenwriter Bill Broyles, an old friend and editor who had almost lost use of his arm in an accident, had written me an invaluable letter. This was my job now, he told me. Forget everything else. If they asked me to do some dumb boring task ten times, I would give them twelve repetitions. That kind of self-discipline and dull repetition came easy for me. I knew how to go to the gym.

At the start, my broken left arm had been a medical inconvenience. Immobilize it; get it out of the way—I had more serious injuries to attend to. But now an orthopedist had to rebuild the wrist with a bone graft, which took me out of rehab for the surgery, and the doctors at TIRR feared the broken arm would hinder my progress. Some exercises and tasks just required the use of two hands. I might hit a plateau and have to be sent home for a while. But I refused to concede this. My bombast often left me chastened. I had to transport myself to and from the sessions on the ground floor. With a standard wheelchair, all I could do was roll in an endless left turn. Theresa and the therapist in charge of supplies found in storage an old chair that a patient could steer with one hand, by gripping and releasing a set of gears. "I want that one," I told them. "I want the exercise." But the one-armed bandit rolled like a wheelbarrow piled with rocks. I needed help from nurses to get from my suite to the elevator, and downstairs the corridor to the gym had a considerable dip in the floor; I couldn't build enough momentum going down to clear the ascent. Pulling with all the strength I possessed, I inched and struggled until someone came along and took pity on me. Some boxer. People raised their gazes from mine because I crept so pathetically along.

But I could never feel sorry for myself at TIRR. On the next machine or mat someone huffed and puffed with injuries far worse than mine. Jim Copeland was a Rice University linguistics professor who had made his life's work penetrating the mysteries of the Tarahumara Indians in northern Mexico. He was also a competitive cyclist who had gotten bashed almost to extinction doing his daily miles in the Houston traffic. Jim was much farther down his road to recovery, yet every movement for him was agony. A flight of stairs and a walkway to an office had been built along two walls of the gym. One day I watched awestruck as Jim's legs gave out climbing the stairs; he got to the top by lifting his hips with shoves of his hands, then on the landing as therapist goaded him to crawl. "I've *got* to walk again," Jim told me. "There's no other way to get to the Tarahumaras."

In the afternoons Theresa put me to work screwing bolts into nuts or kneading therapeutic putty. The most encouraging drill was when she had me sit on one of the raised mats and twist and stretch to catch tosses of a big, soft inflated ball. This was an important test of balance. "Awesome," remarked one student therapist. Theresa was a blonde woman with an infectious trilling laugh. After the exercises that day I sat beside her at a table and watched her fill out a form for me. She came to a line for my status and wrote "Paraplegic."

My reaction was absurd. *Who, me?*

Dorothy and Lila embarked on a gypsy life which shuttled them back and forth from their homes in Austin to the apartment in Houston. Dorothy spent her days in Houston driving around finding me things—workout pants, exercise shoes with Velcro straps instead of shoelaces, and the rescuer of countless evenings, a battery-operated CD player with earphones. Many nights, to relieve me of the bland hospital fare, she brought sacks of food from gourmet delis. Friends made the six-hour round trip from Austin just to cheer me up with conversation and good food. On occasion Dorothy made herself dress up and go out to dinner alone. Near the apartment was a stylish little shopping center. In it was a lively Spanish tapas bar, and one evening Dorothy left her car with the valet, took a table beside the window, ordered a glass of wine and a couple of tapas, and sat quietly reading a novel about a fanciful election in Mexico when the floodgates broke and she started crying—the first time she had wept since the ordeal began. She made little noise but her shoulders shook. Other diners glanced and the waiter hovered, uncertain what to do. Poor things, she thought, so young, so untroubled, and then this middle-aged lady starts losing it in her napkin. The waiter edged uneasily into her view. "Check," she told him. "Just bring me a check."

Patients were assigned an occupational therapist and a physical therapist. Though their responsibilities were complex and often seemed to overlap, my occupational therapist, Theresa, dealt with practical matters like eating, dressing, and negotiating a wheelchair; my physical therapist, Sherry Dunbar, focused on the legs, on trying to help me learn to walk again. Sherry had short brown hair and walked with a brisk and perky sexiness. Throughout my rehab I had several therapists who were attractive women; the profession seems to draw them. The coincidence was good for morale, but I never made any suggestive remarks to them. I heard some of that from other male patients, but what the therapists were doing for me was too important to screw up. Besides, I was a gray-haired man in diapers—not the most virile and rousing self-image.

Every weekday morning Sherry pushed me hard. The first requirement was to set the wheelchair at an angle against a raised exercise mat, lock the chair, clear aside its arm and foot rests, pitch my weight forward, twist my hips, and slide across a smooth plastic board, arriving seated on the mat. Lying on the mat with my shoes off, I would shove my heel forward until my leg was fully extended, then take on the harder task of drawing up my hamstring and pulling the foot back against my buttock. Or I would spread my legs wide on the mat, and in a fanlike motion pull the heels back together. But I couldn't break gravity, the critical element of walking. Trying to lift my foot and leg from the mat, I strained and strained and just couldn't do it.

"Look at you!" Sherry would exclaim when I made some gain, but she reminded me of Jesus Chavez teaching me boxing—she refused to bullshit me. And in a way it was impersonal. When our time was up and I moved on to my hour on the strength machines, she tossed her hair and hurried off to the needs and regimen of her next patient. She was brusque.

"Oh, you gonna walk," one of the veteran nurses assured me. "I can tell by the way they're acting." But the doctors and therapists weren't about to say it. One electrifying hint came when Dorothy was talking about modifications of our home and mentioned building a ramp into our bedroom. "Make sure it's temporary," said Sherry. Dorothy and I glanced at each other, wide-eyed. But the emphasis was on preparing me to go home and function in a wheelchair. My left arm had healed enough that they gave me the kind of wheelchair I would be using. Dorothy had to learn to brake me with her knee going down a ramp and how to pull the wheels up over a curb. Using the slide board, I had to master the difficult transfers between the chair and a soft sofa or bed or the seat of a car.

Because bedsores are so serious for spinal injury patients, twice a night aides came in to turn me over in my sleep, like a baby. I was scrutinized almost every moment, and sometimes I didn't like it. At one point I felt that Sherry and Dorothy ganged up on me. I was alarmingly forgetful, they agreed. "You're a man with two college degrees," Sherry said. "You've written books, you've traveled a good part of the world. And yet I'm having to remind you about some of the simplest things. You act like you've never heard them before."

As Dorothy frowned and murmured in assent, Sherry surmised that when the bullet struck I might have banged my skull on the pavement and suffered an undiagnosed head injury. That angered me, and I'm not sure why. I had a session with the hospital's neuropsychologist. She told me three or four stories and asked me to tell them back to her, which I did. I'm a reporter with a pretty good ear. The psychologist finally concluded it was nothing more than me being bored and heavily drugged. Then she asked me, "What's your greatest fear?"

Her question surprised me, and so did my answer: "That this is going to destroy my marriage."

TIRR had a wise policy that married couples should spend a weekend at home not long before the patient was discharged. Because of the distance to Austin, we got permission to check into a favorite hotel in Houston. As soon as I rolled my wheelchair through thick carpet into our hotel room, I realized I had forgotten something essential when I packed—the diapers or maybe it was the disposable catheters, objects I had not come to terms with possessing at all. Dorothy had to go back out in the heat and traffic and retrieve them.

Saturday afternoon we were reading then lolling in bed. To my utter surprise we found I could have an erection. But I was numb. I couldn't feel the act of love—as shattering a discovery as the one just before had been joyous. We lay quietly, Dorothy's back against me. Not far from my mind was the humiliation of that morning, when I hadn't moved fast enough getting to the bathroom. It is a horror for someone of sound mind to drop shit like a pony or dog. Dorothy started crying now, and in trying to console her I found out that part of it was my selfishness, my thoughtlessness, my forgetting the catheters or diapers the day before. She thought I was avoiding responsibility for the mammoth changes and challenges that lay before us. I had, she said, gotten all too glad to lie around and have people wait on me. We quarreled.

"Are you depressed?" she said.

"I'm starting to be."

"I knew you were going to say that."

The next day, the hottest day of the new summer, I insisted that we go to Jim and Kris Copeland's house for lunch. Jim had been discharged a week or so earlier, and with Dorothy's consent I had accepted the invitation; I thought it would be rude to call now and back out. In the oppressive heat, Dorothy quietly hauled the wheelchair in and out of the trunk. Dorothy and Kris, a stockbroker and young mother, sat at a table and talked about the surliness and self-absorption that had overtaken their husbands. Jim and I talked about pain.

Communication between men and women is hard enough without psychological trauma and debilitating injury. That night I was back in my TIRR cocoon, resting in bed and watching television when Dorothy called. Without spelling it out, she wanted to talk about our weekend together. But I was distant on the phone. I'm not a TV addict, and I know now that I should have turned it off—or at least explained myself and told her I'd call her right back. But it happened that when she called I was transfixed by the drama of the last minutes of Michael Jordan's last basketball game with the Chicago Bulls. As she and I talked Jordan made the impossible play—stole the ball from Karl Malone and seconds before the buzzer hit the title-winning shot.

What a way to go out. What a gifted man!

And of course, what an irresponsible thing for me to do now as a husband and a lover. Dorothy wasn't aware of that basketball game and probably wouldn't have cared if she'd known. All she knew was that once more I had been insensitive to her emotional needs.

In my sessions Sherry tried to get me on my feet by using a tilt board, but just that small change in altitude made me nauseous. Then one day, first with Sherry's help, and then on my own, I discovered that I could stand up, sit down, stand up again! She and another therapist got me to walk the length of parallel bars, supporting myself with my arms on the bars. My right leg was much stronger than the left; I dragged that foot, and the knee kept buckling. They improvised a knee brace with plastic bands, and with my elbows and forearms propped on the padding of their most stable walker, I walked about twenty-five feet, then did it again. A TV crew from Dallas happened to be there that day. The reporter asked me how it felt. My winded reply was silly but honest, straight out of my Texas upbringing: "Like I just scored a touchdown."

The next day Dorothy came in the gym with an anxious look on her face. "You're not ready to go home," she blurted. "I can't take care of you, and you can't take care of yourself." Sherry absorbed this with a nod, then hurried off to tell the doctors. They said perhaps my stay could be extended a week, that Dorothy and I might have another weekend together before I went home. That afternoon they had us meet with a counselor, who proved to be a pleasant, literate woman, a playwright. We both got a lot off our chests that afternoon, talking to the woman. I don't know what Dorothy told her when they were alone. But after our session the counselor told me, "I don't think you're depressed. You spoke right up and defended yourself. If you'd been depressed, you probably would have hung your head and said, 'Oh, I guess you're right.'"

Dorothy was developing a mantra that in other trouble spots would serve us well: "We'll figure it out." As the week passed, our

mood lightened. Being trained to give me a shot in my hip, one afternoon she fumbled the hypodermic, which stuck like an arrow in her
forearm. She and the nurse and I hooted with laughter. Ready or not,
the Friday of my discharge arrived. It was two months and one day
since I had lain in the Mexico City street thinking I was dying.
Dorothy, Lila, and I stuffed clothes and medical supplies in a suitcase
and boxes. Florence, a Jamaican nurse who had grown close to us,
came to say good-bye. "Ah, well, the nice people come and go," she
said, uncharacteristically quiet and shy.

Sherry walked with us as I pushed the wheels of my chair along.
As a good-bye present I showed her that I didn't need the slide board
anymore. I stood up from the wheelchair, grasped the car door, and
swung my hips into the front seat. She grinned and hugged us, then
we were off, but got stalled in the Houston traffic. I reached for
Dorothy's hand and held it, squeezing. Finally we reached the interstate and left the city behind. We rolled the windows down for a few
minutes. The breeze carried a mingled scent of grass, dust, and heat
that was oddly sweet—the smell of Texas summers I'd known all my
life. Godamighty, I was almost home.

Father's Day fell that weekend. Friends had kept the garden I'd
planted alive, and that Sunday, Lila and her boyfriend Greg Wilson came over for our traditional summer feast of pork chops, black-
eyed peas, corn bread, sliced onions, and tomatoes just off the vine.
Dorothy and I liked Greg before my injury, and during my Houston
sojourn he had functionally and emotionally become a part of our
family. With the dogs making the rounds at the table, accepting
pinches of corn bread and sniffing the pork treats to come, it was
Christmas in June, the homecoming of my life.

The house had not changed as much as I feared. Two neighbors,
an architect and builder, had with wood and limestone constructed a

handsome, sloping, winding path from the gate to my office to the front door of our house. A steep ramp down into our bedroom challenged my arm strength as I was going up and braking down. Added to our back porch was a sturdy wood railing that was meant to keep me and my wheelchair from hurtling down a slope into some trees. The top rail was just the right height for me to grip and then stand up. At night I rolled out on the porch and looked up through the branches and foliage at the sky. I had to think all this boded well. I leaned forward and with a heave of exertion stood up. Resting my hands on the rail, I pulled my shoulders back, tightened my buttocks, shifted my weight from one hip to the other, and breathed air that had never circulated in a hospital's sterile space. But then my left knee started wobbling, and with a sigh I lowered myself to the safety of the chair.

Our marriage had always been based on equal division of labor. I was frustrated that I couldn't take my turn going to the grocery store. I wanted to work back into the cooking and cleanup bargain she and I had maintained for years. But in the kitchen I found myself spinning around, hitting a brake, as I tried to move a chicken breast from chopping board to skillet. To clean the sink or load the dishwasher, I had to parallel park. One night I fed the dogs then made cold avocado soup. Nothing to it, yet the two light chores consumed more than an hour. Afterward I looked at the water faucet and glasses in one cabinet behind me, and the whiskey bottle and refrigerator full of ice at the other end of the kitchen. How much trick driving would I have to do to make myself a drink?

The second week home I started outpatient rehabilitation at St. David's Hospital in Austin. It would go on for a year. St. David's had a large pool, and here water played a much more prominent role in my therapy. My first morning of pool exercise, an aide by the pool helped me into another chair and pushed it down a ramp into the water. A physical therapist offered her forearm and asked me to stand up in the chest-deep water, which I did, holding on to the ramp's submerged rail. I was eager to go out in the deep water and swim and float until I found that place where my weight diminished enough that I could stand erect and take some steps. But the therapist said we were going to the shallow end to do my exercises. As the water level fell and my body grew less buoyant, my legs buckled. I flailed and splashed. I needed all the therapist's strength to get me to the side of the pool, which I grabbed like a drowning man. That was a critical point for me, though I didn't quite know it then. I might have given up.

As it always seemed to happen, an angel came along to inspire me and help me along. At seventy-three, George Ferguson had a neatly trimmed white mustache and white hair combed back from a widow's peak. George had been a pilot most of his professional life, then had retired and bought a home on Lake Travis, west of Austin. Soon after that, his doctors told him he had cancer that had metastasized in his bones. He made the grieving, rattled sort of plans you make when you're informed you just have months to live. Then an oncologist persuaded him to try a new chemotherapy, and it worked. But in killing the cancer it almost destroyed his vertebrae.

"A doctor said my spine looked like a collapsed house of cards," George told me. "I wasn't going to blame the doctors. That drug gave me back my life. But I had been a very active man. When it got where I couldn't walk, I gave up. I was on the verge of suicide. Then a doctor told me I ought to start coming here. 'Swim!' I said. 'I can't get out of my chair!' But you know I did," he said with a wink, "and before I knew it, I started getting better. I mean, a lot better. Wasn't long before I threw my walker and crutches and all that stuff away."

The next time he saw me in the dressing room he offered to help me transfer to the shower bench, and I accepted his offer, humbled that I should need help from one so small and pale, but glad to get it nonetheless. "Why, it's terrible such a thing could happen to a big, healthy young man like you," he said later as we sat in front of the lockers. "Your first day I saw you were having all sorts of trouble. I knew how discouraged you were, I could see it on your face. But you just be patient, and keep on coming here, and doing what they ask. You'll be amazed what this water and these folks can do for you."

That week Dorothy and I met my new doctor. David Harris spoke at a rapid clip then would pause and look up, grinning, as if to see if we were still with him. He was dark-haired, enthusiastic, and highly regarded by his peers. He spent an hour talking to us and subjecting me to the tests of strength and sensation that were routine to me now. "I don't blow smoke at my patients," he said, glancing at my legs and wheelchair, then up again. "But I can tell from what I've already seen here that you're gonna be out of that thing by the fall."

The date was July 1, 1998. Just seventy days since I had been diagnosed a hopeless paraplegic. As Dorothy and I rode the elevator to the basement parking garage, I broke the silence. "Well, he sure told us what we wanted to hear."

During the weeks at TIRR, and since I had been home, boxing had seemed to be in my distant past. Richard Lord called and asked me to come back to the gym. He said he could lower the speed bags to the level of a wheelchair. The challenge of working with me appealed to him as a trainer. But I stalled. Dorothy and several friends were already shuttling me back and forth from rehab; I didn't want to burden them with more requests for transportation. But it was more than that. My attachment to boxing was so entwined with my friendship with Jesus. When I was in the hospital we had been able to talk just once, briefly. The fact of his deportation hit me now with a thud. He was in Mexico, and I didn't know if I could ever go there again. How would I ever see him?

One day we were talking on the phone; he blamed himself for my getting shot. "Man, if it hadn't been for me, you never would have been down here."

"Oh, forget that, Jesus. Horseshit. I'm just glad to hear your voice."

He left a short silence. "Yeah. It's good to hear yours, JanReid."

"I'm going to do what I have to do here. You take care of your business, too. There are a lot of good people on your side. We're going to get you back here, where you belong. You and I'll be hanging out again one of these days. Sooner than you think."

I wished I believed it were true.

One day, suddenly, Dorothy and I stared at each other, agape. We were going to New York. It was a *Texas Monthly* assignment, a profile of a celebrity who was not going to be available in Texas anytime soon. As much for our morale, I think, as the editorial needs of the magazine, my colleagues decided to go ahead with the piece and send Dorothy with me. The airline industry takes good care of its passengers in wheelchairs. Still, we almost never got there. In Houston we learned that a large storm system in the East had air traffic backed up all over the country. Flight after flight to New York was canceled. "That's it, I'm outta here," Dorothy said at one announcement.

"Babe, if we don't get to New York tonight, this story cannot get done."

By the time we reached La Guardia the service that was going to pick us up had long since called it a night. I irritated her on arrival by wheeling off in search of a john that did not exist in the baggage area, at least not one with a door wide enough to admit a wheelchair. She thought I was leaving her to lug the baggage alone. With bags piled in my lap, I wheeled after her as she pushed a cart toward the taxi stand. The cabbie helped with the bags but made no move as she collapsed the chair and heaved it in the trunk. But the tension and exhaustion dissolved as we saw and came into Manhattan. Our hands crept into each other's at a stoplight on the East Side. Damn. New York.

The magazine assignment was pleasant, light work. It amounted to little more than one interview. But Dorothy and I had a great escape. The cabbies who watched her sling the collapsed chair into their trunks warmed to us during the rides; they seemed to admire our spunk. One fine afternoon in Greenwich Village I rolled and wobbled across buckled brick sidewalks. Dorothy didn't push the chair; she let me do the arm work. Aimlessly we explored blocks that might have one ramp cut to the street in its four corners, then found that the next block had no ramps at all. We stopped at the sidewalk tables of an Italian cafe and ordered a salad and glasses of wine. Watching pedestrians, I admired their gaits, the strolls and struts. Walking was effortless; they never gave it a thought. Then it struck me that I had to use the bathroom. The floor of the restaurant was built half a step up, and the tables were squeezed close together. Christ. I didn't want to have to catch a cab back to the hotel.

Dorothy thought about it for a moment, then took action. She marched into the restaurant and determined that the ladies' room was large enough to let me stand up from the chair and, propping my hands against the walls, pivot around to the toilet. To the maître d's shock and displeasure she announced loudly that her husband, a customer, needed use of the bathroom and started scooting tables and chairs out of a path from the front door. People half-stood and scuttled aside, intimidated. Soon she pulled the front wheels up, cleared the half-step, and pushed me toward the ladies' room. Face aflame, I looked neither right nor left. She stood guard as I made the maneuver she'd described. Much happier, I swung back into the chair, and we made our way past the maître d' to the street.

"The only time that guy smiled," I told her, laughing, "was when we left."

With that trip I found out I could work again, that I was still a journalist, even in a wheelchair. But more important, Dorothy and I figured things out, worked together. I felt better about our marriage, feared less that events might drive us apart. That afternoon in New York she started trying to hail a cab, always scarce at five o'clock. Finally one stopped. I stood up, grasped the door, and slid into the backseat. This time Dorothy fumbled with the chair beside the trunk, and somebody started honking. A sidewalk waiter leaped off the curb and came running. He expertly mashed the wheels together and swung the chair into the trunk. Grinning, he tapped his chest then pointed his index finger at me, thumb raised in the manner of a child's gunplay. "Quadriplegic, nineteen eighty-four—motorcycle wreck. You can do it, buddy!"

Lila informed us one September night that she and Greg wanted to come over, they had something to tell us. It wasn't hard to puzzle through her unusual formality; they found us all primed to whoop and hug and slap backs when they announced they were getting married in the spring. At St. David's I told my physical therapist, Kristin Murphy, that I wanted to be able to walk down the aisle at Lila's wedding.

Kristin was pretty, cheerful, prone to tennis shoes with brightly colored laces and socks, and though at twenty-nine a couple of gray strands stood out in her glossy black hair, bartenders still asked to see a driver's license to prove she wasn't a teenager. After some frustrating changes of personnel—I got tired of telling a new person the same story every Monday—Kristin had become my regular physical therapist, and we worked together well. From my initial floundering in the pool, she soon had me doing cross steps on lines of tile in the waist-deep water. I cruised around the gym and up a long ramp on a walker. To correct the dropping left foot in my stride, she had me fitted for a plastic brace around my calf, ankle, and heel.

My physical recovery became an unending struggle to get my left leg to catch up with my right. On the exercise mats Kristin had me groaning, stretching muscles that probably hadn't been fully extended since I was a baby. I crawled and walked on my knees, sat and rolled my hips on the big brightly colored inflated ovals called Swiss balls, a difficult exercise of balance. To strengthen my hamstrings I sat on a short stool, dug my heels into the carpet, and propelled myself around the room. One day I pulled myself right off the stool and landed with a *thunk* on my tailbone. Kristin blanched and threw her hands to her face, then scurried to help me. This would require an incident report. But I grinned and shook it off.

At St. David's I moved quickly past the walker. I used forearm crutches that clasp the elbows and have handgrips parallel to the ground. From the start I had said that if I could just reach the point where I walked with a gentlemanly cane, I would consider the battle won. I sensed the nearness of that and nagged Kristin to let me try. At home I kept the wheelchair near my bed at night, in case I had to get up and go to the bathroom. Otherwise I never used it. One day that fall, just as Dr. Harris promised, the wheelchair went away. It was so anticlimactic I didn't even note it on my calendar. I kept the medically engineered cushion for my office chair. I was at my computer working when young men from the rental agency rolled the wheelchair past my window. I waved, they waved, and it was gone from my life.

I invested everything in the struggle to get back on my feet. But in my single-mindedness I sometimes left important matters unattended. Though I tried to keep it from happening, all the focus in our lives seemed to be on me. And I didn't find the ways to help Dorothy as much as she'd helped me. Love's nerve endings weren't forever stilled; I steadily regained sensation where it was most desired. But we couldn't will our intimacy into being the same again, and both of us tried too hard, I think, to convince the other that it didn't matter.

Medical science had developed tremendous aids, if not remedies, for men with sexual injury or dysfunction. The first week we were back in Austin my urologist introduced us to Viagra, and at times I thought that here was a magic pill. Later he got me to try Caverject. The idea of injecting my penis with a needle was appalling to me—it evoked images of the most debased junkies—but then I found out that the procedure was painless, there was nothing to it. And unlike Viagra, you didn't have to think ahead and wait an hour for it to work. Spontaneity, which had always been so important, was once again possible. Still, I knew that my sex drive was feeble. I hadn't had one erotic dream since the shooting, nor had I awakened with a hard-on. Men know these things as nature's gauges, and indeed, blood tests revealed that my body was not making and maintaining a normal level of testosterone. It diminished my energy and raised another concern that had never occurred to me. Both our mothers and other women in our families hurt and stooped from osteoporosis. It was a condition Dorothy feared and took hormones to prevent. I thought it was an affliction of women, the cruelly styled "dowager's hump." But now as I smeared testosterone gel all over my chest and stomach in the mornings, osteoporosis had become my dread, too.

I took about twenty-five pills or dietary supplements a day. How could the consumption of these chemicals be as safe as the doctors claimed? What was it like now to feel normal? Every time I filled a new prescription I pored over the pharmaceutical companies' small print about placebos and side effects, but the medications could alter me in ways that were completely unexpected. A rainy Saturday that first fall brought an annual book fair at the state Capitol building which raised money for the state's libraries; I moderated a panel, and later Dorothy and I went to a fine restaurant with several friends. Whiskey, wine, espresso, and cognac flowed to excess—"Your body really doesn't like that anymore," one doctor at TIRR had warned me—but this was a special occasion. At home, in the spirit of the day and flight of the moment we got a little rowdy. And I found out there is such a thing as *too much* chemical assistance and structural support.

The next morning I rattled on crutches to the bathroom, severely hung over. The mirror relayed a stupefying message below my waist. Dorothy gaped at me and said, "You're going to the doctor." After a phone call I pulled on shoes, some loose workout pants, and a T-shirt. I grabbed a jacket and we set out morosely in gray fog and drizzle. At a clinic, a young nurse on weekend duty quizzed me as delicately as she could, then asked questions about my recent medical history. As she checked boxes and scribbled she cocked her head and raised glances at my forlorn pose.

Nearby, equally disconsolate, Dorothy sat peering intently at a magazine.

The nurse finally laughed and said, "Well, you're our patient of the day."

"Thanks a lot."

Within an hour I would be taking a Valium to deflect the screams of a child in the emergency room, and within three I was in surgery. This was all we needed. I had a bruised ureter and several ruptured blood vessels in my penis. The accident was so rare that both my urologist and the one who performed the emergency surgery winced and said they'd heard of it but had never seen it. The man at his nadir. Here I sit with a broken dick.

(11)

As I drove past the jumble of strip commerce along Lamar Boulevard, I felt the same embarrassed nervousness that gripped me the first summer day I had gone to Richard Lord's Gym. It was silly; I felt like a teenager on a first date. This time I didn't circle the block, but when I parked along the fence of the child care center, I killed the lights and sat for a few moments with my hands on the steering wheel. The sunset played out behind the blunt outline of the gym. I had often heard the gym called a dump, and it was a fair assessment. Dust accumulated on old bags and disabled exercise machines that had been crammed into overhead storage. Strips of duct tape held a patchwork of scavenged industrial carpet to the floor. The ring was spotted here and there with splashes of blood. But in that moment of dying light the scene was magical. A sculptor had made Richard a neon sign, and its logo of an angel's halo stood out in bright yellow below the sky's pinks and blues. It was a warm spring evening; the door to the gym was rolled up. Inside I saw the ring's corner posts and blue ropes, the mishmash of old fight posters on the walls, and the bouncing, jogging forms of people skipping rope.

For more than a year boxing had been cut off from me. I thought and talked about it often, but it was part of my past life, the prior me. When I was in the hospital in Houston, Richard had promoted one of his cards at the Austin Music Hall. Between fights he took the ring announcer's microphone and talked about what had happened to me. Muscular young guys in his T-shirts passed plates down the rows like deacons in a church, and the boxing fans quietly put fifteen hundred dollars in my medical fund. At least once a week I got a call from Joel Elizondo, an Austin flyweight who had retired and now worked the fights as a ringside judge. Joel, a stylish little man with combed-back hair and a thin line of mustache, introduced himself to people by his ring moniker, "World Famous." He took it upon himself to keep my morale boosted and keep me connected with the men and women at the gym. When I answered the phone, he said, "Hey, Champ. It's World Famous. How you doin'?"

As soon as I was back in Austin, Richard called and urged me to come back to the gym. He thought he could help me with my recovery, and I'm sure he could have. He was the most sought-after conditioning trainer in town. But I begged off. I was busy going to outpatient therapy, trying to get back to work, trying to reclaim my life. And in truth I really didn't want to go back there in a wheelchair. I knew I would feel so reduced. But in fitful and bullheaded surges I had gone from the wheelchair to a walker to two crutches and now a single crutch. One night I had pulled my bag of boxing gear out of the closet and beat off the dust it had collected. I examined my mouthpiece, stiff from disuse, and the red headgear I had bought from Greg Curtis for twenty bucks when the magazine staff gave him a new one for his fiftieth birthday. It was definitely a used model; there were faint bloodstains on the padding around the mouth. I wiped off the headgear and put it away, planning to donate it to the gym. In the bottom of the bag I found some leather pads that had finger holes. I had to start wearing them under my hand wraps because I hit hard enough that the twisting punches, the hooks and uppercuts, tore the skin off my knuckles. An editor who worked out at the gym had come to me once and proudly shown me her abrasion the first time she did that. I sat in front of my closet and flexed my fingers in the knuckle pads, and almost by themselves, my hands started moving in a slow shadowbox.

So now I worked up my nerve and stepped out of the car. From the backseat I got my forearm crutch, gripped it with my right hand, and slung the bag across my other shoulder. As I set out I staggered and had to catch myself. I had forgotten how heavy the bag was; or maybe that was the measure of my weakness. As I learned to walk again, I had been surprised to discover that when one leg is much weaker than the other—my left was still frail, the right fairly strong— the crutch or cane is employed beside the strong leg, not the weak one. I was an observer of how people walked, how they ran, how they limped. I now walked like a creature with three legs, only one of my outer legs was a stainless steel pole.

At the door I scrawled my name on the sign-in sheet, looked around, and didn't see Richard, which was really a relief—I had come unannounced and didn't want a hullabaloo. Boxers were jumping rope and stretching. In the ring one young guy thumped a medicine ball against the belly of another who lay flat and grunted with each strike. I recognized a couple of youths, but they were absorbed in their workouts; they paid no attention to me. "I start hitting that bag," said one friend who was new to the gym, "and I can't see or think of any- thing else." And that was part of what I wanted, what I missed. I sidled along the wall to a scarce chair, opened my bag, and pulled out the rolls of red cotton hand wrap. The wraps were well-laundered, but they had absorbed so much sweat over the years that the fabric was stiff as thin leather. I bound them across and around the knuckles, down below my thumbs, a couple of figure-eight wraps to support the metacarpals—ritual with a pleasure all its own.

I propped the crutch in a corner and shoved my bag against it. A speed bag was bolted to the wall within a couple of steps of the chair. I planted my feet and began to try to recapture the rhythm of working the pear-shaped bag. I missed it completely, or grazed it and knocked it rolling around on its swivel, but I didn't frustrate myself. Tacked to the wall before me were a pair of taped hand wraps that one of our valiants had once cut off, dated, and autographed—a win by TKO. On the wall beside these was an illustrated tribute to Alexis Arguello, the Nicaraguan I so admired in the seventies and eighties. The artist showed him dipping his left shoulder and elbow and throwing a perfect uppercut, and I remembered what a graceful athlete Arguello was. In fights he won and lost he always behaved like such a gentleman. As I let my thoughts wander, the skill with the bag came back in spurts. My hand speed would never dazzle anybody, but I loved standing up with nothing supporting me and seeing how long I could keep it going. Ta-*tun*-ta-ta-*tun*-ta-ta.

I worked three rounds on the speed bag, then pulled out my sixteen-ounce gloves and put them on. One of the heavy bags was chained to the ceiling right behind me. At the next bell I turned about, whacked my fists together enthusiastically, and waddled the short distance to the bag. I thought I could keep my hands on the bag for balance and whack it gently, see how it felt. I studied the bag like it was an opponent, then threw out a modest left jab. It was the first punch I'd thrown since the one that almost got me buried. The bag swayed away from me on the chain and then banged me lightly—and put me down hard. Richard's eighteen-month-old son Tiger and I shared the distinction of being the only ones in the gym who had ever gotten knocked down by a punching bag.

"Why are you so afraid of falling?" Dorothy had once asked me, and I replied, "Because I don't know how to get up." She gaped at me, incredulous. I hadn't spoken out, and amid all the other therapy that very practical matter had been overlooked. At the next therapy session, Kristin Murphy had helped me devise an ungainly but reliable technique. But I was so embarrassed now that I forgot. I struggled up on both knees, put my right foot forward, and tried to rise with the strength in my leg, like a normal man. I fell again, grabbing with my arms and gloves at the bag.

I saw a couple of the young boxers watching me. One stepped forward and said, "Sir, do you need . . . ?" He saw my expression and understood that I needed him to leave me alone. I sat on my hip for a moment, breathing grimly, then admitted there was only one way I could do it. I had to start out on my hands and knees. Then I got my feet under me and paused there humpbacked, both gloved fists on the floor. From that point, slowly, I stood up.

The inglorious return didn't keep me from trying again. At first I worked the heavy bag while my right hand held on to the grip of the crutch, throwing left jabs, hooks, and uppercuts. Then I switched hands, pulled on the other glove, and threw right hands only. I was no longer vain about my boxing form. I didn't care what it looked like. The intensity of the workouts was good for me; I drenched myself in sweat for the first time since I was shot. And I found that it was one of the best things I could do for my walking. I was strong enough in my legs to walk; more critical was my loss of balance. The stepping, twisting, and swaying tested my balance continually. But under my sweatpants, I still wore the plastic brace on my left leg. Without it my ankle and knee buckled. I couldn't take for granted the act of pulling on my socks. Setbacks came just as often as breakthroughs, and many times nobody knew about them but me.

I was coming to the end of the most incredible year of my life. In May 1999, Kristin set the date for my discharge from physical therapy. She was confident that along with all the calibrated tests of strength, flexibility, and balance, I had met my real goal—of being able to walk down the aisle with Lila at her wedding. During our last therapy session, I told Kristin I wanted to walk the six-tenths of a mile around the hospital without a crutch or cane. I asked her for constant conversation to keep my mind off all the curbs and cracks that could hurl me down. I stumbled once but finished strong. Dorothy was out of town on a working trip. A friend had built us a short banister that enabled me to get down into the living room, the large windowed space that had first made me want to spend my years in this house. That night in celebration I drank too much wine and fell hard while trying to get up the stairs to the bathroom. I hurt my hip and lay there pissing on myself. After I cleaned myself up in disgust, I again lost my balance, took another hard fall, and thought this time I had broken the leg of Oscar, our ancient, ailing poodle. He was all right, but I sat holding him and wept bitterly and long.

I ricocheted between lows and highs. A few nights after that, Arthur Vance and I put on tuxedos and walked down a sidewalk on either side of the beaming young woman who considered both of us her dad. Greg and Lila's wedding took place in the gardens of a hilltop Victorian granite house that belonged to two of our family's closest friends. Arthur had a silver beard and ponytail, and with my limp and cane I thought we must have looked like old codgers dwelling on past coon hunts and the Battle of Shiloh. Later that night, with a lively band playing on the patio, Lila ran up to Dorothy and said, "Mom, Jan danced with me! I mean, he really danced!" It was true. I couldn't match the beauty of Arthur's first waltz with her, but using the cane for a pivot, I twirled her and we pushed off each other's palms and for a couple of numbers we did a fast jitterbug.

Rehabilitation was up to me now. I had to design and schedule the program myself. Along with walking and stretching, I lifted weights and went to the boxing gym. My shoulders and arms began to fill up my shirts again. In time I walked in the gym with my cane and bag of gear and hung up my cane for two hours. I stayed on my feet during the three-minute rounds but sat down for the one-minute breaks. Then I found I could rest between the rounds standing up. I wasn't boxing. My punches landed on nothing but leather and air. But I was in a fight for certain, and the most bewildering trick of my opponent was pain.

Doctors said the pain I had was "referred" or neurogenic. Some injured nerve in my lower back was sending signals that my brain misinterpreted. When I first came back from Mexico City, even though I was dulled with morphine my legs were so aflame that the brush of a sheet would make me cry out. Specialists brought that under control with a high dose of Neurontin, a drug originally developed to control seizures. Probably I would have to take Neurontin the rest of my life. But it didn't block the other pains, which began suddenly when I was in the rehab program at TIRR. Fluttery spasms traveled up and down my left leg. The climax felt like a combination of a foot gone to sleep, a toe stuck in an electric socket, and an excruciating cramp of muscles that in fact barely twitched. Always I had a sensation of my left leg being burned within by electricity. Then there was a pause, followed by a fiery repetition in my right foot. Sometimes the pain came like a beast I couldn't fend off. Some nights I didn't sleep. Every time I dropped off, that triggered a new pain that woke me up. This went on day after day, night after night. I laughed when I told a psychologist that I called the pains the Wolverine. I didn't even know what a wolverine looked like. She said that personalizing pain is normal.

My masseuse discovered an apparent "trigger point"—I was learning a new vocabulary—by probing the cord of muscle in the middle of my back, to the left of my spine. It set off a tingling sensation that was pleasurable but followed the identical path of the pain spasms. At first this seemed like the breakthrough; the culprit nerve appeared to be at the doctors' fingertips. But no drug or medical procedure could halt the spasms. The doctors encouraged me to try any therapy that sounded reasonable. I tried pepper cream, magnets, acupuncture, hypnotherapy, biofeedback, and, once, a psychic healer named Ta Ta. She asked me to turn off my computer—negative energy, I suppose. For a while I took methadone, a highly regarded painkiller as well as a substitute drug for heroin. Dorothy begged me to stop when my eyelids drooped and I slurred my words at a dinner party. After one doctor's appointment we came home with a drug that was supposed to be fast-acting and efficient because it was delivered by nasal spray. "Do both nostrils," Dorothy said—that was how we took nose spray medicines for allergies. Prominent on the printout we failed to read was the warning: "Do NOT apply twice unless advised by your doctor." Later, on the bed with Dorothy and the dogs, I thought if I lay very still this weirdness might pass. I dozed for a while and awoke as she was stirring from her nap. She looked at me and said in a movie giant's voice, *"Wuuull? Did it WOOOORRK?"*

No, but it scared me. The doctors tried to stimulate healing of fascia that hold the vertebrae together, they tried blocking off my sympathetic nerve system, they injected steroids inside and outside my spinal column. Every procedure they tried sounded so logical. But as soon as the anesthesia wore off, the pain always came back with a fury. As if the Wolverine had a mind and will of its own.

To preserve her own rest and alertness at work, Dorothy now slept most nights in the small bedroom that had been Lila's. "Love you," one of us called, turning out the light. "Love you," called the other. One night when a spasm began at dinner I got up and walked into another room to let it pass. "Thank you for doing that," she said afterward. When she was gone I pulled my left knee to my chest and hissed, cursed, and on occasion I howled. Sometimes our collie Jake was feeling protective, and he came over and poked his long nose at mine. Other times he walked to the office door and stood with his forehead against the glass, hoping to be let out.

Dorothy feared that I just gave up, accepted it as a life sentence. We had an argument one night. Later, when we talked about why it happened, pain was at the heart of it. "I've never really hurt before, not continually," she said. "When I see someone I love hurt all the time, and there's nothing I can do about it, I turn away. I don't hear, I don't see . . ."

But she did see and hear. Crossing a busy street, she often reached for my hand, as she would a child's. It was a loving gesture, and I accepted her grasp. But she was so tired. We both were. A thug and a bullet had dominated our lives for so long. Once when she said something sharp and then came out to my office to apologize, I snapped, "God damn it, I just hurt—okay?" She flinched and a dread came into her eyes that I never wanted to see. I realized on seeing that look that I abused her with my pain.

But pain has a charity, even pain that always comes back. The worst spasms would bring on a whiteness, a gathering into myself, a clenching of my jaws, a shudder. I had to remember to breathe. Yet when the pains were over, within seconds and in a real way I forgot them. With sudden keenness my surroundings leapt back in view. Deliverance opened like a flower, and my mind seized on other things.

When I was at home and the pains came on, I was likely to hobble to a chair and wait for them to pass. But if I was walking or working out, I rarely stopped. I bore down on the left leg and made myself keep moving. Even in the gym in the middle of a round.

At best my footwork now was ponderous. I would never see the day again when I could jump rope or shuffle and skip laterally, in the way that skilled boxers do. The bag didn't pop like it once did, I didn't need the extra pads on my knuckles anymore, and it felt like the punches flew in slow motion. The straight right that I had been so proud of was gone; now it was an awkward stab. It was a matter of reach and balance. If I let it go from a distance I feared my weight would go top-heavy, and I would fall to my knees or land flat on my face. I was timid with the right, couldn't get the coordination back. I couldn't get off, as they say in the game.

But I could still punch. I found that now I hit hardest with my left hook. The power in my body had shifted. So I fell into the combination I'd been working on since I first hung a bag from a log beam in my house in the country. The jab the right the hook. The jab the right the hook. It came back to me. Only a curious change had occurred. Before, I could only circle smoothly to my left. Moving right, I had felt clubfooted. Now, circling to the right was my natural movement, and stepping to the left was hard. That was odd. Was it in my legs or in my brain?

I told Richard about it one day when he was working me with the mitts. His eyes widened, as if in the presence of something vaguely supernatural, then after watching me awhile, he said, "Wait a minute. Let's turn you around here." He positioned my hips so that my right foot was forward. I jabbed and hooked with my right and threw the straight power punch with my left. It flew out and snapped back quickly; the pop against his leather mitts was loud. Boxing left-handed felt strange but intriguing; the routine of the workouts had never offered much variety and change. "You've got a lot more power and speed in that left hand now," Richard said, laughing. "It's made you ambidextrous!"

Sometimes I thought about sparring again—just to prove I could. I still had my mouthpiece. But that was silly. I thought anybody in the gym could just give me a shove on the chest and dump me on the canvas. To the kids in the gym Jesus Chavez was a legend and a face on a few posters on the wall, and I suppose to them I was just this strange old guy that Richard liked to talk to. I had lost count of the years I'd been coming in this dust-caked place. It had grown in size and prosperity. Richard had assumed a neighbor's lease, enabling him to remove a wall and install a second ring. But it wasn't the same for me with Jesus exiled in Mexico. I wondered why boxing mattered to

me anymore. Richard's best fighter now was an undefeated welterweight named Johnny Casas. He had turned pro too late to have a
long career, but he was a master of seeing and working the angles with
his punches, and he took younger guys apart. Johnny had the kind of
high voice you heard in old boxing and gangster movies. One day he
stood wrapping his hands and watched me finish ten rounds on the
big bag. I had fought off the Wolverine a couple of times, and the ef-
fort must have shown on my face. "You got courage," he said. Johnny's
nod was an admission, or readmission, to the club.

(12)

We make friends and choose heroes for reasons firm and private. The reasons are nobody else's business, really, but it's still jolting when they're challenged. As I stood in line in an Austin pharmacy one day, waiting for some refills, a stylish woman who lived in our neighborhood conveyed her belief that my taste in companions was flawed and eccentric. "This boxer in the newspaper," she said. "Now is he the one . . . ?"

"Yes, Jesus Chavez," I replied. "We've become very close. He's a remarkable young man."

"Well, I just looked at the beginning of the story: *boxing*—and, you know . . . I moved on." She shook her head with slight revulsion, and I gave a nod of understanding. She and her husband had been allies in many political campaigns and causes. "His story's not just about boxing," I offered. "It's about immigration policy. Social justice." I shrugged. "In my opinion."

"I've never been able to arrive at a comfortable philosophical position on that," she said. "I mean, we can't just open our borders, can we?"

"I guess not," I replied, sorry I'd run into her and feeling a bit craven.

Jesus was no poster child for immigration reform. He had twice been deported and had twice come back in this country illegally. He was a felon, a convicted armed robber, an ex-convict who was no saint in prison. I couldn't dispute any of those harsh terms or characterizations. I could point to his youth and extenuating circumstances. I wrote that Jesus represented the wan hope of the American criminal justice system—a young male who commits a crime of violence, admits his guilt, accepts his punishment, grows up, and rehabilitates himself. I wasn't just in the thrall of a great young boxer. In fact I didn't know how good Jesus could have been; as the months of his banishment wore on, I feared his chance was passing, that he would never live out his dream and fight for a world title. I couldn't worry much about his boxing career. I was too busy trying to rebuild my own life. But during that time Jesus inspired me as much as any man I knew. I could not imagine being put in the situation he was in—a man without a country. Although I never said it to him, it seemed likely he could never come home again, and I knew how devoted he was to his parents and siblings in Chicago. But he carried on with a cheer and an equanimity that amazed me, and his courage elevated mine.

The Rio Grande had been my portal to a wealth of experience and love. I first asked Dorothy to marry me while standing on one of its bridges. But now I imagined the murky cane-lined river, with the brown plain stretching toward the blue line of Sierra Madres in the distance, and for the first time in my life perceived the border stream as a real divide. I didn't know if I could ever be at ease in Mexico again. Why bother? many friends said. But how else would I ever see Jesus? How could we remain a part of each other's lives?

When I was hospitalized in Houston, one day Joel "World Famous" Elizondo called and said that Jesus was trying his hand at being a promoter in Mexico. "A promoter?" I cried. World Famous explained: "Yeah, well, see, they don't really have a gym in Delicias. Not a boxing gym anyway. They got to train on concrete, and that breaks down the shins." Hoping to raise money to build the kids of Delicias a proper gym, Jesus had gone partners in the promotion with two guys from Alice, Texas. For the fight card they used the basketball gym, and they had to borrow a wrestling ring with sagging ropes and a hole in the canvas that was patched with cardboard. The undercard featured two hunchback brothers from Juárez. One took a shot in the belly and threw up on the ring. Ignoring ticket sellers, the people of Delicias climbed in windows and pushed through doors to watch the show. Afraid of the unstable ring in his main event, Jesus threw a sharp right early at his portly opponent, who at once fell down and took the count. Richard had come back from it just shaking his head. He hoped the rating guys didn't hear about this. Jesus was embarrassed but nonchalant when he called and I started kidding him. "Those guys from Alice, they took off mad," he said, giggling. "Those guys *tore* back to Texas. I'm gonna have to find another way to get that gym built, JanReid. We cleared three hundred pesos. Thirty bucks."

When I was home I called him now and then, and Terri Glanger, now living in Dallas, got him hooked up with e-mail. My most reliable information began to come from Marcy Garriott, who was working hard on "Split Decision," her documentary about Jesus and his case. Jesus was always moving back and forth between his grandparents' place in Delicias and his training base in Mexico City. Not long after I returned to Austin, he returned to Mexico City with Lou Mesorana, the handler and friend who longed to be his manager. Jesus was training for his third fight in Mexico against a veteran named Francisco Martinez Lagunas. Jesus had just begun to check him out—he knew his opponent had a rough-and-tumble reputation and was the father of three—when he saw the newspaper story in the capital. Some *rateros* had tried to carjack Lagunas, and like me, he unwisely tried to fight them. They got rid of Jesus's opponent, shot him dead.

Jesus had to accept the terms of Mexico City. It was then the only place he could get the training and sparring he needed. He told me that he'd learned to dress in tattered clothes and closely watch the routes of cabdrivers. He thought the subways were pretty safe. He said when he was there he mostly just trained and watched movies in his hotel room. Jesus's romance with Terri appeared to be over; yet neither of them could quite let the other go. In October 1998, his American promoters got him a fight in Poland on the undercard of the Polish-American heavyweight Andrew Golota. Jesus won his fight and, in respect for Terri and her family and culture, he took a tour of a Nazi death camp. Jesus retained his North American title in that fight and was still the WBC's number one contender, yet that got him nothing. The game was all about money, American TV money, and no big fight involving an American boxer was going to take place in Mexico. The super featherweight titleholder, Floyd Mayweather, Jr., was an undefeated former Olympic champion. He had looks, charisma, a flashy style, and a supportive consensus of promoters and TV producers; in the manner of Sugar Ray Leonard and Oscar de la Hoya, "Pretty Boy Floyd" was being hyped as an instant all-time great. He had no reason to fight this guy who had all these problems and couldn't enter the United States.

But somehow Jesus kept his spirits up. On New Year's morning, 1999, the phone rang beside my ear and I started to answer, then let it go through to the voice mail. When I played it back the voice of Jesus said: "Hey, JanReid, I just want to wish you a happy and a happy and a happy New Year. I miss you, my man. I'm hopeful you and me can go some rounds in Austin this year." The call had me beaming all day.

But then a few weeks later, the outgoing governor of Illinois waited until his last day in office to turn down Jesus's appeal for a pardon of the robbery conviction. Then the immigration attorney who had been representing Jesus abruptly quit the Washington firm retained by Main Events. No one who really believed in his cause was working the legal system now. From boxing, all I wanted for Jesus was the chance for him to take on his dream: win or lose, just let him have his shot at a world title. I was more concerned about his life after boxing. One day we talked about the possibility he might have to live the rest of his days in Mexico. "You'd be all right," I tried to encourage him. "You could get a good job there, because you speak English."

"Can I carry your bags, sir?" Jesus replied. He covered up quickly with a chuckle. But the remark cut like a knife, because the hotel trades were exactly what had been on my mind.

Jesus now worked with a highly regarded Mexico City trainer named Nacho Beristain. His sparring partners included a former world champion, Goyo Vargas. Jesus had already beaten one Mexican national champion, featherweight Javier Jauregui. But that didn't count much with Mexico City sportswriters because the fight took place in Texas, and Jauregui was a fading talent now. Jesus was ridiculed in Mexico City boxing circles as the *pocho*, the Mexican gringo. His Spanish was imperfect. He grew up among the gringos, he made his reputation among them, he belonged among them. Jesus still had pride, and it was stung. That spring he responded with the biggest gamble of his career.

The son of a distinguished Mexican fighter, Julio Alvarez was now the national champion in Jesus's super featherweight class. Alvarez had been stopped once, and his record of 20–4 didn't match Jesus's 25–1. But Julio was taller and had a broad-shouldered build that made him look stronger than Jesus. He hit hard with both hands, and he had a large following in Mexico City. Beristain told Jesus it would be a serious mistake to fight Alvarez in the capital: The judges' cards were certain to be stacked against him in a fight with Julio. And even if Jesus won, he wouldn't officially be the champion of Mexico because that title was not on the line. If he lost, he would surrender the WBC's North American title and no doubt lose the WBC's number one world ranking. On paper Jesus had nothing to gain and everything to lose. So why did he go through with it?

Machismo is much berated in our culture, the hackneyed province of beer guts and wife beaters; but in Latin America its meaning is nuanced with honor. If Jesus had to live in Mexico, he was determined to gain Mexicans' respect. And he believed he had to do something dramatic, almost desperate, to keep his career alive. "If for any reason I lose that fight," he told Marcy Garriott, "I think that would be the end of the Matador. I really do think that I would want to do something else, rather than finish the rest of my life trying to chase the dream that's not going to happen."

He and I were e-mailing each other during those weeks. One morning I wrote him: "Last night I dreamed a nightmare of a movie, and you and I were the stars. It was someplace in the States, not Mexico, and I was always looking for you. We had wound up in this world that was rock-bottom, man. People living in abandoned wrecked houses on junkyard mattresses. At least it was warm. You were still trying to fight, sort of, but both of us had gone off the deep end. Somebody handed me a pipe and I thought, Wow, is that crack?—and smoked it right then. At least you had good-looking women around. A bunch of us were sitting around on the ground or a floor, and you were telling a story. You were really into this story, and we were all laughing, but you were crazy on something, and it showed. To cool yourself you turned up a bottle of water and poured it on your head. I heard that giggle of yours and jerked partway up, like you do waking up from a bad dream. I thought, Calm down, he's okay, he's in Delicias with his family."

I have no idea what Jesus thought on reading that. I don't know why I felt compelled to share it. I went on that I didn't know what the dream meant; I didn't think dreams meant much of anything—only that he was on my mind a lot.

"You sounded discouraged about boxing in your last e-mail and Marcy said you might retire if you lose this fight. It's supposed to be easier to get you back here if you're a boxer in the news but that hasn't seemed to help yet and I couldn't blame you. Just know that your family and friends are going to love you just as much after boxing. And it ain't gonna turn out the way it happened in my dream. My daughter, who's about your age, is getting married in May—maybe the night of your fight. I see you working this little kid, my grandson, with the mitts in your gym. Wherever it is.

"Win the fight, if there's any way you can. Win all of them you can, then walk away healthy and proud."

Jesus arrived in Mexico City two months before the fight. Nacho Beristain took him up into the mountains for his roadwork, to acclimate him quickly to Mexico City's higher altitude. In the gym he had Jesus sparring with a world contender in another weight class, but he backed off that because both fighters responded to the other's talent and reputation and turned sparring sessions into determined battles—Nacho didn't want Jesus to leave his best fight in the gym. But Jesus knew his training wasn't going well. "I'd start running up a hill and end up walking," he told me, "and I was getting beat up in the gym. I didn't know if the altitude was finally getting to me, or if maybe it was the air pollution. All I wanted to do was sleep."

Two weeks before the fight, Jesus finally got a break. His attorneys in Washington told him that they needed a drug test from him in order to apply for a rarely granted visa that would allow him to train and compete, but not live, in the United States. The test was for illegal drug use—marijuana, cocaine, amphetamines. After a doctor drew the blood, Nacho's nephew, a medical technician, analyzed the results. That night Nacho called Jesus and asked if he was taking sleeping pills.

"No," said Jesus, "I'm not under any medication."

"Well," Nacho said, "you tested positive for barbiturates."

"What is this?" said Jesus. "What is barbiturates?"

He didn't even know what barbiturates were. When he found out, he said it was ridiculous, impossible; he was training for a make-or-break fight. But his blood contained three times the level of barbiturates considered safe. Even by the corrupt standards of boxing this was mind-boggling. It was the stuff of a B-movie. Jesus always ate in the cafe of the small hotel where he stayed in Mexico City. Alvarez probably knew nothing of it, but someone who wanted him to win had been slipping downers in Jesus's food and drinks!

Nacho told Jesus it would do no good to call for an investigation. He would be jeered out of town. The trainer told Jesus he simply had to pull out of the fight. But Jesus said this was too big a fight for him—he couldn't back down. A week before the bout, the boxers in Nacho's gym ran a race. Other fighters pushed and pulled Jesus along, telling him that Nacho would cancel the fight if he didn't make the run; still he finished last. So they went to the boxing authority and its doctor and said he had stomach trouble and couldn't fight on the scheduled date. It was opportune but not surprising that the doctor found an infection in Jesus's stomach. He probably would have found a gastrointestinal bug in any *norteamericano* who'd been living in Mexico two years.

When the month-long postponement of the fight was granted, Julio Alvarez howled, "Tiene miedo," he's scared, and the sportswriters picked up the cry. A cartoon portrayed Jesus with his legs shaking, sweat flying off his head. With bulging muscles, the Julio caricature prepared to drub him. "Poor Jesus," said the caption. "He doesn't *feel* good."

I was one of many people in Austin getting updates of this. The fight and the doping naturally became the talk of Richard's gym. Contractually, Richard was still Jesus's manager, but they hadn't talked to each other in weeks. Richard was convinced that the Mexican promoters and Lou Mesorana were making sure Jesus never got the messages when Richard had called. Finally they talked by phone. "Well, do you want to come down?" said Jesus, moodily.

"Well, do you want me to?" said Richard, moodily.

They were like two bantam roosters, neither one about to yield. I doubted they would work their differences out until Jesus was through as a fighter. In the meantime Richard had a wife and young son, and what had happened to me was fresh in his mind—he was none too eager to spend time in Mexico City. But the fight was scheduled in a larger arena in a safer part of town. Richard agreed to fly down and help work Jesus's corner. When he got there he found his fighter was so sick with a cold, running a fever, that Nacho wanted to cancel the fight over that.

Jesus had every reason to quit and walk away from boxing. I would have. But his pride wouldn't let him. Though he held the North American championship belt, in every other way he was the underdog. The Mexican champion was followed around by a throng of people wearing white T-shirts silkscreened with his name. When Julio, his wife, and young child arrived at the arena the afternoon before the fight, they ran a gauntlet of admirers. "Julio thought I was scared of him," Jesus said. "In a press conference he said, 'I have all my people behind me, I have more than three hundred people backing me up. I'm fighting in my hometown, and I don't feel lonely here.'

And they were like—'What about you, Jesus? You don't have anyone here.' I said, 'I have my mother's blessing and that's more than enough for me.' "

In one of the world's most cynical businesses, Jesus got away with such remarks because people could see the sentiment was genuine. Jesus was an intuitive showman. His looks and manner came across well in the prefight television coverage; young women announced to surprised interviewers they were rooting for Chavez, *claro que sí*. At the fight Julio expected to come into the ring last—it was his town, his crowd—but Jesus exercised his right as the champion and made the challenger enter first. Jesus had been cooking up a surprise for Julio. Not long before the bout, Jesus had gone to see his first bull-fight. He disliked it, thought it wasn't sporting, the bull had no chance. But Jesus understood how the word and image of the bull-fighter resonated in this culture. In Austin, when he styled himself "El Matador," he was paying tribute to his coaches, team, and gym in Chicago. But Mexicans took the nom de guerre seriously. If he were going to assume that name as an athlete, he had better live up to it. An interviewer said, "People are saying that you hate Julio. Is this true?"

For a *pocho*, Jesus managed his Spanish with cryptic lyricism. "At this time I need to maintain the face of a gladiator," he answered. "I think for this same reason, I need to enter the boxing ring wearing a mask, a face of a fighter. After the fight, God will say whatever comes." He said, "I am going to come in as a torero—with a costume of a matador, with the hunger of a matador."

He had bought a torero's black jacket with gold braiding. From the dressing room he walked past the sea of white Julio T-shirts carry-ing a sword wrapped in a red cape. "Everybody was going crazy about it, that was cool," he said later. "I was excited about that. I was still a little worried about the fight."

As he prepared to go out, a friend made up a song rap-fashion and sang it for him:

ting! ting!
the bell has rung
the fight has started
the people are excited
they don't stop yelling
they're for "El Matador"
a guy from Delicias
pride of Chihuahua
and he has to win

Julio's cornermen wore brown shirts with *Campeón Nacional* on the back. When Jesus entered the ring, he stomped his foot loudly, which got the other camp's attention. He held the cape out from his hip and shook it, as if taunting a bull, then flung the cape aside and with a thrusting step pointed the sword at his opponent. Julio, a handsome young man with a straight ridge of nose and strong pointed chin, pointed back with his finger and said, "*Te voy a matar,*" I'm going to kill you. Mexicans respond to pageantry in their boxing, and Jesus had chosen an adroit theme. The man calling the fight on TV picked it up at once, referring to Jesus in the subsequent action not as Chavez—but as Matador! Matador!

In Mexico boxing had everything it once had in the United States. Thrill, suspense, spectacle. Schmaltz and romance, might versus cunning, may the best man win. After the gloves were laced on, the fighters met at midring. As the referee barked his instructions Julio clamped his jaws, thrust his chin out, and tried to intimidate Jesus with his stare. Jesus rolled his head impassively, face shining from sweat and Vaseline, and kicked his feet and shot his hands out, staying loose. The Mexico City fighter seethed. Julio was taller, more muscular, and had a reach advantage—he looked like he belonged in a heavier weight class. Jesus came out circling as always, red gloves high beside his face, forearms out, ready to parry. But then he showed his speed and landed a crisp one-two, the left jab and straight right. Julio came back immediately with two strong-armed rights. Julio's stuff was basic—the jab, the straight right, and a tight hook. He crooked his arm throwing the left when he went lower, attacking the body. From the start Julio sacrificed speed against Jesus in order to maximize his power. He planted his feet widely and launched *cañonzados*, cannon shots in Spanish, bombs in English. He was going for a first-round knockout. Toward the end of the round they came off the ropes and Julio landed four, six, seven unanswered straight right hands. At the bell they spun out of a clinch. Jesus popped him with a right on the back of the head. Julio answered with a contemptuous, illegal, back-hand slap. The referee jumped between them.

Jesus had planned to test his opponent's strength in the first round, and he found the strength was considerable. In the second round the Mexican champ came back with the same strategy, trying for a knockout. Jesus went to work with his staple, the body attack. The first couple of hooks flew wide and wild, but then they began to land, thumping loudly. Julio scored with two more rights, Jesus replied with two fast hooks. Then as they were grappling in close Julio twisted his hips, dipped his shoulder, and threw a hooking punch that caught Jesus square in his love interests—a direct hit to his balls.

Julio winced and made a show of great contrition to the referee, but he was too accurate a puncher and that was too low a blow for it not to be aimed. The referee warned Julio he would take a point away if this continued, and gave Jesus a minute and a half to squat, holding the ropes, then walk and shake it off. Afterward Jesus lunged at him with a hook and missed badly again. Julio made an up-yours, come-on gesture with his right glove, then mugged and taunted him, drop-ping his hands and sticking out his chin.

The low blow questioned Jesus's manhood; and it woke him up. At the bell he walked out and nailed Julio with a right-hand lead. Jesus's pressure backed Julio into the ropes. Jesus must have seen a flaw in Julio's defense; despite his reach disadvantage he was hitting Julio reliably with his right hand lead. A fourth one drove Julio back a step. But at the end of the round Julio banged him low again, this time with a right. The ref ignored it.

Jesus had two cornermen, one speaking English, the other Spanish.

"He'll do that all night," Richard hollered, "unless you make him quit."

"I'm afraid I'll get disqualified if I do it, too," said Jesus.

"Well, you'd better make him respect you."

Julio spent most of the next round with his back to the ropes. Julio wore trunks that were like a bullseye to a boxer throwing body punches; they had a broad stripe around the waist, with a red star over his navel. And gaining confidence and rhythm, Jesus began to land his right hand off the jab. Or he double-jabbed and let the hard right fly. Faint lines began to appear in Julio's eyebrows—cuts. But at the end of the round Julio landed one of his big rights, and the white-shirted contingent stood up, bellowing. It looked like Jesus was more hurt than he was. In a crouch he bobbed and weaved and ducked the flurry of blows. He was experimenting. As he had thought, Julio's height could be a disadvantage. Punching downward, he connected with little but air.

In the fifth Julio no longer looked so much like the raging bull. Both fighters were tiring, but Jesus had his best combination working—a left hook to the ribs or belly, followed by an ascending right hand that had all the power of his leg, hip, and shoulder behind it. For the first time his crowd of supporters shouted the white-shirted Julio down. "*Cha*-vez! *Cha*-vez! *Cha*-vez!" Jesus landed his right hand almost at will. They were deep enough into the fight now that when a hard blow landed, a halo of sweat droplets flew out into the lights. Midway through the sixth Julio thumped Jesus in the ribs with a resounding left hook. The air was knocked out of his lungs, he couldn't breathe. Jesus fell into his ducking crouch, shooting his head left and right, yielding ground and throwing an occasional punch as Julio ran after him, knowing he was hurt, trying to land the big blow that would end it. But Jesus survived, got his wind back, and at the bell he had Julio backed up against the ropes.

The furious fight was just half over.

Julio continued to set his feet wide and throw those three-punch volleys. But the fighter who had looked smaller and weaker continued to bull the other against the ropes. Jesus missed wildly a few times, showing his fatigue, but his combinations had more variety than Julio's. He would be throwing jabs with an occasional right; then he led with a right, hooked high or low with his left, and rattled Julio's jaw with a right uppercut.

Between rounds, horsey girls prissed around the ring in high heels and the blue cotton dresses of Corona beer, carrrying the cards an-nouncing the rounds and using their thumbs and forefingers to tug the hems of their skirts down over the clefts of their buttocks. A string of water, sweat, and saliva hung from Jesus's chin as the bell rang for the ninth round.

Julio got the best of an early exchange of jabs, and Jesus danced and yielded ground. Julio snapped Jesus's head back with a hard right just before the bell. "Three rounds, three rounds," Richard told Jesus on the stool. Richard wasn't saying that to encourage him. He didn't think Jesus could win a decision in this fight. Not in this country, not in this arena. Jesus was hearing in one ear and language that he had better be careful; in the other Richard was telling him to get up in that pocket of danger and knock the guy out.

Jesus came out aggressively in the tenth. He punished Julio inside with short hooks and uppercuts. Jesus appeared unmarked, but both of Julio's eyes were swelling, and blood seeped from the cut in his right eyebrow. When the ref broke them up Jesus threw jabs, followed by rights. He was "sitting down" on his punches, in the argot of the gym, planting his feet and throwing them with snap and power. But Julio kept coming. Jesus jabbed once, then began another left but in a move that looked effortless, he instead threw the right.

Julio walked into Jesus's best punch of the night, and it caught him flush on the chin. His legs buckled, and the seat of his trunks almost hit the canvas—but he had such will and strength in his hamstring muscles that he reclaimed his balance and straightened up. Everyone saw the near-knockdown, but with a magnificent feat of athleticism Julio avoided the automatic two-point advantage it would have given Jesus on the cards. He stuck his tongue out at Jesus and unleashed a barrage of straight lefts and rights. Staying out of trouble, looking for a chance to land another big punch, Jesus kept the strength of his jab rolling out of his shoulder toward those small rips in Julio's eyebrows. The referee stepped in abruptly and waved Jesus to a neutral corner, then led Julio to the ropes. A doctor stood on the ring apron and examined the cuts. Finally he nodded to the ref that Julio could continue. The bell rang before they could tangle much again.

"Good, you got him with that right," Richard complimented Jesus in the corner. "But put him down. Knock him out." In the eleventh they came out trading jabs, then Jesus began hooking to the ribs again. "Up and down, Jesus," Richard yelled. Hurt the body and you'll find the head. Then Julio landed five straight rights—savage chopping blows—to the point of Jesus's left hip. To get away from that punishment, Jesus took a short step to the right, saw an angle of opening, and turned Julio's face upward to the lights, staggering him with a right.

For the first time Julio acknowledged him with a nod.

Then he charged forward and they went after each other like combatants of all species, fighting over food, sex, survival—toe to toe, brawling, then the bell rang and the ref yelled and risked his own health and safety by jumping between them and pushing them apart.

"Last round," Richard said as the girl with the card stepped through the ropes, pulling at her skirt. He was begging Jesus for at least a knockdown: give the judges a reason to go against the hometown boy. But Jesus listened more to his Mexican cornerman. "Ten cuidado," be careful, he warned. Jesus fought him close in. He scored with the hook to the body, then came up with a second hook to Julio's ear. Julio attacked with straight lefts and rights like someone wielding a machete. Yet once more Jesus backed him up, forced him to the ropes. The crowd was on its feet, howling, whistling. Jesus landed another right that flung Julio's head back. He parried the answering volley, allowing the lefts and rights to glance off his forearms, then stung him with another right, square between the eyes.

Then at last the bell.

One of Julio's cornermen gave the fighter a ride on his shoulders. Jesus tried to congratulate Julio. He raised a glove that Julio slapped away. When Julio finished his ride Jesus tried again, but Julio kept his back turned and wouldn't look at him. Jesus walked back toward his corner with his arms raised. The ring filled with people as the judges finished their calculations. With his gloves removed, Jesus forced his way through the cornermen and put his arm across Julio's back, gripped him on the shoulder. Jesus spoke into his ear, and at last leaned over and tried to kiss him on the cheek. Julio hiked his shoulder roughly and gave him a look. What're you doing, man? Get outta here.

A sk me why I love boxing, and I'll show you that tape.

Virtually unknown by the promoters, matchmakers, and television producers who control boxing in the States, that heroic fight and the outlandish events preceding it are reconstructed here. It fell on a Saturday night two weeks after Lila's wedding, and Dorothy and I were enjoying an evening at home, just the two of us, cooking and drinking wine and playing music. The phone rang in the kitchen, and after a while Dorothy got up to check the message. She came back laughing. "Somebody's calling you from a bar."

"A bar?"

"What it sounds like. Go see. I saved it."

I played the recording again—a rustle of static, cutting in and cutting out, then a voice saying something I couldn't understand, then the only part of it that was audible. Marcy Garriott yelling into a cell phone in the Mexico City arena: ". . . and he won! He *won!*"

After a long and dramatic pause the ring announcer had arched his back and said: "Ladies and gentlemen! The winner of this fight, unanimous decision, is Jesus 'El Matador' Chavez!"

Jesus fell to his knees, made the sign of the cross, then stood up with his hands raised. Richard hoisted him on his shoulder and gave him a ride around the ring. Two judges scored it 115–113, the other 115–114. The fight was so close that Jesus may have won it with those two rights just before the last bell. The Mexican judges were innocent of the bias and corruption that even Jesus's Mexican trainer predicted. It would have been so easy and justifiable to let the national champion have it. But for one boxing match at least, they let the best fighter have his due.

Bitterly disappointed, Julio at last came over to shake Jesus's hand, then quickly left the ring. Somebody handed Richard one of the straw cowboy hats that are popular in the north of Mexico, and he stuck it on top of his fighter's head. Jesus looked funny wearing that hat with no shirt, his championship belt gaudy around his middle, sipping a bottle of water. A TV sportscaster thrust a microphone at him and said, "Congratulations. You've shown that you're number one, you showed that you're Mexican." Jesus said it meant a lot to beat Julio in Mexico City, that he had accomplished one of his biggest dreams. He started to say more, then closed his eyes and pressed them with his fingers, holding back tears. Then he raised the two fingers of victory and cried out, "Viva México!"

(13)

The stretch of dirt and rock beneath the jet's wing was as empty and forbidding as any I'd ever seen. I could see nothing green— no juniper, no cactus, not even the lowly creosote bush. That plant scrabbles an existence in the West Texas reach of this desert by contaminating the soil around it and tasting so bad that not even the hungriest and thirstiest beast will browse it. I knew the Texas reach of the Chihuahuan Desert well, and it looked like well-watered savanna compared to this. Some of the stone outcroppings were large enough to be called mountains; the one just below the plane now looked like a neatly combed pompadour. I had been reading a novel about the Mexican Revolution of the early twentieth century. The distances of the Chihuahuan Desert gave history Pancho Villa. In 1916, after Villa's horsemen raided the little bordertown and military garrison of Columbus, New Mexico, U.S. Army general John J. Pershing rolled into Chihuahua on a Punitive Expedition that included howitzers, proto-tanks, even airplanes. The expedition had been ridiculed in the novel I was reading, and I could see why. It may have been a valuable field exercise for the campaigns Pershing would soon undertake in Europe, in World War I, but only generals fattened on the good life in

Washington would think a force so loaded down could catch Villa's mounted guerrillas in rock-hard nothingness like this.

As I waited to board my flight in Austin, I had seen a Mexican artist, a painter of watercolors, who lived with a common friend. Like most Mexicans I knew, he was friendly, solicitous, and in an unstated way, his attitude was protective of me. He was at the airport putting his mother on a plane back to Guanajuato. He introduced us, and I offered a few pleasantries in Spanish, which charmed her. The artist asked me where I was going. When I said "Chihuahua," he grinned and his eyebrows hiked in surprise. He looked around and said, "No one is going with you?"

Chihuahua City wasn't so dangerous a place to go. It was just unusual, off the beaten track. The other passengers on the small commercial jet included none of cowboys, miners, drug runners, and gold-necklaced hustlers who pervade gringo lore in Chihuahua. All the conversation around me concerned some mainstream business. They were technicians and consultants brought here by the economic activity stirred by NAFTA, the North American Free Trade Agreement. None acted too eager to get where we were going.

I occupied a solo seat along the bulkhead, which allowed me to stretch my legs. A number of pain spasms roamed through me on the flight; with the leg room I was able to weather them without squirming and avoid disturbing my neighbors. I had packed without much thought or preparation, stuffing everything in a single bag I carried slung over my shoulder. It grew heavier as I hobbled through the crowd with my cane. Houston has a big international airport, scooter rides for the disabled were unavailing, and I had a tight connection. By the time I reached the gate my leg was on fire. People who have chronic pain are always divided by a tension—wanting help and not wanting to bother. This day I would have flagged a ride. No one could stop the spasms or even explain them in a way I fully understood, but since they began I had made one objective observation: Mundane stress—I've lost the keys, I'm going to miss the flight—set them off 100 percent of the time. But they were bearable. They rose up in me like storm clouds but then they passed. Remembering that was part of my life's work now.

Dorothy hadn't wanted me to make this trip, but she knew she couldn't talk me out of it. I needed to see Jesus—needed to see if the bond I felt really transcended that time in the gym and ring, when he was my trainer and my teacher. Would we still be friends when neither one of us had thrown an uppercut in years? I also needed to put some things at ease within me. I had to keep reminding myself that Mexico was a place, only a place. But now when I watched some travel program on TV, and the camera suddenly scanned across the Zócalo in Mexico City, in my gut I had a sharp, visceral reaction of fear.

Dorothy was not immune to this specter. One night I woke her with one of my pain spasms. She asked me if I was all right, and she moved around for a while, then I could tell from her breathing that she had gone back to sleep. It lasted just a few minutes, then she cried out and fiercely grabbed my arm. I shook her shoulder gently, and she sat up and put her hands to her face. "A man was chasing me," she said. "I ran into a small storage shed. It was clean inside, gleaming. I had all my family jewelry in a little brown box. I stepped out and saw there was a crowd. Then I saw the guy coming again. He pulled out a knife, and I said, 'You're a fat Mexican thug.' He raised the knife to kill me, and I woke up. It was the most vivid dream I've had in years."

This woman had always loved Mexico, had offered and opened it to me as a gift. When Dorothy told me that Mexico was the most foreign place she had ever been, she said it with a fond air of mystery. She shared memories of her first marriage to my friend and mentor, the novelist Billie Lee Brammer. In a Volkswagen van they would drive deep into Mexico's interior, between the cordilleras of the Sierra Madres, where they found only vastitudes of pale earth and sparse stony growth. A hundred twenty-eight kilometers to a gas station.

With dog, clothes, stereo, and all the money they had in the van, on one of those highways they blew out a tire. Like a mirage four campesinos in white appeared from the cactuses. They all carried machetes. After a moment of profound staring, the campesinos came forward to help change the gringos' tire.

She loved Mexico, but then I was shot and crippled there. And just a year and a half later, as I regained my feet and we fought for equilibrium in our lives, we sat at the dinner table one evening in happy anticipation of a vacation in Ireland. The phone rang, and Dorothy learned that her beloved younger brother Houston had died in a nightmarish boating accident off the coast of Cozumel, where he owned a restaurant and bar. "I know Mexico didn't kill Houston," she later said to me, trying to think her emotions through, but then she dreamed about the knife-wielding thug. She seemed inconsolable and terribly alone.

My pains subsided, and for a moment I looked again at the pages of the novel about Pancho Villa. I wasn't going to Chihuahua just to hang out with Jesus and watch him fight. I had begun to write about the hijacking and shooting. I finished one essay by saying a dark beast was loose down there, and I aimed never to feel its breath on me again. I referred to Mexico City, but I knew that I believed and felt that about the whole country. I remembered a time not too many years past when rain was falling and I had walked barefoot, shirtless, and alone through a Mexican village that had no electricity or plumbing. The campesinos I walked among were slash-and-burn farmers in a mountainous jungle. The year could have been 1800 as easily as 2000. I had no fear of them at all. So I was wiser now. But how much had I sacrificed in gaining that wisdom? How much of my loss was courage and self-respect? Maybe I couldn't reclaim a Mexico of mariachi songs and storms of butterflies, but I could face its other nature, and my fear. I always heard that was what made you a boxer— conquering your fear.

.   .   .

The plane's wing dipped low into a turn, and out before us I could see our destination, an oasis of green. In the midst of that wasteland Chihuahua City looked like a mirage. How could a city ever have come to be in that place? Soon we were on the ground, and it didn't look quite as barren as it had from the air. Nor was I totally alone on this trek. If I had been obliged to get around by wit and wile, hailing cabs and riding Mexican buses—as I had planned to do before I got shot—I never would have left Austin. A private King Air turboprop had made its approach and landing right before the descent of our commercial craft, and as I stood in the short line to clear customs, I saw the grin and wave of Marcy Garriott. She and her husband Robert were veteran, accomplished pilots. They had also come to watch Jesus's fight and visit him briefly in Delicias. They had already rented a car and made reservations for us in a motel distinctly tailored to *norteamericano* expectations and tastes.

I had seen the all-but-final edit of "Split Decision." Marcy's documentary told our friend's story in powerful fashion. It would be a smash hit at Latino film festivals throughout the United States. The Garriotts were so low-key and down-to-earth it was easy to underestimate them (as I had on our first meeting in Mexico City). Schooled as an engineer, Marcy had been a vice president in the Bell communications empire. After growing up in the Houston household of an astronaut, Robert considered a career in science, then took an advanced degree in business from MIT; he helped turn his younger brother Richard's gift for creating video games into a giant of that industry. The success of their company enabled Robert to cash out, fly planes and helicopters, learn Spanish, and in his forties do whatever he wanted to do. Richard had sufficient charisma that Merrill Lynch selected him as the subject of a national advertising campaign aimed at young entrepreneurs and investors. Richard believed in Jesus and his

cause, and offered to pay all his legal bills. Though Jesus's boxing career was still stymied, the Garriotts' involvement got him the lawyer
whom many attorneys in Austin had recommended when he was being deported. A law professor at the University of Texas, Barbara
Hines had been overcommitted then and declined his case, to her
eventual regret. She soon fell under his spell as we all had. His case was
so rich with the intricacies and subtleties of immigration law that she
showed Marcy's movie to her students. "More boxing!" they wrote in
their course critiques. Barbara wasn't sure the law had a remedy for
Jesus's troubles, but at least we knew that now his representation
would be reliable and first-rate.

As we rode away from the airport Robert, Marcy, and I chattered
about these things, but I kept turning my head, staring, feeling strange.
On a broad patch of bare earth, with deft footsteps and twists of their
ankles and heels a gang of kids banged a soccer ball outside an adobe
painted aqua. Shorthaired goats watched them with interest, raising
their bearded chins like wise old men. Chihuahua City belonged to
the Mexico I knew along the Texas border—the tinkling of goat
bells, an old man on a ramshackle wagon with a team of gaunt horses,
a street dominated by tire repair shops, and downtown the *zócalo* and a
graceful but slightly forbidding church. All the boxing people were
staying at one hotel. Robert looked over the hotel's garage entry and
decided to leave the rental car parked on the street.

The hotel doorman made a lavish show of presenting me the
ramp for the disabled. We walked into a lobby that had deep plush
carpet and glitzy chandeliers and found Jesus. His smile lit up as he
embraced us, but first he had to finish negotiating with the hotel
manager. In the parking garage thieves had broken into his truck and
torn out his stereo. The hotelman raised his palms and told him not to
worry, he was an honored guest, *un gran peleador*, the insurance would
take care of everything. It didn't turn out that way, of course.

Jesus introduced us to his new manager, a slightly pudgy young man in a brown suit named Fernando Beltran, and I met Lou Mesorana, the American who had effectively expatriated himself in Mexico in order to befriend Jesus and get a piece of his boxing career. Lou told Marcy he enjoyed her movie but added pointedly, with a smile, "I was *conspicuous* in my absence." Marcy smiled and let the complaint pass.

Jesus then took me over to meet his Mexico City trainer, Nacho Beristain. He was a trim man with a sharp nose, a well-trimmed mustache, and a distinguished air. The Garriotts knew him from Marcy's interviews and coverage of the Alvarez fight. In Spanish he greeted them warmly and me politely, but he seemed edgy and distant.

Jesus looked no different to me. He wore running shoes, blue jeans, and a long-sleeved athletic shirt. For a fighter who was criticized for poor defense and letting himself get hit too much, his handsome features still showed no signs of the destruction of his trade. He led us to his room and sprawled on the bed. He watched me walk with the cane and sit down carefully in a chair. It was the first time we had seen each other since the night of the Moi Rodriguez fight.

"So how you doing, JanReid?" he asked me.

"Not bad. I can walk. I drive. I'm working as hard as I ever have. I go to the gym. I can go ten rounds on the big bag, if it's not too hot."

He nodded. "I miss those guys," he said of the men and women who worked out at Richard's gym.

"Everybody misses you."

"Your legs, they still hurt?"

"Yeah. Some."

"That's a tough place, Mexico City. You know Nacho, my trainer, the guy you just met? He got carjacked down there this week. It's the third time that's happened to him."

"You're kidding," said Marcy.

"No. The guy opened the door and put the gun to his head, his temple. Nacho said, 'No, no, don't touch it to my head! It might go off.' He can't sleep at night because he keeps playing it over and over in his mind. Nacho used to be some kind of police; he knows about guns, had one in his car. It bothers him that he let the guy get away with it, that he didn't get to his gun."

How Mexican, I thought. He loses sleep not because of the terror of that experience, but because he surrendered to it—he didn't have the balls to risk and maybe lose his life trying to shoot the *ratero* over a damn car. But I don't know the man, I thought next. People who didn't know me—and some who did—made the same sort of value judgment about me.

Jesus trained in Mexico City and lived there about half the time. The Mexico City boxing press and the Mexican arm of the World Boxing Council had honored the Chavez-Alvarez bout as 1999's fight of the year. Yet Mexico's boxing establishment had not really embraced Jesus's career after his defeat of Alvarez. He was still a *pocho*, a beneficiary of the soft life in North America. There had been no more prime-time exposure on national television. So he fought in Cancún, Baja California, and Chihuahua. One of the times we talked by phone, Jesus had told me he needed money and had gotten the best deal he could get in Mexico—$30,000 on signing, $10,000 a fight, at least six bouts a year. But it never added up to that. Marcy and Robert told me that Fernando Beltran was always making promises. A big homecoming bout in Austin in two or three months. A world title fight with Floyd Mayweather, Jr., by the end of the year. And this very fight the Mexican national hero, Julio César Chávez, was supposed to come to Chihuahua City and accompany Jesus to the ring. It would be almost like a blessing, a passing of the torch. None of it ever happened. Jesus ducked no one but still fought bums. His opportunity and perhaps his talent faded with each passing month.

"They'll fight him till they get him beat," Richard Lord had predicted of the new managers, with his customary cynicism. (Richard and Jesus had formally parted company when he signed the new contract.) "And the Mexican who beats Jesus Chavez," Richard went on, "then they'll have themselves a million dollar fighter." But Jesus had to make a living somehow. He had faith in his new manager, who handled fighters and affairs in Mexico for Top Rank, the promotional company of Bob Arum. It was a high-powered company; in boxing Arum was the principal competitor of Don King. An eventual contract with Top Rank was implied, if not promised. But in the meantime Jesus was fighting in backwater arenas of provincial Mexico. It was a long way from pay-per-view and Atlantic City.

A t dusk a bus pulled up beside the hotel, and along with the boxers, trainers, and other cornermen, we climbed aboard. I found myself seated across the aisle from Nacho Beristain, who smiled and nodded at me as he sat down. I debated trying to talk to him about the carjacking and decided against it. Smoking a cigarette, he seemed tense, pensive, and distracted. When we arrived at an arena, a young man whom Jesus was grooming as an amateur fighter led the Garriotts and me inside. Jesus and Lou referred to the promoter of this fight card as "the Arab." Whatever the man's ethnicity, he was imposing and exotic. He had dark chiseled features and black hair and beard, both of which were razor-cut to moonlike points above and below his face, and he wore a black suit, a black shirt, and a black tie. Jesus's protégé delivered us to the Arab, who glanced at my cane and the video camera that Robert carried, then gave a curt nod to a man who led us to ringside chairs, beneath one of the fighters' corners.

I looked around the oval-shaped municipal arena and thought it was used most often for basketball. The seats filled up quickly, men outnumbering women by about two to one. I saw a lot of Chihuahua's distinctive straw cowboy hats. At one end of the hall a band set up and started playing extremely loud. I thought I could make out someone singing, but it was hard to be sure. The bass line was established by a tuba's *boom poomp! boom poomp!* and the frantic work of the drummer. The band cranked up between every fight and every round. The fight crowd did not drift in, as they do in the United States. Virtually every seat was taken before the undercard began. The fans cheered and rooted as fiercely for the four-rounders as they did the ten-round fights at the end. Marcy poked my arm at one point and gestured upward with her finger. I couldn't believe it. The crowd was doing the Wave. Around and around the small arena they went—standing up, throwing up their arms, then sitting down.

On the bus I had sat beside a handsome fighter who looked supremely bored. He was from Tijuana and seemed to think the night's work was beneath him. His opponent in the six-round middleweight fight was as ugly as a toad. He had a large round face scarred by acne, red clumps of which still gnawed his back and shoulders. When the bell rang he seemed to have no boxing skills at all. The Tijuana fighter danced around him, threw a few flashy combinations, and expected him to crumple. But punishment was fuel to the Chihuahua fighter. The more he got hit, the more earnestly he drove forward, throwing roundhouse punches that outmuscled the dancer and brought his hands down. The campesino's face turned bright red and swelled up from all the punches it absorbed, but the slick Tijuanan backed up, found himself cut off and trapped in a corner—for all his contempt, he was in a fight and steadily getting the worst of it. When the judges announced a draw, the Tijuanan threw up his hands, held his gloves to his face, stomped his feet. He refused to shake the hand of the kid with the face of a toad. The crowd booed the dandy heartily as he stalked toward the dressing room. I agreed with the judges' decision. If anybody won that fight, it was the campesino.

Midway through the card I made my way around the ring, past the defeaning band, to the john. I stood in line and eventually took my turn at the urinal trough. My bladder was full because I had drunk a couple of beers, but I had to really concentrate and at the same time relax to make the pipes work like those of the fellows beside me. I was standing, the thought struck me, in the middle of a packed crowd composed entirely of Mexican men—and liking it! And they liked me, or at least they appeared to. As I rebuttoned the fly of my jeans they grinned and stepped aside for me, nodding respectfully at my cane.

When I got back to my chair, one beside it had been taken by the game, untalented boxer who had fought the six-round draw. His face looked like raw hamburger and his eyes were almost closed by the pummeling he had taken, but he looked very happy. Someone handed him a beer. He looked at me and nodded his welcome and greeting. "Buen trabajo," I told him, raising my beer. He grinned broadly and touched his beer to mine; we were pals.

Two black men approached the corner and climbed the stairs to the ring. Jesus's opponent, Daryl Pinckney, didn't wear a robe over his trunks—just a gray sweatshirt with the sleeves torn out. He stepped through the ropes, let his cornerman pull the shirt off him, then stepped around throwing short punches, loosening up. From Florida, Pinckney had stopped losing fights he was supposed to lose midway through his career; he earned a reputation as a knockout artist and for a while was ballyhooed as a contender. But it didn't happen for him, and now, Richard Lord had told me, he was just making all the money he could before old man time made him get out. I had looked up his record and couldn't believe it: 24-34-3. *Thirty-four* losses?

Old man time had been tapping on his shoulder a good while now.

"Yeah, but he's dangerous," Richard had said.

Jesus stepped through the ropes across the ring. He no longer wore the torero outfit into the ring. He now had a white robe trimmed tastefully in black; it had his name and "El Matador" and "Chihuahua" embroidered on it. Damn, I thought. Jesus's fight wasn't even the main event, but my heart was thudding with excitement. Though he hadn't won over the boxing establishment in Mexico City, the fans from Delicias loved him. They filled a section of the stands and chanted the name of their town as Jesus moved around the ring. Concessionaires

were selling strips of cloth printed in glitter with the names of the top
fighters on the card. Jesus's fans wore them as headbands or whirled
them round and round. Lou Mesorana was in the ring with Nacho
Beristain and Jesus. Lou wore one of the headbands and clapped
his thick hands, smiling. Jesus pointed his glove at Pinckney during
the introductions, then they met with the referee. They were all
business—no glaring or posturing.

Jesus came out biting down on that black mouthpiece, as he always did. He let go a wild roundhouse right that missed by a foot.
Those punches were a signature of his first rounds; I didn't know if he
was trying to lure his opponents into charging, or if it was sheer exu-
berance. He did love to fight. Jesus was back to his old style—pressure,
pressure. With his back to the ropes, Pinckney kept his hands against
his head, his elbows against his ribs as Jesus banged away; then in flur-
ries he fought back. Though Jesus may have slowed down some, his
hands were still fast. Pinckney was skipping laterally in the first round
when Jesus caught him with a hard left jab. Pinckney was suspended
in the air when it landed, so it dumped him on the seat of his trunks.
He shook his head in disgust as Jesus raised his arms and turned to the
crowd. It was a flash knockdown, but it counted on the cards, and
Jesus was all over him as soon as the referee finished the count.

In the second round Jesus continued to maul Pinckney against the
ropes. We could hear the loud thumps of his hooks to the body. It
looked like any second Pinckney would fall. He wobbled and
sagged—playing possum—because he came off the ropes with a swift
right hook that left Jesus on one knee, looking very surprised. It was
only the second time he'd been knocked down in his pro career.

He raised his arms and looked the ref in the eyes, assuring him he
was all right, then resumed the all-out attack. Pinckney continued to
fight back in spurts—it was a thrilling fight—but in the third round he
winced and shook his right hand like something had stung it. By the bell
he thought a bone in his hand was broken, and in the fourth round he

realized the folly of trying to fight Jesus one-handed. When the bell rang for the fifth he calmly sat on his stool. He got up when his gloves were off and bowed to the crowd, who cheered him warmly, then he took Jesus's hand and raised it, walking the winner around the ring. Jesus's young nephew was taking gymnastics lessons, and he saw an opportunity. He slipped through the ropes and then went running across the ring and performed a somersault. The crowd whooped with delight.

After it was over the Garriotts and I decided not to stay in our chairs for the main event. We were going to join Jesus and his family in the dressing room. Marcy and I both heard people yelling at us, and we chose to ignore them. As I made my way with my cane, someone gripped my arm from behind, and it ignited a flash of déjà vu.

Honcho's hand on my arm!

I whirled around in fright—but the hand belonged only to a smiling Mexican man. He and the toad-faced boxer and the people who had been yelling at us pointed at my chair. They were just telling me that I had left my jacket draped on the chair. It was an Italian-made leather jacket I bought the first time Dorothy took me to Paris. It was my favorite garment. I would have been crushed if I'd gone to Mexico and lost that coat.

After the fights, while we sat on the bus waiting for Jesus and the other boxers, I thought about my reaction to the hand on my arm. I was more frightened, perhaps, than the instant I was really in the grasp of Honcho, for I had been hurt by him so badly. But my instinct still was to stand my ground and put myself between Marcy and whoever threatened us. I took that step without thinking—fight first, then flee. Only here there was no threat. Just some people trying to be kind and thoughtful to strangers. My heart had raced and the roof of my mouth had gone dry and metallic—the taste of fear. Yet mixed in with the foolishness I felt as the middleweight handed me my coat was a quiet and private satisfaction. Fear didn't own me, and it never would.

(14)

Jesus's grandmother never watched her grandson fight. With short gray-streaked black hair that she kept brushed away from her pretty, lined face, Hermilla prayed that neither he nor his opponent would get hurt. The exception was the Julio Alvarez fight; she sat in her living room spellbound by the action on TV, drinking beer and smoking cigarettes. "I got very nervous," she said with a shy laugh, hiking her shoulders. Hermilla's home was in one of the nicest parts of Delicias. The streets were broad and paved; the one-story cinderblock homes looked identical in construction, but they were well-painted, and many had chain-link fences across the front. They were homes of the middle class. The difference in the Chavez home was the entryway. On a counter and rack in the front part of her living room, Señora Chavez had an array of packaged candies. She sold nothing else—no cigarettes, no potato chips, just candy. Her candy store meant that she would always know her neighbors, that she would always have children in her home.

The elder Jesus Chavez had a small potbelly, a closely trimmed mustache, and a gap-toothed grin. "My father died very young," he told Marcy when she was interviewing him for her movie. "I think he was forty-four when he died. And he left six of us, seven with my mother. We were already delivering water, because he was very sick, for seven centavos per can. It was barely enough to feed the animals and ourselves. We were many animals! And so we went, until I was old enough to go to the mine. My mother didn't want me to go. She was crying, because she knew what had happened to her husband. The work in the mine is good; it's good but it's not healthy. In 1992 I completed forty-three years with the mining company. That is the daily life of a miner, to be buried in the interior of the mine. He leaves, and he comes back to life."

A fourth member of the family joined us now as we drank Cokes, sat on the sofas and in the easy chairs, and talked. He was Jesus's Uncle Julio. Tall, in his thirties, Julio was the father of the boy who had flipped across the ring after Jesus stopped Daryl Pinckney. Julio was also the relative with whom Jesus had lived when he first came to Austin. The uncle told me that living in Texas had been hard for him. Learning English was difficult. He liked being back here. He said he worked in a *maquiladora*—one of the foreign-owned plants that take advantage of low Mexican wages. He said they manufactured auto parts. He liked his job.

At the rear of their house Señor Chavez had made a small patio of concrete, and on one side of the square had built himself a workshop that contained his large collection of tools. The workshop was his refuge, his private place. On other sides of the patio he had built two apartments consisting of a large bedroom and a bath. Since his separation from his wife, Julio had been living in one of them, and Jesus occupied the other. A wall covered with the fanciful painting of a child was built up from another side of the patio. And in a small pen behind it all was a bleating shorthaired goat that would soon take its turn at the knife and on the coals.

As we talked inside I had noticed that Jesus cocked his head and studied me. "JanReid, that's the first time I ever heard you speak

Spanish," he said when we were in his apartment, where he went to get his keys to his truck. "I was impressed."

"Oh, I'm not any good at it," I said. "I work at it and try, but it's not my gift."

"No. You did good."

It was Sunday afternoon following the fight on Friday. The Garriotts had flown away and Lou Mesorana had gone back to Mexico City. Jesus and I had the day just to fool around. He was concerned and curious about the pains in my legs. I had told him that the whirlpool in my bathtub eased them; he asked his uncle and grandparents for directions to hot springs in the area. They were uncertain, but he decided we were going off to find them.

Jesus had a vehicle that seated four people and was enclosed like a station wagon but felt and rode more like a truck. The thieves in the Chihuahua City parking garage had not only stolen his CD player; they broke out a window and tore up the underside of his dash ripping it out. *Rateros* everywhere, I thought. Outside Delicias, I gazed at countryside that was cut with irrigation channels and shaded with orchards of pecan trees. Though the climate is arid, Delicias is in the river valley of the Rio Conchos, the long Rio Grande tributary. The day before, the Garriotts, Jesus, and I had driven the route of the uphill eight-mile run that he loped along with his Dalmatian Chula on a leash. It went through a pretty village then wound up toward an impoundment of the Conchos, and above the dark blue lake was a footpath up a steep hill of red stone and earth. Unlike many fighters, Jesus didn't listen to music when he was doing his roadwork. Running was his time to think, he said, to reflect and clear his head. When he reached the summit of the small mountain he rested and took in the broad view of the river valley and tawny distances of the nation of his birth. The Conchos heads up in the Sierra Madres Occidental of the Tarahumara Indians, the fabled long-distance runners. In America, Jesus was Chicano, but in Mexico he was mestizo, and the Indian

ancestry that his family talked about was Tarahumara. I had thought
of that, watching Marcy's footage of him running with his dog
through the streets of Delicias. He had a distance runner's long rolling
stride.

He had explored these flatlands on his bike, he said. He and the
kid who looked out for our safety at the arena in Chihuahua City
rode fifteen or twenty miles at a time, meeting people, just looking
around. People in Delicias and some outlying villages knew Jesus
now, asked him for his autograph. "I was very scared when I came
down here," he told me. "But my grandparents took me in just like
they did when my mother was sick and I was ten years old. The apartment I showed you, that was where my Uncle Pepe lived. My grandparents were very sad when I first came here because Uncle Pepe had
passed away just a few months before that. They said, 'Will it bother
you, staying in his place, sleeping in his bed?' I said, 'No, no, of course
not.' For them it's been like one son has gone, and now another son
has come. And JanReid, I swear to you: One night I was lying in
Uncle Pepe's bed, and I felt these arms close around me, and for a long
time they just hugged me. It was him, I think. Letting me know I was
going to be all right."

Past a village of very little charm we found the hot springs. They
looked like the pools formed by irrigation ditches that kids used for
swimming holes, courtship, and beer-drinking in the part of Texas
where I grew up. It was Sunday, and a number of adults and kids
splashed and swam; one family cooked on a charcoal grill. "Nah, I
don't wanta do this," Jesus said abruptly, wheeling about on the dirt
road. He looked at me and grinned.

"Do you like cockfights?" he startled me again.

"I've never seen one," I confessed. Bullfights, dogfights, cockfights—
in a way they were all the same to me. They placed no value on life.
And I was scornful of the latter two. Betting on dogs and chickens in

fights to the death—to me that was low-rent, savage. But I didn't speak up for my principles now. In fact, I was fascinated.

"Maybe I can find us one," Jesus said.

Back in Delicias he drove down an unpaved street. He stopped at a house and knocked on the door. A bald man stepped out on the porch and they talked for a moment, then Jesus motioned for me to come. The bald man smiled and introduced himself as Pancho. He led us through a sparsely furnished house, out the back door. The fenced yard was bare packed dirt. Arranged around the perimeter were several chicken coops. A grizzled white pit bull with a rope around its neck was tied to a steel stake hammered in the ground. Marked with the scars of its blood sport, the dog stood up wagging its short tail until it became apparent Pancho meant to ignore it. The dog lay down and went back to sleep. Northern Mexicans speak Spanish with unusual rapidity, I had learned after tutoring by a Colombian and hearing it spoken by people from other parts of Latin America. From the start I had trouble keeping up with the conversation of Jesus and Pancho, but clearly the subject was cockfighting. The bald man led us over to a place at the rear of the house and pulled a scrap of tarpaulin off a dead white rooster. He picked up the bird by its feet and held it out stiff as a board. This was what had become of his latest fighting cock.

Pancho was the father of one of Jesus's friends. He shook his head, threw the dead bird down, and flipped the tarp over it again. He led us out to the coops, each of which contained a single rooster and hen. Pancho reached in two of the coops and pulled out the fighting birds, getting himself pecked badly enough that blood ran and dripped off the end of his thumb. Ignoring that, he thrust the roosters face-to-face, teasing them and getting them riled. As their heads and beaks shot toward each other, the feathers on their necks fluffed out. Pancho tossed them on the ground and at once we had a cockfight at our feet. They hopped about and flew at each other and bounced off each others' chests with noisy flapping of their wings, but it was like boxers sparring. They didn't wear the steel spurs, so they couldn't kill. Pancho didn't seem too concerned that one might put the other's eye out. He let them scrap for a few minutes, then broke it up and tossed them back in the coops with their hens. Pancho led us back inside the house. The living room walls were decorated with a painting of a bearded Christ, some family photographs, and a framed diploma that Pancho showed me proudly. He was a licensed breeder of *Aves de Combate*.

I congratulated him, and we sat down to what he'd been doing when we arrived—drinking Busch beer and tomato juice. That drew from me a surprised grin. In the bars of Wichita Falls, the drink was a popular tradition called a "red draw." It's not an unpleasant combination of flavors, but when I left my hometown enough people stared and turned up their noses when I made one that eventually I lost the habit, though I sometimes ordered one when I went there, for nostalgia's sake. Pancho was the only person I'd ever encountered who had no connection to Wichita Falls and mixed tomato juice with his beer. We drank and talked for two or three hours. It was the first time I had ever drunk with Jesus. I certainly didn't disapprove; I used to think that Richard Lord's never-stop emphasis on training was going to burn Jesus out. But I had to concentrate so hard to keep up with their Spanish that my attention lapsed at times and I got a little bored. I slowed down on the red draws—my paraplegic kidneys and bladder didn't appreciate large quantities of beer. Pancho was an animated storyteller. At one point he pointed at his blue eyes then ran his palm over his bald head and said he wished he could meet the gringo who was responsible for him! We shared his laughter. I think Jesus must have told Pancho what happened to me in Mexico City, for he said, "Yo soy un hombre pobre. Pero todo lo que tengo es suyo." I am a poor man, but all I have is yours.

Pancho's wife made us delicious quesadillas from fresh tortillas and a crumbly white cheese called *quesa fresca*. Jesus's grandfather stopped by for a couple of beers and cigarettes with Pancho. The sun went down and it grew dark outside. Jesus got a little drunk. I discovered why we had stayed so long. Some men were coming by in a while to look at Pancho's birds. They might be buying, they might be selling. When Richard Lord and Jesus were beginning to disagree, Richard often said of his fighter: "You know how he is when he sets that jaw. . . ." Actually I didn't know what Richard meant by that; but when the men showed up at Pancho's house I noticed that Jesus's right jaw was clenched. He too was bored, he had money from his fight, but no sweetheart to share his good times with, and he wanted some excitement. I wouldn't lose sleep over watching a cockfight, but there was a surliness in Jesus's manner that I hadn't seen before, and it made me nervous.

He followed the older men out in the backyard and asked them if there was going to be a fight. They told him no. He showed the visitors money he'd earned from stopping Pinckney and offered to pay them for two of their best cocks. Then we'd put on the steel spurs and watch them fight. The two men glanced at each other. Two cocks they'd bred and trained and groomed, and this young *pocho* wanted to watch one kill the other? They turned him down.

When we left Pancho's house it was eight o'clock or so. I told Jesus I was a little tired and thought I'd turn in early. He agreed quickly and seemed a bit contrite. It mattered a great deal to him that I had come to Mexico to see him, and he wanted me to have a good time. He said, "Let me show you one more thing about this town."

Near the business district he pulled up to a building marked only by some neon above the entrance. We walked into a time warp of plush red velour and polished hardwood beams. The bar was the shape of a large horseshoe. Three or four people sat on stools drinking beer and tequila. Pool tables with leather pockets occupied some rooms that Jesus and the barkeep, who spoke English well, escorted me through. On every wall were framed photographs of entertainers and athletes. Louis Armstrong, Marlene Dietrich, Jack Johnson, Cantinflas. Wood-burning stoves of ornate metalwork sat here and there, stacks of neatly chopped firewood at the ready. Near the entrance to the dining rooms, where all the tables were set but the room was darkened, light shone on the framed cover of an old *Texas Monthly*. Evidently the magazine had once plugged the place in a travel story. We walked through a door and came out in a large tiled square with a fountain. I realized the place was a hotel and asked the man how many rooms he had. "Forty-three," he said proudly. But except for the interior of the bar, no lights gleamed anywhere. The place was mind-boggling, a hugely expensive movie set. It had a distinct air of desolation and abandonment, yet there was no dust, no cobwebs. I was profoundly confused.

Jesus and I took stools, ordered shots of tequila, and ticked the glasses before we drank. A man in his sixties came over and said hello to Jesus in English. He appeared to be criollo, a Mexican of European blood. He wore an expensive sportcoat. The man congratulated Jesus on his latest win and said he was confident Jesus would win the world championship. Jesus thanked him, introduced him to me, and the man bought us another round. The only other man in the bar sat nearby with a fiftyish woman whose cheeks were rouged and hair was bleached blonde. A nice pair of legs were crossed on the stool. She looked us over, blew a stream of cigarette smoke, and smiled. The man with her slid off his stool and approached us, putting his hand against the bar to steady himself. In Spanish he gushed his admiration for Jesus, patted him on the back, then left his hand there. He touched the fighter's short black hair, then tried to pull his face close. Jesus laughed and fended him off with a polite forearm.

The owner said maybe we'd enjoy our drinks more on the other side of the bar. The old queen raised his hands and muttered apologies, apologies, and wobbled back to his drinking partner. I sat beside my friend and grinned at his embarrassment. "Is that the first time a gay guy's ever hit on you?"

"No," he said with a laugh, eyebrows shooting up. "But it's the first time one's ever kissed me!" He chuckled again, remembering. "In Austin, Terri used to tell me, 'Gabriel, gay men just *adore* you.' Great. All I need."

As we drank, a number of women drifted into the bar, dressed up and carrying purses. I finally understood the place. Tourism was a hapless venture in Delicias; no one came here except for business or family reasons. Trying to keep up his overhead, the hotelier had turned this fabulous place into the town's whorehouse. A wooden-faced prostitute walked through the door, and before entering the bar she made the sign of the cross.

"Damn," Jesus said, considering his tequila glass. "Crossing herself every night she comes to work. Hoping she won't get AIDS."

I didn't remark that I'd seen him make the sign of the cross when the bell rang and he had to go to work.

The next morning I was having breakfast in the motel's coffee shop when he came to pick me up and take me to the airport. Jesus had loaded me down with gifts—the gloves, now autographed, he had worn against Daryl Pinckney, bottles of his grandmother's homemade red and green salsas, and a beautifully shaped and labeled bottle of sotol. It's similar to tequila and rawer grades of liquor made from the agave plant, except sotol is a different desert plant with nutritious flesh in its bulb root. I knew of sotol liquor by reading accounts of the nineteenth-century frontier. I imagined it to be like pulque, the vice and doom of *pobrecitos*. But Dorothy and I would find that this clear stuff was tasty. We also established, though, that it should not be consumed like cognac, just because we poured it in snifters.

As I finished my eggs and coffee Jesus sat with his elbow on the table, grinning. A middle-aged man in a coat and tie came over to our table and introduced himself. He asked Jesus if he would have a word with some men at a nearby table. When Jesus returned, I checked out of the motel and we carried my possessions to his truck. He said on the way out of town, "Those men said they'd like to help me get that gym built in Delicias."

"I noticed them before you came in. They're like men in every small town I've ever lived in. They own the tractor dealership, the drugstore, the insurance agency. They have breakfast at the same place every morning. They talk and gossip, and then they go run their businesses. They run the town, in a way. They can probably help you raise money for that gym."

"Yeah, except they told me that they're PAN, and the people in power here are PRI," he said of the Mexican political parties. "Which makes it harder."

"You never know. PAN might win."

"I don't know what the parties are about, what they even stand for. I like it here in many ways. You're free in Mexico, you have personal freedom. People in the United States don't understand that. But this is a very corrupt country."

We rose from the orchards and river valley into Chihuahua's stark ranching country. "There has never been a world boxing champion from Chihuahua," Jesus said after a while. "If I get a title fight, I'll be the first."

"There's never been one from Austin, either."

He looped his wrist over the steering wheel and smiled. "You remember I told you I was born in the town where Pancho Villa got killed? People still talk about Pancho Villa here. When the American soldiers invaded Chihuahua, chasing Pancho Villa, they wore green uniforms. People here didn't like being invaded, and they still talk about that, too. They didn't know much English, but they would yell out, 'Hey, Green. Go!' and point to the border. They say around here that's where the word 'gringo' came from." Jesus shrugged and grinned. "I don't know if that's true."

I was buoyed by my solitary trip to Mexico. I didn't know if Dorothy and I would ever care to travel there again. Other countries in Latin America have beauty and charm, without the risk. But I no longer felt destroyed by Mexico. I had gotten back up on the horse that threw me.

And I was not quite so worried about Jesus. I didn't know if he would ever be allowed back in the United States; he was a bit of flotsam on a tidal wave of history and law. America would get over its fear of Latino immigrants, but maybe not in time for Jesus. At six or eight thousand dollars a fight he was making fair money in Mexico. He could have made a home for himself in Oaxaca, Zacatecas, or Guanajuato, places where attractive young Mexicans, Americans, and Europeans spill each night through the streets. But he chose dry and homely Chihuahua. Jesus knew and I now understood that he might not have survived his exile if not for the comfort and company of his family.

Others worried about him after the Pinckney fight. He was slow to get back in training. He didn't go off on wild benders, but he was drinking more than usual. Unsavory guys wanted to be his entourage. We heard that his grandfather had a talk with him: Okay, he had taken a break, now it was time to get back to work. Delicias was a small town. If he was going to be a champion, he must conduct himself like one.

I knew Jesus was centered not because he returned to Mexico City and the boxing gym. It was when his new lawyer, Barbara Hines, asked him to write a letter. She took his case on its merits, but as she did with all her clients, she asked him to write her about what he hoped to gain from the legal action. He procrastinated, and I sympathized—writing was not a skill that came to him easily. But Jesus bore down and at last delivered his lawyer the following letter:

"There are many reasons why I want to come back to the U.S. One of the most important ones is my family. I miss them very much and I wish I had the chance to only visit them every once in a while.

"My friends in Austin, I get lots of mail from them and they wish just as much as me that I will get to come back. Some people probably think that it's mainly for boxing and to make money but that's not what it's all about. I think that there are more important things than money. Family, friends, and to finally get back to where I was raised and to where I know how to live best.

"I have learned to love Mexico very much and I love to be with my family here. My boxing is going well but I don't know anything else here in Mexico other than boxing.

"I don't know exactly how this country works politically and I think it will be hard to find something after boxing.

"I love my Chicago family and friends and all my friends from Austin. I only wish I can finally find my way back home."

(15)

The morning of New Year's Eve, 1999, Dorothy was shaking my shoulder; my groaning had once more awakened her. It was dawn, judging from the light. She said, "Do you have any pain medicine?" I murmured and pointed at the chair beside the low-slung bed. On it was a glass of water and the vial of Vicodin. She said, "Why don't you take it?" She rolled over on her side and jabbed at her pillow. The reason I haven't already, I thought, is that I was asleep.

Dorothy and I had agreed we couldn't face our usual Christmas— the ten-foot tree and the big party that friends had come to expect. The death of her brother that fall weighed heavily on our moods. Then she read one day that the French were going to set off ten thousand flashbulbs on the Eiffel Tower at midnight of New Year 2000. She said, "Oh, honey, we've got to see that."

Through friends we had rented two apartments in the Marais, the fine little neighborhood on the Right Bank, and spent a week in each. The first apartment was just two blocks from the Seine, and the day we arrived we bundled up, crossed the short bridge, and prowled the little shops and cafes on the Ile St.-Louis. The apartment was so small it was like living on a boat. But everything had its place;

everything worked. The kitchen was up to any meal one might want to cook, and the triangular bathtub was just big enough for me to crawl in. At a market we had bought an eighteen-inch Christmas tree and spent a good part of a day and night decorating it. We had cooked a Christmas dinner of roast veal and rosemary potatoes, and called Greg and Lila in Austin and my mother and sister in Wichita Falls. Mother couldn't help being a little worried about this, my sister reported. After what happened to me, she didn't think we ought to be gallivanting around in foreign countries. Dorothy and I laughed and tried to persuade her that Paris and Mexico City were not the same places at all.

The second apartment was a four-story walk-up, which didn't bother me. The physical therapy had left me well-schooled on getting up and down stairs. This apartment was the residence of a French businesswoman. It was larger, lived-in, full of interesting books and records. The bed was an ordinary mattress set upon a raised wood frame. I knew firm beds were supposed to be good for human backs, but this one was like a rock slab for my hips. I woke each day remembering what it had been like to be paralyzed. With a painful wrench of my hips I rolled over on my side and lowered my feet to the floor. It took a hot bath and an hour or so to get me fully mobile.

That New Year's Eve morning Dorothy had gotten up, dressed, and left the apartment after our brief exchange about the pain pills. She walked south on Rue de Turenne, shoulders braced against the gray, penetrating cold. We had stayed a little too long, she worried. There had been so much time walking, walking, with her trying to stay warm and me slowly bringing up the rear. She had watched me go taut-faced and stiff-legged, leaning heavily on the cane, when the spasms grabbed me. She doubted I could make the hike necessary to see the fireworks show. Earlier, in a coffee shop one afternoon, I had spread out our map and calculated how far we would have to walk to reach open spaces and have a good view of the Eiffel Tower. I didn't say, but my quiet and my blank-eyed expression must have conveyed the truth. Walking both ways it was a little over four miles.

Dorothy looked in a few shops for more Christmas presents she wanted to take home, then at one of the markets bought a bouquet of lavender roses, which she would leave in a vase for our host. She walked up the coiling wood stairs, let herself in the apartment, and the day turned. "It was your smile," she said. "You looked up and smiled."

Off a small park, Place des Vosges, we had lunch in a cafe that seemed to draw closer as each table was claimed and we ate the rich food and drank a bottle of red wine. But the small table next to us could have been yards across, judging from the body language of the French couple. She was blonde, trim, pretty, and she dined in the European manner, holding her fork with the tines down. He wore a white turtleneck and a cashmere blazer. His gaze drifted toward other tables and the shadowy forms of people walking outside, beyond the condensation on the windows. She spoke occasionally, and he responded with stretches of his mouth and tilts of his leonine head. He tried to pour her more wine; she stayed him by placing her palm on the glass. Happy New Year. I hoped Dorothy and I never struck such a ruined and distant pose.

After the walk we warmed ourselves in the apartment with our backs to the radiators. The tugs of a nap drew us toward the bed as soon as the coats and mufflers were put away. We awoke about the same time and lay still for a moment, our heads on the pillows, watching each other. I unclasped the top buttons of her gown. In time we were gasping and twisting out of clothing, eyes closed then opening for glimpses of the love contours we had known so long and well. We wanted to make it through these bomb blasts in our lives, and that was one of the times I knew we would.

Long after darkness fell, we began to put on layers of cotton and wool for the cold night out. "Ready?" said Dorothy, standing up on her toes to touch her lips to mine.

"Let's hit it," I said. We set out a little after ten p.m. The subways were running all night and free, and we thought we should at least give them a look. In the St.-Paul station we saw two cars arrive and pass. They were so packed that when the doors opened, release of the pressure shoved people outward, and they had to grab and brace to avoid being ejected on the platform.

"Nah," I announced. We walked back up the stairs, and as we stepped back out on the sidewalk we were amazed to see a small white sedan pull up to the Metro stop's cabstand. Here we didn't give possibilities of danger a thought; Dorothy waved and ran over. The taxi driver, a young Korean woman, said in English, "I will take you as close as I can. But you must have small change."

Dorothy showed her a denomination of francs that satisfied her, and the car shot through a commercial district then on down the long street, Rue de Rivoli, that runs beside the Louvre. The driver let us out at a traffic barricade. We walked around the corner of the palace turned museum, and the long open space of the Jardin des Tuileries opened before us. Across the Seine, splendidly aglow in orange, was the Eiffel Tower. I looked at Dorothy. Tears were streaming down her cheeks.

We could have seen the show well without taking another forward step. But it was only ten-thirty, so we began to wander slowly with the crowd. We stopped now and then and rested with our forearms on the low wall above the Seine. We passed a line of buses where a large number of police stood in loose formation, talking and smoking. On this night they were almost unnecessary. It was such a gentle crowd; hundreds of thousands of people were said to be on the streets, and all night I didn't see one unpleasant incident.

The tower was a magnet—we couldn't get close enough. Taking our time, we walked about a mile and a half. I would make three more on the way home and finish feeling strong. Finally the tower loomed so close it seemed pointless to go any farther. We set up a comfortable vantage point along the river wall. An ongoing game kept balloons batted up, over, along the way. I heard languages I couldn't begin to identify. As the moment grew close I didn't know what to expect. Then the flashbulbs went off, and a human roar erupted that exceeded any I had ever heard. On the tower the flashbulbs zipped up, down, and across the spans and supports. A thick cloak of fireworks began at ground level and slowly worked its way upward, throwing starbursts of every color all over the sky and somehow igniting ropes of explosion that whirled out and around the tower. Dorothy was aiming and clicking her camera. "Babe, don't take pictures!" I yelled through the tumult and detonations. "Look!"

Another night in Austin, fourteen months later, felt almost as festive and unreal. "*Cha*-vez! *Cha*-vez! *Cha*-vez!" the crowd began to chant.

After three years the dam of unforgiving had broken. Jesus had told me about his pivotal appointment with immigration authorities at the U.S. consulate in Juárez, Mexico. "There was a long line of people, JanReid. I went to the lady in charge and right away she said, 'You've got a problem, well, everybody here has a problem. You're not any different just because you speak English. Go back to the back of the line.' So I did and we all made our way for two and a half hours. They gave me a physical, and they asked me to talk to a psychiatrist. He was really pretty nice. He asked me if I'd ever been in prison, and I told him I had, and we talked about that. At the end of the interview he told me he was a boxing fan. He shook my hand, wished me luck, and said he was glad to have me back." The long exile ended with Jesus on the banks of the Rio Grande, signing autographs for employees of the INS. He was a permanent resident again. Jesus could travel freely now. He had a Green Card.

This was no inside fix by the movers and shakers of pro boxing.

To the contrary, when Jesus's homecoming bout was announced, the promoters and TV producers had seemed a bit startled; suddenly here stood this guy with twenty-nine straight wins and three years as the number one contender. It didn't hurt that I championed his cause, nor that Marcy Garriott made a heartfelt movie about his odyssey. It happened because a young video game magnate, Richard Garriott, was able to finance the work of a dedicated activist, Barbara Hines, who knew every nuance of the law—and because in every dealing with the INS, Jesus impressed officials with his honesty and his character.

Still, like Muhammad Ali when he declined the military draft during the Vietnam War, because of politics Jesus had lost three years of his athletic prime. I don't contend that Jesus had as much talent as Ali, but in the months leading up to the Troy Dorsey fight in Atlantic City, boxing insiders seemed to have little doubt that Jesus was destined for a world title. In the ensuing three years he had fought only one opponent of his caliber, Julio Alvarez, and his skills seemed to erode as he fought the string of Mexican journeymen. Now almost no one in boxing thought he could beat the super featherweight champion, Floyd Mayweather, Jr. Despite his ranking, Jesus had become a nonentity in American boxing. At one point *USA Today* ran an overview of boxing that placed him thirteenth among super featherweight contenders. Outside Texas he was an unknown—just another Mexican fighter.

But no fight was as hard as the one Jesus had just won. Now he had a life after boxing, and in Austin it was his hour. Texas politicians and well-dressed women preened near the ring and TV cameras. An event was being planned in which the Texas legislature and Governor Rick Perry would grant a symbolic pardon to Jesus for his illegal walks across the Rio Grande bridge. For the first time, the University of Texas had allowed one of its arenas to host a boxing match. Boxing promoters and ESPN producers were astounded by the electricity and noise and the size of the crowd; few boxers in America were able to put seven thousand people in the seats. Dorothy and I were at ringside with Marcy and Robert Garriott. Nearby were John Spong, David Courtney, and Mike Hall—the friends who had gone with me to Mexico City. People were wearing mock torero hats to welcome home El Matador. They might have been mistaken for Mickey Mouse ears. I saw Sean Curtin, the old Irish trainer from Chicago, amused by the foolishness and loving it. Jesus's sister Lidia, a newlywed, rushed up to me in her excitement and planted a fragrant kiss on my cheek. Maybe nowhere else in America—but in Austin, Jesus was back on top.

In the ring, up in the lights above us, a svelte former world champion, Tom "Boom Boom" Johnson of Detroit, moved around with a blue robe and look of grim intention on his face. Johnson was thirty-six, but he had fifty wins, and this fight was his chance to get back in contention and in the money. Then the music began and everyone was jostling, shoving, trying to get closer for a look. Jesus and his entourage came down the aisle beside our seats. Men behind him waved flags of Texas, Mexico, and the United States. And with them, dressed to the nines, was the immigration lawyer, Barbara Hines, who wouldn't have been caught dead at a boxing match two years earlier; now she sashayed along holding up his North American championship belt. "By golly," she had told me, "you just don't know how life is gonna surprise you." When she came back to her seat Dorothy and I asked her about the scene in the dressing room. "There were thirty guys and me. It was so *male*." The crowd parted for an instant, and then I saw Jesus, beaded with sweat and wearing a black robe, resting his red gloves on another's shoulders. He glanced and recognized me and threw me a grin.

Then the bell rang and he was above us, champing on that mouthpiece, hands held high. "What's this, John L. Sullivan?" Dorothy laughed about his stance. A few months earlier she had told me never to waste another boxing ticket on her. Now she was yelling like the rest of us. Boom Boom Johnson stepped smartly, juked with his shoulders and head, tried to drive Jesus back with his jab. But he couldn't land his power combinations, and Jesus's pressure was unrelenting. By the end of the fourth round Johnson was gasping, his gloves on the ropes, before he sat down. The body shots just took too much. In the eighth he chose not to answer the bell. Richard Lord picked up Jesus by the waist and carried him around the ring, the fighter beating his fists in the air and yelling back at the adoring crowd.

After it was over, a network boxing analyst, the sometime trainer Teddy Atlas, acknowledged the rousing show but said with mild condescension, "Floyd Mayweather is special." The champion from Grand Rapids, Michigan, was twenty-three, he was lightning fast, and he had the patina of an Olympic gold medal. He was projected and endowed by the powers of boxing as a multimillion-dollar fighter. Top Rank now held the promotional rights to both Mayweather and Jesus (no acknowledged conflict of interest, this being boxing). Until now Top Rank executives had referred to Jesus as "the mandatory." Until the Austin crowd grabbed their attention they didn't even afford him the respect of a name. Jesus was twenty-eight, which is not young for a boxer. He wore a brace on one knee, which had a torn ligament; he'd gotten kicked by a bull while helping some people brand their cattle in Delicias. The official line out of Las Vegas, where he was supposed to fight Mayweather, was that Jesus had no chance.

But three months later the outcome of such a title fight, if it happened, seemed not so preordained. Hoping to impress an HBO TV audience and a crowd in his home of Grand Rapids, Michigan, Mayweather hurt his hands, danced, and pat-patted his way with light jabs to a decision against a game but little-known challenger. "Mayweather's lucky he didn't get Chavez tonight," said one of the TV announcers. The night Mayweather was booed in his hometown, Jesus had stolen the champion's show in a twelve-round brawl against

a Californian named Juan Arias. Jesus had demonstrated everything—
jabs, left hooks, straight rights, uppercuts, and stamina. But he still
took too many punches, and Richard Lord, now Jesus's second cornerman, said of his opponent: "Arias could have knocked him out at
any time, and he was trying to."

Their relationship largely mended, Jesus trained a great deal in
Richard's gym, benefiting from some grueling sparring with Johnny
Casas. Jesus's lead trainer now was Houston's Ronnie Shields, who
had groomed Evander Holyfield and Pernell Whitaker at the peaks of
their careers and was one of the best in boxing. Shields had briefly
trained Jesus before the deportation, and on the HBO debut his touch
showed; it may have been the best performance in Jesus's career. Still,
late in the fight Jesus weathered a jolting hook then resumed slugging
with Arias. It was a risky exchange, for Jesus was well ahead on the
cards, and afterward Shields reprimanded him: "I know you're a warrior, Jesus, but I don't want to see any more of that." Richard told me
that in the locker room, after the unanimous decision, "Jesus's hands
were swollen up like grapefruits. He wanted to go over and see Arias.
They just looked at each other, then at their hands, and laughed.
What's a handshake when you've been through something like that
together? It's a bond that nobody can understand outside boxing."

After the Arias fight, *USA Today* again put Mayweather at the top
of its world rankings, but added, "El Matador was sensational." Jesus seemed happy, although he was hindered by his Mexican contract, and it remained to be seen if he would make any money in
boxing. For now he was content with having a new car and, for the
first time in his life, his own apartment. In Austin I was clumping
along a sidewalk one day when Billy Gammon, the insurance executive who had first lured me out to Richard's gym, called out and trotted up to say hello. As we talked about Jesus's uncommon journey,

Billy reflected, "It's funny how the 'matador' business started with a high school English teacher and a gym in Chicago. But Jesus comes as close as anyone we'll ever see around here to having the kind of courage it takes to be a real matador."

I wondered if I'd cry when he finally got beat. Probably. And then start begging him to quit. He was risking his life, his mind, in there—consider the sad state of Muhammad Ali. Physically and emotionally I was pretty much through with boxing, I believed. Yet one day I was working out and thought, Go on, do it—nobody's going to ask you to. I had mentioned sparring once to Julian Henry, a man about my age who had been training hard and pairing off with the young boxers almost daily. Suddenly I was pulling on the groin cup and smearing Vaseline across my cheeks and nose. I stepped through the ropes like Frankenstein on stilts and Julian took it easy with me. Later I realized how few punches he had thrown. I staggered once in the sparring and swung my arms to keep my balance. But for two rounds I was back in there; I was relaxed and I landed some blows to Julian's headgear. "You didn't look bad," one man said afterward, with a narrowed gaze. Maybe it was a ridiculous thing to do, but for the rest of that evening my mood soared. I wish Jesus had seen it.

Still, when I thought of him now, it was not in Richard's gym, under TV lights, or on the dusty plains of Chihuahua. The INS had first allowed him to come back in the country when his mother fell ill in Chicago. On the way back to Mexico he came through Austin, and a number of us went out to dinner with him. It was a misty night, the sidewalks and pavement were slick, and after dinner he walked me to my car. I could tell he debated whether to take my arm as I stepped down from a curb. All the prohibitions born of being told what it was to be a man fell away. Beside my car, we stood for a moment hugging each other. He loomed so large in the ring that I often forgot how short he was. I sighed and rested my chin on the top of his head.

.   .   .

It was a fine and fitting reunion to see David Courtney, John Spong, and Mike Hall at Jesus's homecoming fight and then help them close down a bar. One reminder of our friendship was as constant in my life as my car keys. David had been rummaging in a junk shop when he found a cane that someone had painted orange. He stripped it, stained it, found someone who could carve my initials into the grip, and to its front he had tacked on a *milagro* in the form of a human leg. The tokens are a Mexican tradition; in Spanish the word means "miracle," and the small crafted bits of copper or silver are entreaties for a blessing, or at least good luck. David gave it to me when I was ready to give up the more supportive crutch, and this cane felt just right. Its strength would take whatever weight I had to put upon it, and it was exactly the right height.

When I was still in the wheelchair Dorothy and I had gone to a play with David and John Spong and their dates. Toward the end of the drama a couple of blanks were fired loudly from a pistol, and I saw John flinch and turn pale. The noise took him back to that street in Mexico City; he still reckoned with that terror, too. John and I talked often—about music and writing and his airy two-story house in the hills south of Austin. "I didn't call you about walking in on a rattlesnake in the living room at three in the morning?" John asked. "I must have woke up everybody else." His country place made me nostalgic for my rustic cabin long ago. But not all our enthusiasms were shared. After Jesus's fight with Boom Boom, John sipped a beer, shook his head, and quietly told my wife: "I don't know about boxing, Dorothy. I just don't get it."

In addition to his magazine work, Mike Hall had his following as a singer and songwriter, and finally I talked him out of a couple of his records. One featured a thirty-eight minute track about a man's dream of the Spanish Civil War. Mike sang over and over in a deadpan mantra: "Life is all right, for the time bein'." Good, rowdy rock and roll welled up for a time, then came a squawk of such loud and abrupt discordance that I couldn't help jumping. "You listened to all of it?" Mike said, laughing. "A friend of mine was driving when that came up, and he thought he'd had a wreck." Mike was devoting energy and creativity to music again; when he got some extended time away from his job at the magazine, he and his sidemen made good money and played to rapt houses on quick tours of Europe. The enthusiasm of Europeans kept a lot of American musicians in the business. His new band was called Mike Hall and the Woodpeckers. Their first record was *Dead by Dinner*.

Our interchange as friends was never constant. Dorothy and I had a wedding party at our house for David and his bride. Mike held his wedding in Alpine, Texas, because the band had a gig out there. And John's romance looked solid and serious to me. The women partners in our lives recognized the importance of our friendship. It was a curious bond we shared. After a while we hardly spoke of Mexico City. A woman who thought the episode was a variety of madness peculiar to men asked if I would do the same thing again. I didn't answer because the replies were complicated and contradictory. No, of course not, because even if I wanted to, I would never again have the ability to do something so reckless and violent. But, yes, I'd risk taking another bullet, if that was the only way those guys would still be walking around. And I knew they would do the same for me.

Epilogue

Many Mexicans—and residents of Mexico City—have told me that a cop or ex-cop shot me. They had no evidence, yet they made the accusations with complete assurance. If anyone in the United States doubted the menace of the police in Mexico City, the doubts should have been dispelled by the death of Frederick McPhail, a twenty-seven-year-old New Yorker murdered seven months after I was shot. A Mexican coroner ruled that McPhail drank himself to death, which was true; except that Mexico City cops forced him to guzzle straight vodka until he passed out, after first drawing all available cash out of his credit cards. The case was cracked because the youth's father knew his son was not a heavy drinker. His persistence led to an ATM camera which showed the killers using one of the credit cards while still in uniform. A pair of cops heard the jig was up on their patrol car's radio; they jumped out and left the car with the motor running. Detectives later found three of them working illegally on a construction site in a small town near Austin, and a speedy extradition whisked them back to Mexico City. More than a dozen Mexico City cops were charged with the robberies that led to the murder.

In my case no arrest was ever made; to my knowledge there was no investigation. A sinister e-mail from Mexico City appeared one day: "We can find the guys who did that to you." Someone trying to make a buck. I replied curtly and never heard from that person again. Though the Ministry of Tourism has contacted me several times, I have never spoken with one law enforcement official in Mexico. I don't know what to believe. But I knew I had to go back.

Several weeks after I was shot and Red Duke's jet flew us out of Mexico City, Roberto Castañeda, the Mexican surgeon who first worked on me, called us in Texas to see how we were doing. I had no memory of him, but he told me in his tentative but almost perfect English that we had a certain bond. When I wrote about the experience I mentioned the doctor, his embrace of Dorothy and Lila, and his plea when they said good-bye: "Please don't hate my country."

After some hesitation I sent him the essay and a letter. Dr. Castañeda wrote back: "I knew about your article. Obviously, I read it in detail and enjoyed it very much. Unfortunately you said terrible things about México City, but it is understandable. My personal opinion is that the article shows México City exactly as it is. It is a tragedy that our city can be so dangerous. Sometimes we do not see things because we are accustomed. I distributed copies among doctors and friends, asking for their opinions. Majority of them think that you wrote the crude reality of our city. However, let me tell you that some of my friends who read it, considered it a little bit exaggerated. I am sure that time is going to heal some of the bad feelings that you have about this city. But fortunately you think that we did a good job with your emergency situation, and specifically that we treated you and your family very kindly, and I feel very happy with that comment in your article and in your letter. Let me tell you that I read your article exactly on the 'Doctor's Day' in October and that was the best present I have ever received. . . . Please continue being in touch with me."

.   .   .

Because it was Sunday the traffic in Mexico City was light, and it was a beautiful day. For a few days in June 2000, Dorothy and I had been staying at a resort near Cuernavaca that Roberto recommended. He had invited us to come to a family celebration of one child's baptism and another's confirmation; it was a touching gesture, and an honor. I looked out and thought how serene and untrammeled the countryside looked so near the huge city. The driver delivered us to the hotel where members of Roberto's family were staying, near Chapultepec Park. We rushed inside, checked in, left our bags in storage behind the desk, and took the sedan provided by the hotel. It was a short drive to the restaurant, the driver said, and in good English he commenced with touristy chat. When we arrived we found the whole restaurant had been taken over by the Castañedas' celebration. When we walked inside Dorothy cried out and threw her arms around a man who hugged her just as exuberantly. The man I had heard so much about wore a suit and owlish black glasses. He looked the part of a prosperous and confident young doctor.

Roberto turned to me and I said, "Finalmente!"

"Sí, sí. Finalmente!" he said, shaking my hand, and then we embraced.

Gripping my arms, he inspected me and said, "You look a lot better than you did the last time I saw you."

"I bet."

He turned with us then to a group of people who were coming forward to meet us. The tables were covered with white cloths; pink balloons lay and were batted about; a mariachi band played. Roberto's nine-year-old daughter, who had been confirmed into the Catholic faith that morning, ran about in a white dress with flaring petticoats, enjoying her day of constant attention and making the most of it now that church and parental strictures were released. Her hair lightly reddened with henna, Roberto's wife was warm but shy toward us, for she spoke little English. Two of Roberto's sisters lived in Boca Raton, Florida. One was married to a stockbroker, the other to an orthopedist. They were thoroughly and proudly Americanized. Amid the chatter Roberto said to me quietly: "I must ask you. The trimming of your small intestine. Did you ever have any problems with that?"

"No. None at all."

"I thought not," he said, smiling proudly, for he was speaking of his work.

Handed a glass of champagne, I talked to Roberto's older brother, Javier. He was a pleasant man fast growing bald. "At the university I studied physics and mathematics," Javier told me. "But now I have a company that installs air-conditioning systems. I'm a technician."

He shrugged and I nodded. With a smile he said, "You wrote that you would never come to Mexico City again. But here you are."

"Yes, and enjoying it very much."

"Mi casa es su casa," he said. I acknowledged his family's hospitality with a toast to the room with my champagne glass. But there was an insistence in his smile. "Mexicans are a peaceful people. Do you know, in my whole life I have never struck another man with my fists."

My hand jerked slightly; the wine sloshed as I raised it to my mouth.

Across the room Roberto was telling Dorothy: "Your husband has to let this thing go. *Let it go.*"

"I know," she said. "He knows."

Too soon the hour was over. They were moving on from the children's religious celebration to a wedding. Friendly people crowded around us saying good-bye. Roberto pulled me aside. "You have to find the place that can treat you for your pain. In your country

I'm sure it exists. The pain is too much with you. I can see it in your eyes."

Outside, taxis were zooming into the drive, picking people up, and shooting onward. I did exactly what I was supposed to do: I asked the maître d' of this classy restaurant to call us an appropriate cab. "Con seguridad," I said.

"Claro," she said, of course. A green and white Nissan pulled in the drive. Dorothy and I looked at the maître d'. She nodded and held out her hand to the cab. And like sheep led to slaughter, we got in.

The driver had a surly expression and said nothing to us as he sped away. I realized this was *exactly* the kind of cab my friends and I had taken at Plaza Garibaldi. The backseat even felt the same. I looked quickly at the sun visor on the passenger side. There was no registration credential—only a grimy business card. The driver was going very fast, turning right, turning left. *Good God!* I'd done it again, only this time I'd dragged my wife with me! My heart was pounding. I said nothing, just looked at the doors to see how to lock them. They couldn't be locked from the inside! Dorothy meanwhile cursed the heels on her shoes and looked for door handles that would let her *out* of the cab, so she could run. Then the driver careered back out on the Paseo de la Reforma, cut a hard right, and jerked to a halt beside the doormen of our hotel. He swung his flat, unknowable eyes at me, indicating the fare and expecting a good tip.

For part of our trip the Ministry of Tourism offered to provide a driver, so we came to be riding one day with an attractive, well-educated young woman named Hortensia. She drew the assignment because she spoke English so well. The driver, Jaime, spoke no English, but he navigated the daunting freeway traffic very well. I looked out the windows and blinked. Because of the smog, I had never before seen the mountains from the city. A communications officer for the ministry, Hortensia had a thick shock of dark brown hair, arched eyebrows, and a sharp, distinctive nose. She looked at me and asked mildly, "What happened to you?"

I told the story quickly. At the end she shook her head and said, "The same thing happened to me."

"What?"

"Yes," Hortensia said. "It was on a workday, middle of the week. I had an appointment about ten blocks away, so I just hailed a cab. I knew, the minute the driver left the curb. I don't know what it was about him—I just knew. I kept hoping for a stoplight, so I could jump out. But it was just like with you and your friends. When the driver stopped, these guys jumped in the seat with me. They didn't do anything to me, except one of them had a gun that he kept poking in my ribs. But they kept talking about what they were *going* to do to me, which was almost as bad. 'You rich bitch,' things like that." She shuddered. "It was terrible. They had me four hours."

"Four hours!" I cried.

"Yes. I had credit cards, and they took me to ATM machines. I was so scared, I couldn't remember the PIN numbers. I kept saying, 'Look, leave me alone, just a minute. Let me think.' But they were right up in my face and ears. 'You rich white bitch. . . .' They got about eight hundred dollars from me. When they finally put me out of the car, I had no idea where I was. Someone let me use a phone, and I called my boyfriend, but I was so terrified I could barely speak. I had nightmares for months."

From a friend who had come to my bedside in Mexico City, I had a map with the place where I'd been shot circled in ink. Persia Street. Jaime kept studying the map and trying to reconcile it with his knowledge of the city. A couple of times he stopped the van, got out, and went to talk to taxi drivers, taking the map with him. He drove on, and then he saw a police squad car parked beside a curb. He stopped again and took the map to them.

Jaime must have told them some of the story, for in another flare-up of Mexican surrealism, we found ourselves speeding toward my crime scene with a police escort, red and blue lights flashing. After delivering us, the cops didn't stick around. I gave them a wave of thanks as they killed the lights and drove away. Persia was a short street. My comrades in Austin had said the taxi driver left a freeway, which I remembered, then he drove a couple of blocks, turned a corner to the right, and stopped. I saw there was only one place it could be. I walked out to it in a light rain. Dorothy and Hortensia maintained a distance.

I used to fear physical pain. Now I feared things left unfinished. In the journey I had found a courage and optimism I never knew I possessed. But bravery and sanguinity flagged as I grew older and understood what it had done to my health. Some women friends had said they envied Dorothy when they heard she was the reason I fought to stay alive. I knew our marriage had wobbled under the day-to-day strain. I wondered if I could have changed it, could have spared her, spared us. Remembering that night, I decided I could not. David had the pluck to break and run, and he was probably safe. But Mike and John were caught between the angry *pistoleros*. They were in dire trouble, and so was I. In a split second of instinct and decision I looked a killer in the eye and did what I could to stop him. What a terrible, costly way of proving my manhood—in the old vernacular, I could finally say I had balls.

But that myth cheapens it. Of the hundreds of letters I received after the shooting, the one I cherished most came from Mike's sister, who wrote: "Michael hasn't talked much to me about what happened to y'all on the morning of April 20. However, from the little he has told me, he believes that your actions saved his life, as well and John and David's lives. Maybe no one will ever know for sure, but I feel so strongly that if it weren't for you, and your selflessness, and your act of bravery, I wouldn't have an older brother anymore."

I can be proud of what I did. That's no sin.

Persia Street lay in a strange part of town. Its strangeness, Dorothy later realized, lay in the fact that it was so empty. Everywhere else, Mexico City imposed a continual crush of people. On Persia no one was home. I saw one store at the next corner, and a couple of school-girls walked past in blue uniforms, carrying umbrellas and books. But all the other doors to the street were locked shut. Two trucks rested on the sidewalk in states of disrepair, but no mechanics worked on them. I asked Jaime, who had walked with me, if this was a dangerous place. He wagged his hand, the gesture of *más o menos*, more or less, not too bad. More dangerous, he said, were barrios to the south.

I had come here to find only quiet and the soft rain on my face and hair. What I desired most was release. And indeed Honcho's face was fading; I don't know if I would recognize him if I walked up to him on the street. There will always be his kind, snatching at the thrill of murder, in every place on earth. Honcho has no presence in my dreams. I've never dreamed about him, and I doubt I ever will. But I won't forget the faces of those people who came out from their houses, sad and stricken in the haloed light. I wish they could know that in time I got up and walked away from his bullet. In my way I won that fight.